REVOLUTIONARY DEISTS

REVOLUTIONARY DEISTS

EARLY AMERICA'S RATIONAL INFIDELS

KERRY WALTERS

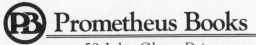 **Prometheus Books**

59 John Glenn Drive
Amherst, New York 14228-2119

Published 2011 by Prometheus Books

Inquiries should be addressed to
Prometheus Books
59 John Glenn Drive
Amherst, New York 14228–2119
VOICE: 716–691–0133
FAX: 716–691–0137
WWW.PROMETHEUSBOOKS.COM

15 14 13 12 11   5 4 3 2 1

Library of Congress Cataloging-in-Publication Data

Walters, Kerry
    Revolutionary deists : early America's rational infidels / Kerry Walters.—[Rev. ed.].
        p. cm.
    Rev. ed. of: Rational infidels.
    Includes bibliographical references and index.
    ISBN 978–1–61614–190–5 (pbk. : alk. paper)
    1. Deism—United States. I. Walters, Kerry S. Rational infidels II. Title.
BL2747.4.W35 2010
211'.50973—dc22

                                                        2010014741

Printed in the United States of America on acid-free paper

For John X. Jobson,
who loved the eighteenth century

CONTENTS

INTRODUCTION

For some eighty-five years—between, roughly, 1725 and 1810—the American colonies and early Republic were agitated by what can only be described as a revolutionary movement. When most people today think of this period in the history of the United States, they think of the political revolution that simmered, eventually erupted, and culminated in the break from England and the establishment of the American Republic. That revolution is not our subject here, although there are obvious connections between the two. Instead, this book deals with a revolution in religious and ethical thought, one that started modestly enough in the beginning but swelled to inflammatory militancy toward the eighteenth century's end. In the process, it helped to change the way in which American religious leaders practiced theology, as well as influenced the direction of popular religious sensibility. This revolution, which was the first major widespread challenge to Christian orthodoxy in America, was spearheaded by a group of thinkers who can be called "rational infidels." These men defended a religion of nature and reason known then and now as deism.

Deism was that religious worldview which sprang from the Enlightenment's emphasis upon reason, natural philosophy (or what today would be called science), and experience. Its central tenets can be easily summarized, in spite of the fact that there was a certain degree of diversity in the thought of its individual proponents. Deism insisted that reality is the creation of a perfectly benevolent and rational deity—the "Supreme Architect"—whose divine rationality and goodness are reflected in his handiwork. Physical reality, for the deists, conforms to universal, immutable, and absolute laws of nature set in motion by God. The discovery and comprehension of these laws is within the reach of the human mind which, like everything else in creation, is imbued with vestiges of the divine rationality. In coming to know reality, humans also gain a deeper appreciation of the Divine Architect's character, since it is through natural law that he reveals himself. Moreover, the highest form of worship of the Deity is in the exercise of those godlike qualities that he has bestowed upon humanity: reason and benevolence. A rational and empirical investigation of nature, then, is the basis of "true" theology, and the examination of one's conscience as well as the virtuous treatment of fellow humans is the foundation of all ethics.

Had the American rational infidels stopped here, it is unlikely that their thought would have sparked the religious revolution it did. After all, an increasing number of eighteenth-century conservative and liberal Christians, from Cotton Mather and Jonathan Edwards to William Paley, were sympathetic with the claim that God reveals himself in his handiwork and that, consequently, one approach to the divine was through the investigation of the natural world. But the deists went much further by insisting that the rational study of nature was the *only* avenue to an understanding of the Deity. Consequently, they dismissed—sometimes systematically, sometimes polemically—the supernaturalist doctrines of miracles and special revelation, argued that neither Scripture nor ecclesial tradition possessed divine authority or internal consistency, and refused to accept either the divinity of Jesus or the orthodox trinitarian definition of the Godhead. Such doctrines, they charged, violated ordinary human experience and were antithetical to the dictates of reason. Belief in them, they said, not only kept mankind in the shackles of superstition and ignorance but also insulted the majesty and dignity of God.

Even more radically, many (but not all) of the American deists also argued that the Christian religion exerted a pernicious moral influence upon humankind. It vitiated virtue by convincing humans that they were utterly corrupted by original sin and hence incapable of improving themselves through their own efforts. It encouraged intolerance and the persecution of dissent by claiming to be the one true religion. It hampered progress in the sciences as well as retarded social justice by doctrinally promoting ignorance and institutionally repressing freedom of thought and expression. Christianity, in short, was seen by the deists as more than just a perversely irrational theology. In their judgment, it was also a fundamental obstacle to the improvement of humankind and the amelioration of social and political injustices.

Given the connection they saw between theological belief and social justice, the rational infidels also directed their energies to the reformation of what they regarded as those social and political institutions that bred intolerance and stunted the progress of reason and human felicity. In politics, each of the deists was ardently republican, believing it was the duty of the state to protect the "natural" rights of freedom of conscience and equality of opportunity. In their eyes, humans could flourish only in a social environment that allowed them the widest possible latitude for self-expression and rational inquiry. Consequently, the American deists' campaign for religious freedom was paralleled by agitation for the elimination of those social institutions that were obstacles to the creation of such an environment. They denounced slavery, the abuse of Native Americans, the subjugation of women, and religious persecution of freethinkers and members of dissenting sects. They insisted upon absolute freedom of the press and universal education, and vigorously opposed both implicit and explicit collaboration between church and state. In short, the American deists sought to liberate the conscience as well as reason, the individual as well as society. For them, there was no significant distinction between ecclesial and political oppression. Both were unwarranted incursions upon the human spirit that promoted ignorance and subservience, and hence violated the God-given faculty of reason.

In their own eyes, the deists were champions of a rational and humanistic religion, and prophets of a coming age of reason in which humans would finally liberate themselves from the shackles of tradition and enjoy the fruits of progress. In the eyes of their orthodox theological and political opponents, they were loathsome apostates, traitors to the ways of both God and religion, and disrupters of the established social order. But regardless of on which side of the debate an individual fell, one thing was clear to the eighteenth-century mind: the gauntlet these rational infidels threw down before Christianity could not be ignored. Orthodoxy in the United States would not reel again from such a sustained onslaught against its cherished beliefs until the late nineteenth-century debate sparked by Darwinism.

This study makes no claim to being a systematic history of American deism. Such a treatise still remains to be written, and would be at least twice the size of the present volume. Instead, my aim here is more modest. In the pages that follow, I've attempted to capture the heart of the American deistic worldview by examining the thought of its primary champions: Benjamin Franklin, Ethan Allen, Thomas Jefferson, Tom Paine, Elihu Palmer, and Philip Freneau. The six middle chapters of this book are devoted to a summary and critique of their separate positions. Predictably, there is a good deal of overlap in the thought of these six rational infidels. Each of them, after all, approached the issue of religion from more or less similar starting points, and each of them was fundamentally loyal to the deistic worldview. But having acknowledged the continuity of their thought, it is also necessary to point out that each of their reflections on deism bears the stamp of the individual man. Franklin's ideal of rational religion had a focus and tone different from that of Palmer's or Freneau's, in spite of the fact that all three of them agreed on a good many central issues. Likewise, Jefferson, Allen, and Paine each concentrated on different avenues of exploration, although they concurred on basics. Consequently, in discussing the contributions of these six deists, I've chosen to highlight the uniqueness of their individual perspectives by focusing on those emphases that render each of them distinctive thinkers.

Franklin's deism, for example, is primarily characterized by a curious ambivalence born of his struggle to accommodate certain aspects of the Calvinist ethos with natural religion. Ethan Allen's singular trademark as a deist is the fact that he was the first American to author a book-length defense of natural religion. Cumbersome as his treatise is, it spotlights him as the pioneer of American deism. Thomas Jefferson's special deistic focus centered on what he took to be the purity of Christian ethical teachings stripped of their unacceptably supernaturalist presuppositions. Tom Paine's forte was polemical debate. He was neither an original nor especially penetrating thinker, but he did possess a memorable rhetorical talent for savaging the claims of orthodox Christianity, which earned him the reputation, in his day as well as ours, of being *the* deistic iconoclast. Elihu Palmer, the eloquent, renegade Presbyterian minister, did more than any other American rational infidel to turn deism into a nationwide and militant movement. Along with Jefferson, he was the most philosophically sophisticated of the American deists, and penned a comprehensive treatise on natural theology that became a bestseller in the young Republic. Finally, Philip Freneau carved a niche for himself in the pantheon of American deism by praising nature and nature's God in lyrical poetry which both reflected his commitment to rational religion and anticipated nineteenth-century romanticism. In focusing upon the distinctive and unique contributions of each of these men, my aim has been to paint a scenario which does justice to the broad scope of American deistic thought without sacrificing either its richness or its depth.

The six portraits of American deists which comprise the bulk of this volume, then, provide an account of deistic sensibility in the eighteenth and early nineteenth centuries by focusing upon the individuals behind the movement. In the first chapter, however, I set the stage for the middle portraits by speaking in more general terms. There I discuss the general characteristics of the Enlightenment ethos which gave birth to natural religion. I also sketch the historical and intellectual factors which gave rise to and uniquely stamped American deism (as opposed to British or French deism) and demonstrate how threatened orthodox believers were by American deism's challenge to Christianity.

In the final chapter, I conclude the discussion by examining the reasons for the eventual demise of American deism as a national movement, as well as reflect upon the legacy it bequeathed to subsequent American thought. As will be seen, the deistic ideal of a rational religion began to lose currency as the eighteenth century gave way to the nineteenth. Infidelity would continue to challenge orthodox Christianity in the nineteenth century, but it differed in both emphasis and style from the Enlightenment-based rationalistic approach of the deists. Part of the reason for deism's ultimate demise was the increasingly obvious simplicity of its views of God, knowledge and human nature. But, curiously, another explanation for its failure to sustain itself as a widespread popular movement is that it succeeded so well in ameliorating the dogmatic supernaturalism of orthodox Christianity in America that it reduced the need for its own continued existence.

Two points about my approach should be mentioned here. First, I've tried to let the six American deists speak for themselves as much as possible, and consequently have not hesitated to load the text with generous quotations from their works. Most of the primary sources used here are long out of print, and hence inaccessible to both the lay and even scholarly audience, and I thought it important to resurrect their voices (along with their occasional eccentric spelling and grammar). But my treatment of American deism is not purely narrative—supposing, of course, that such an enterprise is even possible. I have also tried to interpret and philosophically appraise the central claims of Enlightenment deism. This interpretation is of two kinds. First, I have reflected upon the strengths and weaknesses of specific arguments defended by individual deists in each of the six middle chapters. In addition, I've devoted a good part of chapter 8 to an analytic examination of the strengths as well as the weaknesses of Enlightenment deism in general.

Second, as the reader will notice, I've provided biographical sketches of all the deists treated here except Benjamin Franklin and Thomas Jefferson. The omission of biographies in these two cases is neither an oversight nor an arbitrary decision on my part. Franklin and Jefferson are household names in America, and few individuals are totally ignorant of at least the broad outlines of their careers and personal lives. Moreover, there is an abundance of secondary biographical literature available to any reader who wishes to explore the matter more fully. But the lives of Allen, Palmer, Freneau, and (to a point) Paine are much less well known, and there is a relative dearth of information available about them as persons. Consequently, I thought it necessary to provide the reader with a brief summary of their lives in order, as it were, to fill in the gaps.

INTRODUCTION TO THE REVISED EDITION

The first edition of this book, then titled *Rational Infidels: The American Deists*, appeared nearly twenty years ago. Published by a small press, the book's initial printing quickly sold out, and I was gratified that its reception by both scholars and general readers was favorable and even enthusiastic. Unfortunately, the press that released it went defunct before a second printing could be arranged.

At the time it appeared, *Rational Infidels* was the only book-length treatment of American deism. Nearly two decades later, somewhat to my surprise, it still is. In the intervening years, I've received hundreds of requests from people who wished to read the book but were unable to locate a copy of it. So it's with great satisfaction that I offer this revised version to the public. I'm very grateful to Steven L. Mitchell, editor-in-chief of Prometheus Books, for his enthusiastic support for the project.

In preparing this new edition, I found myself both pleased and mortified—pleased that the substance of my analyses of the American deists still, in my opinion, holds; but mortified that my prose was sometimes irritatingly prolix. My only excuse is that I was a relatively young scholar when I wrote the book, and (like many young scholars) too fond of my own words. In this revised edition, then, I've allowed most of my original interpretations to stand, but I've done my best to smooth out infelicitous sentences and clean up my worst lapses into wordiness. I've also added section titles throughout each chapter and updated the notes to reflect recent scholarship. I hope that all this makes the book more reader-friendly.

In this age of the Internet, many (but by no means all) eighteenth-century books written by British and American deists are more readily available than they were twenty years ago. But for the reader who wishes a convenient compendium of the pertinent writings of each of the deists discussed here, I recommend my anthology *The American Deists: Voices of Reason and Dissent in the Early Republic* (Lawrence: University Press of Kansas, 1992). It was intended as a companion volume to *Rational Infidels*, and serves *Revolutionary Deists* equally well in that capacity.

Revolutionary Deists is dedicated to the memory of a dear friend and astute student of the eighteenth century: John X. Jobson. John embodied the range of interests, high regard for reason, and love of learning that characterized the Enlightenment. All of us who knew him are better for it.

CHAPTER ONE

THE "AGE OF LICENTIOUS LIBERTY"
DEISM IN AMERICA

When Alexis de Tocqueville published the second volume of his massive *Democracy in America* in 1840, one of the aspects of the culture of the early Republic that he examined was religious sensibility. De Tocqueville, a French Catholic, was intrigued by Christian belief in the United States. He was particularly impressed with its pervasiveness. "The religious atmosphere of the country was the first thing that struck me on arrival in the United States," he says. Elsewhere, he marvels that "America is still the place where the Christian religion has kept the greatest power over men's souls. . . . [T]he sects in the United States belong to the great unity of Christendom, and Christian morality is everywhere the same." But even more amazing to de Tocqueville than the ubiquity of Christian sentiment was his perception that Americans regarded Christianity as "necessary to the maintenance of republican institutions." He noted that any politician who dared attack Christian belief would suffer a swift public fall, and that witnesses in courts of law who denied belief in the existence of (the Christian) God would not be sworn in, "on the ground that [they] had destroyed beforehand all possible confidence in [their] testimony." His conclusion was that "for the Americans the ideas of Christianity and liberty are so completely mingled that it is almost impossible to get them to conceive of the one without the other." Consequently, he suggested, "Religion, which never intervenes directly in the government of American society, should [nonetheless] be considered as the first of their political institutions."[1]

De Tocqueville's appraisal of the role of Christian belief in early nineteenth-century America provides us with a fascinating portrait of religious sensibility in the early Republic. But when read against its broader historical background, this snippet of Americana becomes even more intriguing. It is obvious that de Tocqueville's 1840 description could, with a few qualifications, equally well describe American religious belief today. It may be that a greater number of citizens now than in de Tocqueville's time have reservations about the literal truth of many Christian doctrines, but it is a fair estimate that few political figures who publicly confess such infidelity will enjoy long public careers. (In a 2007 poll, for example, over half of surveyed Americans said they would not vote for a presidential candidate who professed disbelief in the existence of God.)[2] Moreover, although the doctrine of separation between church and state has continued to withstand periodic judicial challenges, it is also the case that the notions of liberty and democracy are still inextricably associated in the public mind with Judeo-Christian values. It is as true today as it was one hundred and fifty years ago that religious conviction—or at least rhetorical appeals to it—is a sustaining element in Americans' attitudes about civic and political responsibility as well as about personal character. As such, it is still a "political institution"—in, of course, de Tocqueville's sense.

But if one moves backward in time from de Tocqueville's 1840 description of Christian belief in America, a rather startling discovery surfaces. Barely a generation before de Tocqueville traveled to America, a century-long revolt against Christian belief was at its high point. Had an eighteenth-century de Tocqueville visited America sometime between, roughly, 1725 and 1810, he would have received a much less homogeneous impression of religious sensibility in America. In those years, orthodox Christian belief was systematically and at times savagely criticized by a group of thinkers who called themselves "deists." Influenced by the Enlightenment's championship of reason and science, the American deists rejected the supernaturalist worldview of conventional Christianity. They denied the possibility of revelation or miracles, refused to acknowledge that Jesus was divine or the Godhead trinitarian, and in many instances they even insisted that the moral precepts spelled out in the New Testament were unworthy of either God or man. In place of the Christian faith, they defended a religion based upon the dictates of reason and conscience, and argued that God revealed himself not through the moldering pages of Scripture so much as through the panorama of natural law. The deists would have agreed with de Tocqueville that religious sensibility should be a guiding force in the establishment of social mores and political institutions, but would have vehemently insisted that such sensibility springs from the religion of nature, as they frequently called their perspective, and not from Christian dogma. For them, orthodox Christianity was one of the primary historical obstacles to the progress of both government and science. It was an "infamy," a "despotism," a form of "mental lying," which enchained the human spirit in superstition, ignorance, and fear. It was a tyrant to be deplored and overthrown, not the salutary spiritual standard applauded in *Democracy in America*. In short, religious belief in eighteenth-century America was not at all the pervasive and rather complacent Christianity that de Tocqueville encountered in 1840. Three generations of deists, whom their orthodox contemporaries lambasted as "infidels," saw to that.

Although deism in America erupted into a national and militant movement toward the end of the eighteenth century, its early and middle periods were relatively sedate. Early American intellectuals such as Benjamin Franklin were sympathetic to the idea of rational religion, but wary about publicly trumpeting their infidelity. There are several explanations for this reticence.

First, early and mid-eighteenth century sympathizers with deism's rejection of supernatural religion were often somewhat ambivalent in their endorsement of the new way of thinking. Most of them agreed that orthodox tenets of American Calvinism such as the utter depravity of humans were unacceptable because they were offensive to human reason and dignity. But because they lived during a period in which orthodox Calvinism's worldview was so pervasive, many of them were unable to completely throw over the trappings of supernaturalism. Franklin, for example, continued to believe in the possibility of special providences, holding that the Deity could and occasionally did supernaturally intervene in human affairs. Later deists rejected such lingering fidelity to Christian doctrine. But deistically minded Americans in the early years of the eighteenth century, caught as they were in the sometimes confusing transition period between Calvinism and the Enlightenment, were not as unambiguously confident. Deism in the first half of the century, then, was often an uneasy amalgamation of Enlightenment-based natural religion and Calvinist-inspired supernaturalism. The theological ambivalence felt by its early supporters made them reluctant to defend publicly a religious model about which they themselves, to one degree or another, were unsure.

Moreover, early sympathizers with deistic rationalism hesitated to go public because of their fear that dissemination of the new way of thinking would undermine social stability. Many colonial intellectuals attracted to deism were also suspicious and contemptuous of what they tended to think of as the "mob." They feared that a diminution of the normative and ecclesial authority of traditional Christianity would open the floodgates of anarchy. The "common" people, in their estimation, were too boorish and unlettered to appreciate or profit from a religion founded upon reason and nature, and therefore needed artificial and institutionalized standards to control their behavior. The deists thought it better to allow the mob to retain its faith in conventional Christian beliefs until such time as it was better educated and hence more receptive to the dictates of rational conscience. Until that day arrived, deism was best confined to the genteel drawing room and the gentleman-scholar's study. This fear of the socially disruptive effects of natural religion's demolition of Christianity was expressed as late as 1786 by Benjamin Franklin, when he advised a correspondent against the publication of a popular tract on deism.

> I would advise you, therefore, not to attempt unchaining the Tyger, but to burn the Piece before it is seen by any other Person; whereby you will save yourself a great deal of Mortification from the enemies it may raise against you, and perhaps a good deal of regret and Repentance. If men are so wicked as we now see them *with religion*, what would they be *if without it?*[3]

Franklin's advice is especially revealing, because it also hints at the third major reason for American deism's early reticence: "You will save yourself a great deal of mortification from the enemies it may raise against you." Franklin was quite correct, even as late as 1786. The American colonies had a long history of religious intolerance. In 1658, for example, the Pilgrims of Plymouth Colony enacted an anti-Quaker law that mandated "No Quaker Rantor or any other corrupt person shall be a freeman of this Corporation." A few years later, three "incorrigible" members of the Society of Friends were hanged by the Puritans in Boston. The southern colonies also enacted equally draconian laws against religious dissent. In the early eighteenth century, Virginian legislators decreed that disbelief in the authority of the Bible was illegal, and disqualified non-Christians from holding public office. Blasphemy, which included as minor a transgression as the profession of doubt about scriptural authority, was a jailable offense. Nor did other colonies, with the exception of Rhode Island, brook dissent. Georgia, South Carolina, North Carolina, New Jersey, and New Hampshire each required that members of their assemblies be Protestants in good standing. Even Pennsylvania was no exception. An act passed in 1700 required inhabitants to either attend church services on Sundays or show they worshipped privately in their homes. Violators of this early "blue law" risked a hefty fine.

These and similar pieces of legislation predictably served as disincentives for public confessions of deism, which most American Christians, regardless of their particular sectarian allegiance, regarded as outright atheism.

Repressive laws against religious dissent were gradually expunged from the books toward the end of the eighteenth century, largely due to the tireless efforts of legislators such as Jefferson, Madison, and South Carolina's Charles Pinckney. But even then, freethinkers who publicly advertised their apostasy suffered social opprobrium as well as sanctions. Ethan Allen, who in 1784 published his *Oracles of Reason*, the first full-blown American defense of deism, was castigated by the faithful as "one of the wickedest men that ever walked this guilty globe." Tom Paine, whose militant book *The Age of Reason* came out in 1794/5, was contemptuously dismissed as a "drunken atheist" and "detested reptile." Thomas Jefferson, an intensely private man who never publicly discussed his deistic sympathies, was branded an "atheist and fanatic." Even after the likelihood of legal persecution had diminished, it was an act of almost foolhardy bravery to admit to deistic leanings.

Still, as the century progressed, deistic sentiments became more prevalent and their holders more outspoken. American colleges were the first settings to be infected by public infidelity. As early as 1759, Ezra Stiles, alarmed at what he perceived as the frightening extent to which skepticism had encroached upon the academy, lamented that "Deism has got such Head in this Age of Licentious Liberty" that colleges had no choice but to acknowledge its presence and "conquer and demolish it."[4] By the end of the century, "licentious liberty" was even more entrenched in American colleges. Yale, for example, had earned a somewhat exaggerated reputation for free thought. Lyman Beecher, who became a student there in 1793, later recalled that the "college was [then] in a most ungodly state. The college church was almost extinct. Most of the students were skeptical. . . . That was the day of the infidelity of the Tom Paine school. Boys that dressed flax in the barn, as I used to, read Tom Paine and believed him. . . . Most of the class before me were infidels, and called each other Voltaire, Rousseau, D'Alembert."[5]

Nor was Yale the exception. Apostasy raged at any number of other institutions of higher learning. Virginia's College of William and Mary was known as a training ground for "infidelity."[6] In 1799, the College of New Jersey (Princeton) had "only three or four [students] who made any pretensions to piety."[7] A 1789 alumnus of Dartmouth College recalled that his fellow students had been "very unruly, lawless, and without the fear of God," and lamented that ten years later "but a single member of the class of 1799 was publicly known as a professing Christian."[8] Even Harvard became enmeshed in free thought. William Ellery Channing, who graduated from there in 1798, sadly recalled: "[the college] was never in a worse state than when I entered. . . . The tone of books and conversation was presumptuous and daring. The tendency of all classes was to skepticism."[9] Officials at Harvard obviously shared Channing's concern. In 1791, the college's overseers publicly banned and burned Gibbon's *Decline and Fall of the Roman Empire* because of what they perceived as its uncomplimentary interpretation of early Christianity. Three years later, when young William Channing matriculated, each incoming student was presented with a copy of Richard Watson's *Apology for the Bible*. This treatise was a polemic directed against the "Tom Paine school." The very fact that Harvard officials felt compelled to make Watson required reading reveals the extent to which young college-bound men at the end of the century were fascinated by and attracted to the religion of nature.

Deism's influence in the American colleges was more intense, perhaps, than in the general populace. But even there, infidelity became increasingly obvious—and, to the faithful, worrisome—as the century drew to a close. Newspapers, journals, magazines, and broadsides published scores of articles on deism, many of which spawned additional scores of furious or delighted responses. Elihu Palmer, a blind renegade minister, is largely responsible for moving deism from academic enclaves to the popular forum. Beginning in the early 1790s, Palmer launched a nationwide crusade for deism which, ironically, had all the rhetorical fervor of an old-fashioned religious revival. He stumped the Eastern seaboard from Maine to Georgia, touting the religion of nature and harshly condemning Christian doctrine and ethics. In addition, he founded deistical societies in state after state to continue spreading the word in his absence, and edited two deistical newspapers, each of which enjoyed wide circulations. The first, called *The Temple of Reason* (1800–1801), exerted such influence in the Middle Atlantic and Southern states that John Hargrove, a Baltimore minister, felt obliged to found *The Temple of Truth* as an orthodox antidote to Palmer's perniciously spreading appeal.

Palmer's second journalistic foray, the *Prospect*, ran from 1803 to 1805, and likewise attracted a large readership. The extent of its circulation is suggested by the fact that its subscribers were requested to pay their rates to agents in Newburgh, Rhinebeck, Philadelphia, and New York City. Thanks to the efforts of Palmer and other militant infidels, deism at century's end had thrown aside its earlier reticence. Doctrinal ambivalence, genteel qualms about the socially disruptive consequences of deism, and fear of persecution vanished in a wave of enthusiasm for nature's God. The widespread popularity of deism at this time is indicated by the following outburst of frightened rage by one Rev. Robert Hall in his 1801 publication *Modern Infidelity*:

> The efforts of infidels, to diffuse the principles of infidelity among the common people, is another alarming symptom peculiar to the present time. [Earlier deists] addressed themselves solely to the more polished classes of the community. . . . [But now deism,] having at length reached its full maturity . . . , boldly ventures to challenge the suffrages of the people, solicits the acquaintance of peasants and mechanics, and seeks to draw whole nations to its standard. [10]

Deism-inspired infidelity, in short, was no longer the preserve of the cultured and educated. It now belonged to the masses, and embroiled the entire Republic in a debate as incendiary as it was far reaching. Through either personal reading or word of mouth, few people in these years were unaware of the deistic challenge to Christian authority.

Ironically, the Christian establishment's rather hysterical reaction to the spread of deism only served to keep the movement in the public eye. Men of the cloth relentlessly blasted the "new infidelity" from their pulpits, unwittingly arousing their parishioners' already lively curiosity about this threat to orthodox hegemony. Pamphlet after pamphlet was churned out by ministers eager to warn the unsuspecting about the "Antichrist" rearing up in their midst. Doubtless, many of these tracts achieved their intended purpose, but it is also the case that some of them backfired. Young Ben Franklin, for example, was converted to deism after devouring several anti-deistic polemics.[11] Ministerial volleys such as the Reverend Uzal Ogden's thunderous charge that deism "more became a lunatick, than a person in the enjoyment of his rational sense!" titillated and intrigued the average person, prodding him or her to learn more about the religion of nature.[12] One clergyman, belatedly recognizing the unexpected consequences of such publicity, gloomily predicted that "our Zion must die without an helper" while deistic infidels laughed at her "dying groans." Likewise aware that clerical denunciations were shoving deism center stage, the Methodist Episcopal Church urged a national day of fasting and prayer in 1796 to recall the country to its senses. The general assembly of the Presbyterian Church followed suit two years later, adding with typical Calvinist earnestness that divine wrath would smite the United States unless she turned away from deism.[13] But all such attempts to stem the tide of deistic infidelity proved fruitless. Elihu Palmer certainly exaggerated when he boasted toward century's end that there were "thousands and tens of thousands of deists" in America, but he was not off by much.[14] True, the movement would eventually burn itself out by 1810, but until that time, Ezra Stiles and other Christian champions were quite justified in seeing the period as an "Age of Licentious Liberty." One can only speculate how de Tocqueville would have reacted to the religious climate had he visited America in the eighteenth century's final decade. But one thing is certain: his impressions of American religious sensibility would have been quite different than they were a generation later.

THE NEW LEARNING

The natural religion defended by deists in both America and Europe was a product of the Enlightenment, that period in Western thought which is roughly coterminous with the eighteenth century. The period is also called the Age of Reason, an appellation immortalized by Tom Paine, the most iconoclastic of the American deists. But like so many other striking labels, this one is somewhat misleading if taken as an unambiguous description of the Enlightenment ethos. It is true that the era's temperament was firmly grounded upon the principles of reason and science, or what the eighteenth century commonly referred to as "natural philosophy." But it is also the case that several of the period's most prominent philosophers—Rousseau, for example, comes immediately to mind—do not comfortably fit this conventional mold. Consequently, in thinking about the Enlightenment as an intellectual movement, it is more accurate to view it as a generally pervasive attitude, a basic worldview orientation, than a uniform system of specific beliefs and propositions. As Carl Becker correctly points out, the Enlightenment ethos was a "climate of opinion" that allowed for a wide latitude of individual perspectives, not a monolithic school of thought.[15] As will become apparent in subsequent chapters, the rich diversity of opinion encouraged by the Enlightenment's climate is especially striking in American deism.

Still, in spite of the wide divergences of opinion among Enlightenment thinkers, most of them were in solid agreement over fundamental methodological and philosophical issues, and it is possible therefore to speak of the movement in somewhat general terms. This near unanimity in regards to basic principles stemmed from the period's enthusiastic endorsement of the thought of three seventeenth-century thinkers: Francis Bacon, Isaac Newton, and John Locke. The influence of these three men upon Enlightenment thinkers in general and American deists in particular can hardly be exaggerated. Together, they laid the foundations for a new way of thinking about knowledge, reality, God, and society that propelled Western thought into the so-called modern era. Enlightenment savants were so impressed by this perspective that they tended to call it the New Learning, the implication being that it once and for all had supplanted the "old learning" of bygone centuries.

Francis Bacon (1561–1626) laid the first cornerstone of the New

Learning by defending what he and many of his followers considered to be a new logic.[16] This system was first outlined in *The Great Instauration* (1603) and further elaborated in the *Novum Organon* (1620). In both of these works, Bacon severely criticized the traditional Aristotelian model of "syllogistic" logic for what he took to be its overweening formalism. The "old" organon, he maintained, ignored ordinary experience of the physical world and concentrated exclusively on the deduction of logical implications from abstract first principles. The arguments generated from such a method, Bacon conceded, are logically impeccable, but they lack any concrete applicability or "scientific" utility. Because the major premises upon which the old logic grounds its deductions are a priori and untested, drawn from hidebound tradition rather than empirical investigation, the conclusions to which they give rise are abstract—and hence vapid—speculations possessing neither explanatory nor practical value. As such, according to Bacon, "demonstration by syllogism" lets "nature skip out of its hands."[17]

In place of the old Aristotelian model of deductive logic, Bacon proposed a "new" organon which derived its first principles from the concrete data of experience rather than a priori speculation. The old system erred in incestuously manipulating nothing but words and propositions in its search for deductively airtight conclusions. The new system, on the other hand, proceeded inductively, scrutinizing physical phenomena, inferring probabilistic generalizations, experimentally testing and retesting these inferences against physical data, and then mathematically formulating the generalizations that held up as expressions of natural law. This methodological emphasis upon experience, Bacon assured his readers, not only provided a more solid foundation for human knowledge than the formalistic Aristotelian approach, but also infused an instrumentality into logical reasoning, thereby providing humans with a practical calculus by which to manipulate and subdue nature. For Bacon, as well as his eighteenth-century admirers, logical analysis became synonymous with what today would be called applied science. Knowledge, as Bacon said, is empowering, and his "novum organon" promised to provide the key to such empowerment. As he put it in *The Great Instauration*:

> The art which I introduce . . . is a kind of logic; though the difference between it and the ordinary [or syllogistic logic] is great; indeed

immense. For the ordinary logic professes to contrive and prepare helps and guards for the understanding, as mine does; and in this one point they agree. But mine differs from it in three points especially, viz., in the end aimed at; in the order of demonstration; and in the starting point of the inquiry. For the end which this [logic] of mine proposes is the invention not of arguments but of works; not of things in accordance with principles, but of principles themselves; and not of probable reasons, but of designations and directions for works. And as the intention is different, so accordingly is the effect; the effect of the one being to overcome an opponent in argument, of the other to command nature in action.[18]

Bacon's call for a logical methodology that took experience rather than abstract speculation as its starting point struck a responsive chord in his contemporaries. It appealed to them partly because it conveniently supplanted a model of logic which, although traditionally honored, was increasingly perceived as methodologically inadequate. But even more significantly, Bacon's system of inductive reasoning was endorsed wholeheartedly because it promised to unravel the mysteries of the physical order—a realm that was fast becoming an object of fascination for the seventeenth- and eighteenth-century mind—and in addition claimed to be the necessary conceptual tool for the continuous "invention of arts." It bequeathed to the modern era a heady vision of steady scientific progress that appealed to the savant as well as the early capitalist.

The advantages of Bacon's new logic over the syllogistic model were dramatically illustrated by the natural philosophy of Isaac Newton (1642–1727). In both his *Philosophiae Naturalis Principia Mathematica* (1687) and *Optics* (1704), Newton provided the eighteenth century with a systematic description of physical reality that demonstrated to everyone's satisfaction the superiority of Baconian observation, experiment, and mathematical calculation to Aristotelian speculation. Newton himself claimed to be following the path Bacon had blazed. As he proudly observed in describing his methodology, "*Hypotheses non fingo*"— "I do not feign hypotheses."

In keeping with his endorsement of Bacon's rejection of a priori first principles, Newton insisted that the "whole burden" of natural philosophy consists in an empirical investigation of physical "forces" from which the observer infers lawlike generalizations.[19] Starting, therefore, with a careful study of the obvious phenomenon of force or motion, Newton worked to construct a systematic model of physical reality that showed the material order to be explicable in terms of insurmountable and uniform natural laws. The axioms of this natural philosophy were a far cry from the a priori assumptions favored by pre-Baconian thinkers. They were "deduced from phenomena and made general by induction" . . . a process, Newton asserted, that provided "the highest evidence . . . a proposition can have."[20] Such deductions revealed that physical reality is best envisioned as a clockwork mechanism of complex intricacy whose parts function with a uniform and immutable precision that allows for neither spontaneity nor change. As Newton rather laconically put it, "Nature is very consonant and conformable to her self."

While Newton's natural philosophy reinforced the eighteenth century's confidence in Bacon's method, it also convinced the Enlightenment savant that reality was eminently knowable because completely rational—what other word could better describe a network of causes and effects whose operations are uniformly lawlike, immutable, and mathematically expressible? Moreover, this demonstration of reality's intrinsic knowability underscored the Baconian insistence that science is properly most concerned with the "invention of the arts." Newton's grand cosmological mapping of physical reality assured the eighteenth-century natural philosopher that there is no limit to either scientific knowledge or technological progress. The key to nature and nature's ways had been discovered, and the universe now revealed itself as a new continent to be explored, mined, and subjugated. It is little wonder that Alexander Pope later celebrated both Newton and the New Learning's natural philosophy with the famous couplet: "Nature and Nature's laws lay hid in night; God said, Let Newton be, and all was light." In praising Newton in such lavish terms, Pope spoke for his entire generation.

But Newton's achievement went beyond revealing to the eighteenth-century mind the ubiquitous rationality of reality and the accompanying promise of scientific progress. His cosmology also bestowed meaning upon reality by pointing to the existence of a divine First Cause, a Primordial Architect who served as the initial impetus as well as exemplar of the clockwork universe. The lawful nature of physical reality, said Newton, is too striking to suppose it to be the product of mere chance. Instead, "this most beautiful system of the sun, planets, and comets could only proceed from the counsel and dominion of an intelligent and powerful Being."[21] This Being, affirmed Newton, revealed itself in its creation. To discern the characteristics of physical laws, then, is by inference to learn something about the Deity's nature. Cosmological arguments for the existence of God, as well as attempts to infer divine nature from an examination of physical reality, certainly predated Newton. Both ancient philosophers and scholastic theologians had accepted the possibility of such demonstrations by analogy. But Greek and medieval thinkers, to the Enlightenment mind, had speculated in a vacuum because they operated without the benefit of a clearly demonstrated natural philosophy. Newton, however, supplied such a cosmology in his *Principia*, thereby grounding the assertion of divine existence on a scientific foundation that the New Learning's adherents took to be as forceful as it was irrefutably clear.

Bacon proposed a new inductive logic, thereby liberating humankind from the stultifying abstractions of syllogistic reason. Newton charted nature's laws, thereby demystifying the cosmos. John Locke (1632–1704), the third luminary of the New Learning, focused upon the nature and scope of human reason, ambitiously undertaking to elucidate "the original, certainty and extent of *human knowledge*, together with the grounds and degrees of *belief*, *opinion*, and *assent*." Moreover, he did so by appealing to the Baconian ideals of observation and experiment—or, as Locke put it, by proceeding from the "historical, plain method" of inquiry into "the original of those ideas which a man observes."[22] With Locke, the final foundation stone of the Enlightenment's New Learning was laid.

In his *Essay Concerning Human Understanding* (1690), Locke argued that the "ground of belief" is experience, not innate ideas or a priori first principles. The human mind, in fact, is nothing but a potentiality (the famous tabula rasa) for the absorption of information derived from the five senses. All human knowledge, from the most immediate to the most abstract, ultimately stems, then, from the raw material of experience: sense data, or what Locke referred to as "simple ideas." More complex ideas are generated from simple ones by the mental function of association: the intellect compares sense data, classifies them on the basis of their similarities and dissimilarities, and ultimately, in good Baconian fashion, infers lawlike generalizations from the classifications. As Locke put it,

The mind makes the [simple] ideas received from particular objects, to become general; which is done by considering them as they are in the mind, such appearances, separate from all other existences, and the circumstances of real existence, as time, place, or any other concomitant ideas. This is called *abstraction*, whereby ideas, taken from particular beings, become general representatives of all of the same kind, and their names general, applicable to whatever exists conformable to such abstract ideas.[23]

In keeping with the earlier Baconian model of logical method, then, Locke postulated that beliefs are the product of inductive generalizations. It follows that the truth of any knowledge claim is tested by either an appeal to ordinary experience or the logical coherency of simple idea associations. But Locke went beyond Bacon by suggesting that such a procedure is not merely a valuable methodological device but also a model of rationality itself. In any area of human investigation, legitimate beliefs are ultimately founded upon experience and logical coherency. Consequently, meaningful discourse, whether it be scientific, philosophical, or theological, is always grounded in experience and logic. Human reason neither can, nor should, seek to go beyond these two standards. Consequently, appeals to mysterious criteria such as innate ideas, much less subjective psychological certainty, are unnecessary as well as misleading. Even knowledge supposedly supplied by divine revelation is answerable to the standards of experience and reason. If putative revelatory beliefs violate either of the two canons, they are prima facie candidates for rejection. Locke, a more or less orthodox churchman, saw the theological implications of his thesis, and awkwardly hedged his bet by insisting that "genuine" instances of revelation were "above" rather than "contrary to" reason.[24] But his empiricist analysis of the nature and extent of human reason cast grave doubts upon the verisimilitude of beliefs that claimed divine origin.

Locke's analysis of the nature and capacity of human reason was greeted by the eighteenth century as a discovery every bit as important as Newton's natural philosophy. The Newtonian system demonstrated that physical reality operated under the guidance of immutable natural laws. Similarly, Locke's psychology showed human reason to also be lawlike in its operations, and hence parallel in nature to the very reality that served as the source of its raw material. An obvious symmetry was posited, therefore, between mind and reality. Reality in and of itself is perfectly graspable by a rational mind, and human intellects are rational. The enthusiastic optimism to which Bacon's novum organon had given birth was thus nurtured and brought to maturity by the panrationalism suggested by Newton and Locke. No invention, no technology, was beyond the scope of human endeavor. It was indeed the best of all possible worlds.

The impact of Bacon, Newton, and Locke upon eighteenth-century thought was definitive. Together, these three men defined the parameters of the Enlightenment ethos by introducing a new way of looking at reality—the so-called New Learning—which would serve as the eighteenth century's standard of investigation as well as appraisal. Their contributions systematically defended experience and reason, rather than aprioristic, syllogistic speculation, as the twin foundations of human knowledge. Their insistence upon the empirical origins of all human knowledge catapulted natural philosophy into the spotlight, and convinced subsequent philosophers that scientific methodology was capable of disclosing the nature of social as well as physical reality. After all, it seemed reasonable to conclude that humans and societies, being a part of nature, are likewise guided by nature's laws. Their rejection of traditional methods and explanations instilled in the Enlightenment a healthy skepticism of authority in any area, scientific, political, or theological. As Kant put it, their thought served as the catalyst for "man's release from self-imposed tutelage" to arcane and archaic lore. "*Sapere aude*!—Dare to reason! Have the courage to use your own minds!—is the motto of enlightenment."[25] Finally, the New Learning formulated by Bacon, Newton, and Locke bequeathed to the eighteenth-century mind a deeply optimistic faith in the inevitable perfection of human knowledge, scientific invention, and, by implication, society. The doctrine of panrationalism, which was the underlying assumption of the Enlightenment worldview, guaranteed that a perfect parallelism held between the intellect and reality, and that, in principle as well as practice, the physical realm was ultimately susceptible to human dominion. D'Alembert accurately captured this optimism in the following paean to the New Learning:

The discovery and application of a new method of philosophizing, the kind of enthusiasm which accompanies discoveries, a certain exaltation of ideas which the spectacle of the universe produces in us—all these causes have brought about a lively fermentation of minds. Spreading through nature in all directions, like a river which has burst its dams, this fermentation has swept with a sort of violence everything along with it which stood in its way.[26]

D'Alembert's exuberant cry touched a responsive chord in all adherents of the New Learning, and especially in the American deists.

BRITISH DEISM

The "lively fermentation of minds" spawned by Bacon, Newton, and Locke was soon apparent in all areas of intellectual endeavor, and religious inquiry was no exception.[27] Some churchmen were horrified at the theological implications of the New Learning. Although Newton privately professed an acceptance of miracles and Locke retained faith in special revelation, their respective systems seriously undermined the likelihood of rational belief in either. This became increasingly obvious to their defenders as well as to their critics, and often prompted the latter to reject the New Learning outright.

But theirs was the minority opinion. Most clerics saw Baconian logic, Newtonian physics, and Lockean psychology as supporting evidence for the existence of the Christian God. In their estimation, the lawlike orderliness of the cosmos as well as of the mind clearly pointed to the necessity of an intelligent and benevolent Supreme Architect. Consequently, many churchmen, particularly in Britain, adapted their beliefs to the New Learning by positing a distinction between "natural" and "supernatural" or "revealed" theology. The former generally focused on naturalistic design arguments for the existence and attributes of God. The latter concentrated upon distinctively Christian dogmas—the Trinity, the divinity of Jesus, miracles, and scriptural revelation—which were incapable of being discovered by the light of experience or understood by human reason. Following Locke's suggestion in the *Essay* that revelation should be defined as "above" rather than "contrary to" reason, the "liberal" theologians of the eighteenth century insisted that Christian dogma was likewise above reason rather than contrary to it, and hence complemented rather than contradicted natural theology's claims. Thus Samuel Clarke (1675–1729), one of Newton's close associates, argued that Christianity's supernatural revelation was congruent with natural theology, even if its dicta were necessarily based on faith and hence outside the purview of rational discovery.[28] Similarly, George Cheyne (1671–1743), a fellow of the Royal Society, argued that the inherited taint of original sin hindered human reason from acquiring on its own an adequate knowledge of God. Consequently, natural religion needed the aid of divine revelation.[29]

But in spite of its self-assuredness, liberal theology's marriage of natural reason and supernatural revelation was an uneasy one. Apologists such as Clarke and Cheyne, who enthusiastically absorbed the New Learning while retaining their faith in Christian dogma, tended to give away with one hand what they took with the other. They willingly endorsed the assumption that reality was an immense mechanism operating in accordance with rational and immutable laws of nature, and hence was capable of being fully understood through experience and human reason. But they pulled back—arbitrarily, in the eyes of some— when it came to traditional Christian dogma, thereby insinuating that the previously postulated lawlike character of reality wasn't really so immutable or rational after all.

This tension provided the impetus for the emergence of British deism, a movement that attempted to formulate a "pure" religion of nature by expunging from it elements of Christian supernaturalism. The campaign was launched by John Toland (1670–1722), who published his *Christianity Not Mysterious* (1696) one year after the appearance of Locke's liberal tract *The Reasonableness of Christianity*. Much to the embarrassment of Locke (who publicly disassociated himself from deism), Toland claimed to base his arguments upon the New Learning's empiricist model of cognition. Taking the bull by the horns, Toland argued that a credible natural religion must display logical consistency even at the expense of traditional Christian articles of belief. He therefore discounted the possibility of miracles and divine revelation, the former because they were contrary to experience, the latter because it was beyond the reach of reason and therefore not bona fide knowledge.

The deistic Supreme Craftsman was as rational as his creation, and Toland considered it unworthy as well as illogical of the Archetype of Reason to communicate in less than rational ways or to violate the system of natural laws he had established.

Anthony Collins (1676–1729) agreed with Toland and surpassed him in his attack upon supernatural religion. Arguing that the pure religion of nature and reason had been perverted by superstitious priestcraft, Collins's *Discourse on the Grounds and Reasons of the Christian Religion* (1724) indirectly attacked ecclesiastical authority by arguing that Sacred Scripture, the basis of that authority, was irrational and incomprehensible. While Collins directed his attack specifically against biblical prophecy, his contemporary Thomas Woolston (1669–1733) took on the doctrine of miracles. In his *Discourses on the Miracles of Our Saviour* (1727–1729), he concluded that the New Testament's account of Jesus' miracles is as "broken, elliptical and absurd" as any tale "told by any imposter . . . in religion,"[30] and that even the early Church Fathers interpreted scriptural miracles in only a figurative way.

A rash of deistic treatises denouncing the claims of revealed Christianity appeared in subsequent years.[31] Although they weren't terribly acute from a philosophical or theological perspective, they stirred up enough controversy to keep the movement in the public eye. But undoubtedly the most influential one was written by Matthew Tindal (1657–1733). His *Christianity as Old as the Creation* (1730), which quickly became known as the Deist Bible, was of all the British deistic works the best reasoned and most comprehensive defense of the religion of nature. Tindal argued that revealed theology (as opposed to natural theology) was not based on the "Nature and Reason of things," but rather on superstition and wishful thinking.[32] He offered as an antidote to supernaturalist confusion the following rule: If any putatively revealed truth differs in even the slightest detail from experience or reason, it is to be condemned and rejected.[33] This represented a radical break with Locke's liberal attempt to salvage Christian revelation. For Tindal, there was no appreciable distinction between a proposition "above" and a proposition "contrary to" reason. One was perhaps a bit less mysterious than the other, but neither ultimately proved satisfactory to a rational mind. Moreover, Tindal denied the divinity of Jesus, claiming that the notion was an invention of priestcraft. He insisted that the Scriptures demanded veneration of an ethically unworthy deity who displayed caprice, jealousy, and arbitrary cruelty in his dealings with humans, and he concluded that true religion—the religion of nature, stripped of all priestly superstition—was both logically and ethically superior to Christianity.

The deistic movement in Britain, then, carried the New Learning precipitated by Newton, Locke, and Bacon to its logical conclusion in the realm of theology. It rejected revealed religion as contrary to human as well as divine reason, and insisted that the "Great Book of Nature" and the "Light of Reason" were better guides to a knowledge of both God and morality than scriptural or priestly dogma. Although frequently accused of atheism by their contemporaries, the British deists were not disbelievers so much as religious and ethical reformers. They accepted the existence of a Supreme Architect, and argued that his presence was demonstrable through reason and experience. They took as their task the methodological critique of an ideology—supernaturalist Christianity—which they believed had subverted the original reasonableness and purity of religious sentiment. In doing so, they posed a radical threat to orthodox religion's hegemony, a threat which far surpassed the liberalizing tendencies of eighteenth-century Christianity. An indignant Jonathan Edwards accurately captured the deists' radical point of departure in his *History of the Work of Redemption* (1773) when he said they

wholly cast off the Christian religion, and are professed infidels. They are not like the Heretics, Arians, Socinians, and others, who own the Scriptures to be the word of God, and hold the Christian religion to be the true religion, but only deny these and these fundamental doctrines of the Christian religion: they deny the whole Christian religion. Indeed they own the being of a God; but deny that Christ was the son of God, and say he was a mere cheat; and so they say all the prophets and apostles were; and they deny the whole Scripture. They deny that any of it is the word of God. They deny any revealed religion, or any word of God at all; and say that God has given mankind no other light to walk by but their own reason.[34]

DEISM COMES TO AMERICA

New ideas that arise from and agitate cosmopolitan worldviews trickle down only gradually to provincial settings, particularly colonial ones. The arrival of the New Learning upon the American shore was no exception. The impact of the new worldview launched by Bacon, Newton, and Locke finally began to influence the thought of American men of letters toward the end of the first quarter of the eighteenth century. The famous Dummer gift of books to Yale College in 1714 introduced the New Learning to a curriculum that still focused on instruction in classical languages and taught a meager natural history comprised of undiluted Aristotelianism. But after the Dummer gift, the New Learning quickly spread throughout the colonial colleges. By midcentury, students as well as a handful of reading laypersons were familiar with, even if still somewhat confused by, the new way of thinking.

The attempts of liberal British Christians to accommodate their theology to the New Learning also arrived in the colonies during the first half of the eighteenth century. Clarke and Cheyne's works were widely read, as were John Tillotson's *Principles of Natural Religion* (1675) and William Wollaston's *Religion of Nature Delineated* (1722). The influence of liberal Christianity upon American religious thought was far reaching, cutting across sectarian boundaries and favorably influencing even such redoubtable champions of conservative biblicism as Cotton Mather. Some colonial theologians immediately recognized that the New Learning posed a potentially grave threat to orthodoxy, but most of them, like their British counterparts, interpreted it as evidential support for the claims of supernatural religion. Harvard College, one of the colonies' mainstays of theological propriety, was so impressed by the New Learning that it inaugurated the Dudleian Lectures in 1755 for the express purpose of "the proving, explaining, and proper use and improvement of the principles of Natural Religion."[35]

The clause in the Dudleian statement of purpose mandating natural religion is revealing, for it underscores the fact that the works of British deists had also arrived on the American shore by 1755. Sympathetic as they might have been to liberal Christianity, American churchmen were scandalized and outraged by the denials of Christian doctrine they discovered in writers such as Toland, Collins, and Tindal. At midcentury, the tracts of the British deists were primarily read only by the American upper class and intelligentsia, although Pope and Addison, both of whom defended anemic versions of deism, were two of the colonies' favorite authors. But as the century progressed, deistic tracts began to be read by a wider audience, first in college circles, then by the general public. Pulpit condemnations of the "godless" religion of nature, which increased in frequency as well as intensity as the years rolled on, also fueled the growing curiosity about the strange infidelity that had been imported from Britain. Soon, the champions of American orthodoxy, correctly or incorrectly, saw the dissemination of deism as a very real threat indeed—a perfidy which, if unchecked, would destroy the American New Jerusalem and usher in, as Ezra Stiles put it, an age of licentious liberty.

In retrospect, it appears that orthodox clergy in America tended to overestimate the range and influence of deistic "infidelity," misreading what in fact was a relatively short-lived current as a tidal wave of permanent apostasy. But for all of their hysteria, colonial and early republican churchmen were correct in being alarmed at the reception that deism received in America. American deism as a movement endured scarcely two generations, but during that time it attained a wide and sometimes explosive following. The reasons for its startling popularity are many and complex. But, speaking in broad terms, it may be hazarded that rational religion captured the popular imagination to the extent that it did because the American environment was ripe for it. Three factors in particular prepared the way for deism in the colonies and early Republic: the Calvinist tradition against which it reacted, the steady infiltration into North America of French Enlightenment ideals, and the experience of national independence.

The theological worldview of John Calvin (1509–1564) was a staple in American Christianity during the seventeenth and eighteen centuries. The New England Congregationalist tradition, founded by dissenting "Puritans" of the Massachusetts Bay Colony, most obviously was based upon Calvinist tenets; but so were, in various degrees, other Protestant denominations such as Anglicanism, Presbyterianism, and even Quakerism. Calvinism, in short, set the tone for Christianity in the colonies. To belong to most of the mainstream Protestant sects was to subscribe, to one degree or another, to its precepts.

Although Calvinist-inspired theology was not a monolithic set of beliefs unanimously accepted by all sectarians, most mainstream Protestants in eighteenth-century America endorsed at least some of the so-called five points of Calvinism ratified by the Synod of Dort in 1619. These five essential doctrines were: (1) *unconditional election*, the assumption that God freely chooses whom to save and whom to damn, without in any way basing the divine decision on considerations of individual merit or "works"; (2) *limited atonement*, the principle that Christ's sacrifice guarantees the salvation of some—the "elect"—but not all; (3) *total depravity*, the scripturally based tenet that all humans, by virtue of Adam's fall, are inherently and utterly corrupt; (4) *irresistible grace*, the assumption that humans are completely helpless to participate in their salvation, and that spiritual rejuvenation, if it comes, is a freely given grace from God which the individual is powerless either to choose or reject; and (5) *perseverance of the elect*, the doctrine that humans imbued with grace are incapable of falling from that state. At least in the context of American Calvinism, the nuclei of doctrinal belief were divine predestination and individual corruption. God decreed from the beginning of time who would be saved and who condemned. Human actions in and of themselves, consequently, do not merit salvation, nor is human reason capable of understanding the mysterious cosmic blueprint. The best that depraved humans can do is to constantly search their souls, humble themselves, and patiently await the signs that indicate if they are elected for salvation. As the Puritan divine Jonathan Mitchell put it: "Pursue and follow home in self-examination, by applying and considering the Scripture-evidence of a state of Salvation, and searching whether they be found with thee."[36]

The intense psychological and emotional stress that such an uncompromising theology inflicted upon its adherents surfaces time and again in the introspective musings of seventeenth- and eighteenth-century American Calvinists. But alongside Calvin's gloomy theological condemnation of both human nature and reason was a more optimistic but equally intense emphasis upon cultivation of the mind. Calvinist clergy were noteworthy among American clerics for their training in languages, theology, and, in the eighteenth century, natural philosophy. Their sermons were often learned (sometimes tiresomely pedantic) discourses that sought to educate as much as to edify congregations. In short, as Perry

Miller has put it, American Calvinism was a sometimes uneasy mixture of anti-intellectual piety and meticulous rationalism.[37]

The tension generated by American Calvinism's bifurcated attitude toward human reason was only highlighted by the arrival of the New Learning at the beginning of the eighteenth century. The advocacy by both liberal Christian and Enlightenment savants of reason and experience as sufficient foundations for knowledge of things secular and divine soon exerted its influence upon Calvinist speculation, prompting it to stress its rationalistic strain at the expense of its pietistic one. Calvinist divines began to gravitate from revealed to natural theology, and to so emphasize the role of human rationality that many of them, such as Ebenezer Gay (1696–1787) and Ezra Stiles (1727–1795), came dangerously close to affirming that humans, by the use of unaided reason, could come to know God's will and save themselves through their own efforts.[38] This confidence that individuals could participate in their salvation through freely chosen good works came to be known as "Arminianism."[39] Its rationalistic challenge to orthodox Calvinism's insistence upon predestination and human depravity prompted some Calvinist clergy to renounce their Puritan heritage and return to the more liberal Anglican church. But most of them remained in the Calvinist fold and attempted, sometimes awkwardly and sometimes ingeniously, to accommodate the New Learning to the *Institutes of Christian Religion* and the Westminster Confession.

The crisis toward which American Calvinism's tense acceptance of both piety and rationalism propelled it came in the 1740s, with the intercolonial religious revival that has come to be known as the Great Awakening. Sparked by enthusiasts such as George Whitefield (1714–1770), Gilbert Tennent (1703–1764), and Jonathan Edwards (1703–1758), the Great Awakening was a last-ditch effort on the part of orthodox Calvinists to derail Arminianism and rationalist challenges to the traditional Puritan "Scheme of Grace." Insisting that the Christian faith had been poisoned by ungodly defenses of human reason and freedom of determination, the leaders of the revival called for a return to a religion of the heart that stressed the traditional pietistic standards of internal spiritual regeneration and rejuvenation. Introspection, fear, and self-abasement, not reason or works, were the necessary conditions for salvation. The utter depravity of human nature, the helplessness of individuals to save themselves through either good intentions or efforts, and the irremedi-able inability of reason to fathom the ways of God were emotionally defended in fire-and-brimstone sermons calculated to whip listeners into a frenzy of horror and submission that would draw them back to tradi-tional piety.

Embroiling New England as well as the Middle Atlantic and Southern colonies, the Great Awakening seemed just the antidote to liberal ten-dencies for which the faithful longed. And, in fact, it did restore, at least for a while, widespread religious fervor. But it failed in the long run to stem the tide of either liberal Christianity or natural religion. Even more to the point, it led to consequences that, ironically, actually nurtured the growth of deism in America.

There are two reasons for this unintended and undesired conse-quence of the Awakeners' efforts. First, their revivalist message inadver-tently encouraged the very Arminian tendencies they wanted to forestall. Even as Edwards in his pulpit and Whitefield in his open field preached the orthodox doctrines of predestination and utter depravity, they also exhorted their listeners to make the effort to throw off sloth, open them-selves to divine grace, and work toward their own conversion and ulti-mate regeneration. It is difficult to see how the Awakeners could have avoided this mixed signal, since the very purpose of a revival is to encourage sinners to mend their evil ways and return to a godly state. But it is precisely this message of spiritual self-determination, conveyed with gripping eloquence and fiery passion, that sank in—especially since many of the Awakeners' auditors were already leaning toward Arminianism from sheer weariness with traditional Calvinism's bleakness. The Awak-eners' unintended espousal of Arminian autonomy, then, undercut the very fidelity to doctrinal literalness they hoped to revive.

Moreover, the Great Awakening polarized and brought to the fore-ground the conflict between rationalism and traditional piety that had been brewing for the last few decades. Many colonials, attracted by the New Learning but bound by emotional ties to Calvinism, had tried to keep a foot in both camps by explaining away fundamental differences between the two worldviews. After the Great Awakening, in spite of its unwitting bow to Arminianism, such compromises became increasingly difficult. Battle lines were established unambiguously between tradi-tional orthodoxy and liberalism, pietism and natural theology. They split what hitherto had been a more or less solid Calvinist hegemony into several doctrinal splinter groups. The Great Awakening, then, paradoxically ended the Calvinist-inspired ideal of a theologically homogeneous Zion in the Wilderness. It was not so much a successful revival of Calvinism as "the dying shudder of a Puritanism that refused to see itself as an anachronism."[40]

The almost suicidal theological convulsions of the Great Awakening prepared the way for the subsequent popularization of deism in America. First, the splintering and dissolution of the earlier Calvinist hegemony created a climate of theological and speculative ambivalence that rescued American deism from the necessity of self-protectively adopting the harsh and uncompromising infidelity of the French savants. True, deistic sensibilities were savaged by the American Christian establishment, and secular penalties for heresy remained on the law books well into the first years of the young Republic. But for all that, American deists were spared the relentless secular and ecclesial persecution their Continental counterparts endured. Angry and militant colonial and early republican deism certainly was. But the demise on the American shore of orthodox hegemony for the most part prevented it from sliding into paranoic hysteria and thereby alienating moderate sympathizers.

Second, the legitimization of liberal theology that the Great Awakening unwittingly helped to foster enhanced receptivity to later deistic defenses of a religion of nature. Many observers of the emotional frenzy fanned by the revival were horrified and disgusted by such displays of passionate enthusiasm. The perceived irrationality of such examples only underscored their Enlightenment-tinctured distrust of enthusiasm. Moreover, the revival's renewed emphasis upon the increasingly distasteful doctrines of human depravity and predestination highlighted in their estimations the merits of the New Learning's humanistic alternative of self-determination and rationality.

Finally, the spiritual and philosophical vacuum created by the erosion of widespread fidelity to Calvinism's orthodox worldview provided a point of entry for new religious perspectives. Given the fact that the climate of opinion was already sympathetic to the claims of rationalism and liberal religion, the uncompromising naturalism of deism, which stressed reason, human dignity, and ethical responsibility, was seen by many as a logical and saving foundation upon which to construct a new religious system. The deistic Temple of Reason and Humanity, in short, arose from the rubble of the orthodox New Jerusalem.

Reaction to the Calvinist ethos, as well as the sectarian splintering that followed the turmoil of the Great Awakening, were fundamental in shaping a climate receptive to deism's call for a religion of nature and reason unburdened by supernaturalism and doctrinal intolerance. But there were other winds blowing throughout the American colonies that likewise encouraged infidelity. One of these gusts was the importation of French thought to the American shore.[41] The French and Indian War in midcentury helped to introduce the hitherto rather insular colonies to hints of French radical thought. Ethan Allen, for example, claimed to have discussed free thought with several French prisoners of war he encountered during this time; he was impressed (and perhaps even initially shocked) by their cavalier dismissal of Christian doctrine as well as by their scathing contempt for the clergy. A steady flow of French New Learning, represented by the writings of *philosophes* such as Diderot, Voltaire, d'Alembert, and Volney, continued to trickle into the colonies throughout the rest of the century. Americans such as Franklin, Jefferson, and Paine all spent time on the Continent, and while there imbibed a rather heady religious radicalism that they subsequently brought back with them upon their return to America. Finally, toward century's end, the example of the French Revolution, with its vision of a secular state in which freedom of conscience was a primary ideal, excited the imagination of liberal-minded Americans. Admittedly, the influence of French religious radicalism was less pervasive in the colonies than that of British deism, if for no other reason than the burdensome obstacle of language, but the radical mood of the French *philosophes* did infect American thought to a certain extent, particularly in the colleges. It will be recalled, for example, that Yale students in the 1790s were in the habit of calling one another Voltaire, Rousseau, and d'Alembert, clearly indicating a certain amount of hero worship on their part for these religiously radical savants.

The gradual importation of French infidelity appears to have influenced American deism in at least two ways. First, the harsh anticlericalism of French *philosophes* provided a shocking but exhilarating example to many American thinkers chaffing under what they took to be an unjustified degree of ecclesial influence. Even after the disrupting effects of the Great Awakening, clergy in the colonies and early Republic exercised what today seems an almost unbelievable amount of spiritual and moral authority. In addition to serving as the intellectual leaders of the community, they often assumed the roles of social and political watch-dogs, condoning or condemning lifestyles and norms from the vantage point of a privileged spiritual position. French anticlericalism, with its mocking denunciations of priestly venery and ecclesiastical corruption, helped erode the sacrosanct aura surrounding the American clergy, just as the British New Learning called into question its defense of orthodox dogma. Both tendencies encouraged the overt criticism of institutional-ized Christianity so effectively hurled by the American deists. Franklin, for example, mocked Protestant sects and their ministers for what he saw as a self-satisfied and supercilious intolerance of opposing perspectives. Jefferson, at least in his private correspondence, savaged the ignorance of churchmen. Allen, Paine, and Palmer were less reserved. Each of them attacked the American clergy in both print and public speeches, con-demning them for their self-serving manipulation of parishioners. Of all the leading American deists, only Philip Freneau tended to shy away from clergy-baiting, although at times, in his youthful poetry and a few late essays, he likewise indulged in clerical denunciations. The French influence, in short, served as a catalyst for radical intoxication on the part of the American deists. They tended to adopt their philosophical and sci-entific ideas from the British tradition founded by Bacon, Newton, and Locke, but their angry and sometimes militant attitude toward estab-lished religion and its purveyors came in large part from the French.

But the French example influenced the climate of American deism in another way as well, a way that is connected with the impact upon Amer-ican infidelity of America's own revolutionary break with England. The American War of Independence, although initially sparked by dissatisfac-tion over what the colonies saw as an unwarranted usurpation of their legal rights by Britain, soon matured into a struggle for a republican form of government that would guarantee the ideals of political equality and fair representation. (As will be seen in chapter 4, one of the most influ-ential catalysts of this growing regard for republicanism was the deist Tom Paine.) As the war progressed and the colonies became increasingly aware of the struggle's broader implications, a rather heady atmosphere of liberation from traditional ways of thinking began to set in that impacted religious issues as well as political ones. When Paine characterized the struggle as a time that tried men's souls, he referred to more than just the political upheaval. He also meant to imply that American thought was going through a transition period which, like all births, was unsettling and occasionally painful as well as exhilarating. In the minds of many colonists, the ideals of political liberty and self-determination came to encompass the ideals of freedom of conscience and personal autonomy in matters religious. It is not surprising that many of the period's leading thinkers and statesmen were convinced deists as well as ardent patriots. In their minds, the two convictions were inseparable. The one threw off the chains of political bondage, the other struck away the shackles of ecclesiastical dominion. Elihu Palmer spoke for them when he insisted that political and churchly authority were "twin despots," historical collaborators in a pernicious campaign to control body and spirit.

The American struggle for independence and the subsequent formation of the Republic, then, gave birth to a climate that was especially favorable to the liberating message of the New Learning. They fostered a social attitude of intellectual as well as political liberty that refused to be bound by hallowed tradition in either the political or religious arena. The French Revolution of 1789 only served to further fan this flame of independence, convincing many American thinkers that republicanism was on the march and that the entire Western world would embrace it by throwing over both secular and religious tyrannies. But the example of the French Revolution also imbued American deism with a vision of humanistic ideals that, although certainly present in the American experience, were neither as dramatic or pervasive. The American Revolution was essentially a political movement. But its French counterpart, with its cry for fraternity as well as equality and liberty, was social as well. The goals of the French Revolution—goals which had a profound influence on the subsequent nature of American deism—encompassed more than just the establishment of a new political structure. They also sought to inaugurate radical and far-reaching changes in the status of social and individual existence, changes which ensured that freedom of thought, economic opportunity, and release from traditional class structures would come about. The French ideal, in short, did not rest content with political emancipation. It struggled for the emancipation of humans by providing them with an environment best conducive to their individual well-being and flourishing.

This intensely humanistic direction, in which human conscience rather than superstition was the ultimate standard of measurement, exerted an immense influence on the thought of the American deists. Deism emerged in America before the French Revolution, and undoubtedly would have continued had the events of 1789 not occurred. But the example of the French Revolution unquestionably helped to radicalize the movement, nudging it in the direction of social as well as religious militancy. Such militancy would reach its culmination in the career of Elihu Palmer, who campaigned for, among other things, universal suffrage, the abolition of slavery, and legal rights for women. Thus, while it is obvious that a great deal of the hostile reaction to American deism was sparked by its denial of orthodox Christian dogma, it is also the case that the radical nature of its social and political agenda likewise stirred up a great deal of conservative anger and fear. Deism in the young Republic was seen as more than just a campaign against Christian orthodoxy. It was also viewed by its enemies (and even by some of its more moderate supporters, such as Benjamin Franklin), as a potentially revolutionary force that threatened to undermine the established social order. It is not surprising that the later American deists were sometimes referred to as Jacobins by their political and religious opponents.

Deism in America, then, was shaped by a number of intellectual and social factors. From Britain, it acquired the philosophical foundation of the New Learning as represented by Bacon, Locke, and Newton. Similarly, American infidelity learned a great deal from British liberal Christianity—so-called natural theology—as well as from the writings of British deists proper. French radicalism helped to turn the attention of American deists to social issues by imparting to them a humanistic concern for the well-being of individuals laboring under the stultifying effects of unjust social and political institutions. The examples of the American and French revolutions encouraged the deistic regard for republicanism, and convinced at least the more militant deists that true freedom of conscience was attainable only in a secular society that guaranteed liberty from political as well as ecclesial repression. Finally, the dismal memory of Calvinism's antihumanistic religious credo, as well as the gradual breakup of the Calvinist hegemony in the eighteenth century, provided both an incentive and an opportunity for the dissemination of deism's message of a religious sensibility based upon reason and nature. Each of these factors helped create a climate that in turn shaped the nature and course of deism in America, a climate that stamped upon it a distinctive character. Less radical than French atheism, which in part was shaped by its background of overpowering church and state oppression, but more militant than the staidly liberal character of British deism, American deism in retrospect can be seen as occupying the middle ground in eighteenth-century free thought. It advocated religious and social reforms that undoubtedly struck contemporary observers as radical in nature, but it stopped short of the total overthrow of the established order championed by the more radical proponents of French thought. It sought the liberation of mind and spirit, but always within the boundaries, as Elihu Palmer put it, of "reason, righteous and immortal reason."

DIVERSITY AND CONVERGENCE IN AMERICAN DEISM

The preceding pages have provided a sketch of the historical, philosophical, and theological backdrop against which American deism should be examined. Although I have necessarily painted this background in broad, sweeping strokes, it should be kept in mind, as mentioned earlier, that neither the Enlightenment ethos nor American deism was a monolithic movement. Instead, both of them are more properly regarded as general orientations that allowed for a good deal of individual diversity and difference of emphasis on the part of their spokespersons.

In the chapters that follow, this diversity-in-unity that characterizes the temperament of American deism will become apparent. All of the figures treated in them were unique individuals who approached the religion of nature in slightly different ways. Franklin and Jefferson, for example, can be viewed as early moderate deists who were extremely reluctant to trumpet their infidelity in the public marketplace—Franklin because he was fundamentally ambivalent about his deism, Jefferson because he was almost obsessively self-protective about his personal religious views (as well as politically astute enough to recognize their unpopularity with the electorate). On the other hand, Allen, Paine, Palmer, and, to a lesser degree, Freneau, were militant champions of deism and equally outspoken critics of Christian supernaturalism. None of them suffered from Franklin's deep-seated reservations. Nor were they reluctant to expose themselves to the recriminatory backlash that public defenses of deism inevitably brought.

In addition to their diversity in tone and style, the American deists to be examined focused their analyses of rational religion in different directions, depending upon their respective personalities, abilities, and particular interests. Franklin's approach emphasized the rationality of ethics and the need for sectarian tolerance, in addition to a rather unsuccessful attempt to harmonize certain features of traditional Calvinism and the New Learning. Jefferson deplored Christianity's supernaturalism, but insisted that its ethical pronouncements were both sublime and genuinely "deistic" in tenor. Ethan Allen, in his own cumbersome and sometimes tedious way, concentrated on showing that deistic religious sensibility could be justified through metaphysical demonstrations (or, in the eyes of some, pseudo-metaphysical demonstrations). Paine, the most obviously iconoclastic of the American deists, philosophized with a hammer, gleefully focusing most of his energies upon demolishing the sacred cows of religious as well as political orthodoxy. Palmer, in many respects the most influential of the American deists, settled for nothing less than a grand systematization of the deistic worldview, and in the process elaborated a cosmology as well as an ethical system based exclusively upon naturalistic principles inspired by the New Learning. Finally, Philip Freneau, the last of the mainstream American deists, poetically sought to impress upon his readers the majesty and benevolence of the American deists. His fidelity to rational religion was expressed not through the technical language of science and philosophy so much as through the lyrical language of the heart. Moreover, like Franklin before him, Freneau was a man caught between two opposing worldviews, and the tension sparked by this situation imparted a certain amount of ambivalence to his thought. Franklin, the first of the line of American deists, sought to effect an uneasy alliance between Calvinism and Enlightenment New Learning. Freneau, the last of his line, attempted a similar marriage between the New Learning and early nineteenth-century romanticism.

But the diverse approaches of individual American deists should not blind us to the common thread of agreement that runs through and hence unifies their thought. The shades of difference in their personal convictions, tones, styles, and emphases notwithstanding, all of them were in solid agreement with the fundamental tenets of natural religion. They all agreed that reality is rational, defined by immutable and absolute natural laws; that these laws were set in motion by a Supreme Architect whose nature is essentially reflected in creation; that humans are likewise imbued with a spark of the Divine Reason that permeates reality, and hence are capable of understanding that reality; that natural philosophy, established upon the foundations of the work of Bacon, Newton, and Locke, is the key to comprehending and subduing physical creation; that to understand reality is to understand the Deity, since the latter's true revelation is to be found in his handiwork; and that the highest form of worship humanity can offer the Supreme Architect is rational inquiry and virtuous behavior.

Moreover, each of the American deists was opposed, uncompromisingly, to supernaturalist religions in general and Christianity in particular. They insisted, for example, that the latter's central tenets—revelation, miracles, eternal damnation, the depravity of human reason, the divine authorship of Scripture, the divinity of Jesus, and the triune nature of the Godhead—are unworthy of the Deity's dignity and an assault on the rationality of humans. Furthermore, they agreed that historical Christianity had bred an atmosphere of ignorance, fear, superstition, and intolerance that retarded social development, militated against the well-being of individuals, and hampered the progress of science. The demolition of Christian supernaturalism thus represented for them more than an end to irrationality and a perverted theology. It also signaled the beginning of a new epoch—an epoch of reason—in which humankind, freed from the bondage of centuries, would at last come into its own.

The "age of licentious liberty" which Ezra Stiles claimed was ushered in by the American deists, then, is better described as one of "rational infidelity." It sought to replace old religious and political sensibilities with new models based upon the pellucid findings of reason and natural philosophy. The heyday of this rational infidelity only lasted some two generations. For all practical purposes, it ended in 1811, with the collapse of *The Theophilanthropist*, the last deistic newspaper to be printed in America. But the demise of deism as a national movement did not mean that it had no lasting effect upon the religious sensibilities of the United States. Its legacy was immense, even if not as pervasive as its advocates, from Franklin to Freneau, would have wished. In the final chapter of this work, we shall return to this issue by examining the reasons for deism's eventual decline as well as its subsequent influence upon religious thought in America.

NOTES

1. Alexis de Tocqueville, *Democracy in America*, trans. George Lawrence (New York: Doubleday Anchor, 1969), pp. 290–93, 295.

2. *The Gallup Poll*, 2007 (Lanham, MD: Rowman & Littlefield, 2008), p. 75.

3. Benjamin Franklin to Anonymous, July 3, 1786 (?), in *Benjamin Franklin: Representative Selections*, ed. Chester E. Jorgenson and Frank Luther Mott (New York: Hill & Wang, 1968), p. 485.

4. Letter to Thomas Clap, August 6, 1759, in folio volume of Stiles Mss.,Yale University, p. 460. Quoted in I. Woodbridge Riley, *American Philosophy: The Early Schools* (New York: Dodd, Mead, 1907), p. 217.

5. Lyman Beecher, *Autobiography and Correspondence*, vol. 1, ed. Charles Beecher (New York: Harper & Brothers, 1866), p. 43.

6. William Meade, *Old Churches, Ministers and Families of Virginia*, vol. 1, (Philadelphia: Lippincott, 1910), p. 75.

7. John Johnston, *The Autobiography and Ministerial Life of the Rev. John Johnston, D.D.*, ed. James Carnahan (New York: M. W. Dodd, 1856), p. 30.

8. Quoted in G. Adolf Koch, *Republican Religion: The American Revolution and the Cult of Reason* (New York: Henry Holt, 1933), p. 242.

9. W. H. Channing, *Life of William Ellery Channing* (Boston: American Unitarian Association, 1880), p. 30.

10. Robert Hall, *Modern Infidelity Considered with Respect to Its Influence on Society* (Charlestown, MA: Samuel Etheridge, Printer, 1801), pp. 44–45.

11. Benjamin Franklin, *Autobiography*, in Jorgenson and Mott, *Benjamin Franklin: Representative Representative Selections*, p. 16.

12. Uzal Ogden, *An Antidote to Deism*, vol. 2 (Newark, NJ: John Woods, 1795), p. 280.

13. Koch, *Republican Religion*, pp. 275–82.

14. Kerry Walters, ed., *Elihu Palmer's 'Principles of Nature': Text and Commentary* (Wolfeboro, NH: Longwood Academic, 1990), p. 258.

15. Carl Becker, *The Heavenly City of the Eighteenth-Century Philosophers* (New Haven: Yale University Press, 1965), esp. pp. 1–32.

16. For a full treatment of Bacon's "new" logical method as well as his criticisms of Aristotelian and medieval scholastic logic, see Kerry Walters, *The Sane Society Ideal in Modern Utopianism: A Study in Ideology* (Lewiston, NY: Edwin Mellen Press, 1989), pp. 75–143.

17. Francis Bacon, *The Great Instauration*, in *The Works of Francis Bacon*, vol. 1, ed. Spedding, Ellis, and Heath (Boston: Houghton, Mifflin & Co., n.d.), p. 41.

18. Ibid., pp. 40–41.

19. Isaac Newton, "Preface to the *Principia*," in *Newton's Philosophy of Nature*, ed. H. S. Thayer (New York: Hatner, 1974), p. 10.

20. Isaac Newton to Cotes, 1713, in Thayer, *Newton's Philosophy of Nature*, p. 6.

21. Isaac Newton, *Principia*, bk. 2, in Thayer, *Newton's Philosophy of Nature*, p. 42.

22. John Locke, *An Essay Concerning Human Understanding*, ed. Peter H. Nidditch (New York: Oxford University Press, 1979), bk. 1, ch. 1.

23. Ibid., bk. 2, ch. 2.

24. Ibid., bk. 4, ch. 18.

25. Immanuel Kant, "Beantwortung der Frage: Was Ist Aufklarung?" in *Immanuel Kants Werke*, vol. 4, ed. Ernst Cassirer and Hermann Cohen (Berlin: 1920–22), p. 174.

26. Quoted in Ernst Cassirer, *The Philosophy of the Enlightenment*, trans. Fritz C. A. Koelin and James P. Pettegrove (Boston: Beacon Press, 1965), pp. 3–4.

27. The rest of this section is adapted, with a few modifications, from my *Elihu Palmer's "Principles of Nature": Text and Commentary*, pp. 18–22. Additional sources that discuss the New Learning, the Enlightenment, and religion include James Byrne, *Religion and the Enlightenment* (Louisville, KY: Westminster John Knox Press, 1997); Peter Gay, *The Enlightenment: The Rise of Modern Paganism* (New York: W. W. Norton, 1995) and *The Enlightenment: The Science of Freedom* (New York: W. W. Norton, 1996); Knud Haakonssen, *Enlightenment and Religion: Rational Dissent in Eighteenth-Century Britain* (Cambridge: Cambridge University Press, 2006); Peter Harrison, *"Religion" and the Religions in the English Enlightenment* (Cambridge: Cambridge University Press, 2002); Jonathan I. Israel, *Radical Enlightenment: Philosophy and the Making of Modernity, 1650–1750* (New York: Oxford University Press, 2002); and J. B. Shank, *The Newton Wars and the Beginning of the French Enlightenment* (Chicago: University of Chicago Press, 2008). Two useful anthologies are Paul Hyland, *The Enlightenment: A Sourcebook and Reader* (New York: Routledge, 2001) and Isaac Kramnick, *The Portable Enlightenment Reader* (New York: Penguin, 1995).

28. Samuel Clarke, *A Discourse Concerning the Unchangeable Obligations of Natural Religion, and the Truth and Certainty of the Christian Revelation*, in R.

Watson, *A Collection of Theological Tracts*, vol. 4 (London, 1791), pp. 109–295. See also Clarke's *Discourse on Natural Religion*, in L. A. Selby Biggs, *British Moralists, Being Selections from Writers Principally of the Eighteenth Century*, vol. 2 (Oxford: Clarendon Press, 1897), pp. 3–56.

29. George Cheyne, *Philosophical Principles of Religion: Natural and Revealed* (London, 1715).

30. Thomas Woolston, *Discourses on the Miracles of our Saviour*, vol. 2 (London, 1728), p. 48.

31. For an exhaustive treatment of the minor British deists, see vol. 1 of Leslie Stephen, *History of English Thought in the Eighteenth Century* (New York: G. P. Putnam's Sons, 1908). See also James A. Herrick, *The Radical Rhetoric of the English Deists: The Discourse of Skepticism, 1680–1750* (Columbia: University of South Carolina Press, 1997) and Diego Lucci, *Scripture and Deism: The Biblical Criticism of the Eighteenth-Century British Deists* (Bern: Peter Lang, 2008).

32. Matthew Tindal, *Christianity as Old as the Creation; or, The Gospel a Republication of the Religion of Nature* (London, 1730), p. 52.

33. Ibid., p. 60.

34. Jonathan Edwards, *History of the Work of Redemption*, in *The Works of Jonathan Edwards*, vol. 1, ed. Edward Hickman (Boston, 1834), p. 599.

35. Josiah Quincy, *The History of Harvard College*, vol. 2 (Cambridge, MA, 1840), p. 139.

36. Quoted in Perry Miller, *The New England Mind: The Seventeenth Century* (Cambridge, MA: Harvard University Press, 1982), p. 53.

37. Ibid., p. 66.

38. See Robert J. Wilson, *The Benevolent Deity: Ebenezer Gay and the Rise of Rational Religion in New England, 1696–1787* (Philadelphia: University of Pennsylvania Press, 1984) and Edmund S. Morgan, *The Gentle Puritan: A Life of Ezra Stiles, 1727–1795* (New York: W. W. Norton, 1983).

39. So called after the Dutch theologian Jacobus Arminius (1560–1609), who argued that humans are not totally passive in their regeneration, thereby challenging the Calvinist doctrine of utter depravity and helplessness. See Gerald O. McCulloh, *Man's Faith and Freedom: The Theological Influence of Jacobus Arminius* (Eugene, OR: Wipf & Stock, 2007).

40. Alan Heimert and Perry Miller, eds., *The Great Awakening: Documents Illustrating the Crisis and Its Consequences* (Indianapolis: Bobbs Merrill, 1967), p. xiv. For a detailed analysis of the Great Awakening and its impact upon colonial religious sensibility, see Alan Heimert, *Religion and the American Mind: From the Great Awakening to the Revolution* (Cambridge, MA: Harvard University Press, 1966); Thomas A. Kidd, *The Great Awakening: The Roots of Evangelical Christianity in Colonial America* (New Haven, CT: Yale University Press, 2009); and

Frank Lambert, *Inventing the "Great Awakening"* (Princeton: Princeton University Press, 2001).

41. For a detailed account of the influence of French radical thought on American deism, see Herbert A. Morais, *Deism in Eighteenth-Century America* (New York: Russell & Russell, 1960), chs. 2–4. For additional accounts of deism, Enlightenment thought, and religion in eighteenth-century America, see Ernest Cassara, *The Enlightenment in America* (Lanham, MD: University Press of America, 1988); Robert A. Ferguson, *The American Enlightenment, 1750–1820* (Cambridge, MA: Harvard University Press, 1997); David Holmes, *The Faiths of the Founding Fathers* (New York: Oxford University Press, 2006); Henry May, *The Enlightenment in America* (New York: Oxford University Press, 1978); John Meacham, *American Gospel: God, the Founding Fathers, and the Making of a Nation* (New York: Random House, 2007); the first three chapters of James C. Turner, *Without God, Without Creed: The Origins of Unbelief in America* (Baltimore: Johns Hopkins University Press, 1986); and Steven Waldman, *Founding Faith: Providence, Politics, and the Birth of Religious Freedom in America* (New York: Random House, 2008).

CHAPTER TWO

THE AMBIVALENT DEIST
BENJAMIN FRANKLIN

B enjamin Franklin (1706–1790) has become an American institution. Every schoolchild is familiar with the Horatio Alger–like rags to riches story of his boyhood and youth, his electrifying experiment in a thunderstorm with kite and key, his arithmetical calculus for the cultivation of virtue, his venerable status as the voice of experienced wisdom at the deliberations of the Continental Congresses, and the pithy, homespun aphorisms with which he adorned the pages of *Poor Richard's Almanac*. Franklin is an integral part of Americana. If it is sometimes difficult to separate fact from fiction in considering his career—a difficulty exacerbated by his often imaginative autobiography—it makes no matter in the minds of many. For Franklin's life is the stuff of which folklore is spun, and folklore's proper function is to edify, instruct, and entertain, not to report.

Still, elusive as he is, there is an actual person behind the legend. While part of the difficulty in tracking down the real Franklin has to do with the mythological trappings he has acquired over the last two hundred years, another part is a result of the fact that in many respects he was an individual who, throughout his long life, oscillated between opposing and sometimes incompatible perspectives. The real Franklin was an often ambiguous admixture of intellectual polarities and tensions. This is not to suggest that he was unique in this regard. Each of us, to one extent or another, wavers between antipodal perspectives. But few of us are as richly endowed or historically influential as Franklin.

Nowhere is Franklin's ambivalence more apparent than in his religious views. He was, he tells us, "religiously educated as a Presbyterian" and raised "piously in the Dissenting way."[1] But he early on began to doubt the rigid and gloomy doctrines of Calvinism, and was converted at the tender age of fifteen to the natural religion of deism—a conversion, ironically, brought about by reading anti-deistic tracts. "It happened that [these tracts] wrought an effect on me quite contrary to what was intended by them," he tells us; "for the arguments of the Deists, which were quoted to be refuted, appeared to me much stronger than the refutation; in short, I soon became a thorough Deist."[2] But from deism, Franklin quickly moved to a forbidding Newtonian-inspired mechanism, which left little room for God and none for human freedom, and by 1725 had published a defense of this position entitled *A Dissertation on Liberty and Necessity*. He soon regretted this work, and returned to a more moderate form of deistic belief. But even then his religious ambivalence lingered. He accepted the central tenets of deism, but never was able to disabuse himself of a somewhat lukewarm fidelity to certain aspects of Calvinist tradition. He continued, for example, to non-deistically defend the possibility of special providences, or God's direct intervention in the realm of immutable natural laws, and during the turbulent years of the Great Awakening he found himself emotionally overpowered (although intellectually repulsed) by the fundamentalist preaching of revivalists such as George Whitefield. He was an ardent champion throughout his entire life of freedom of conscience. Yet four years before his death, he was so frightened by what he saw as the disruptive possibilities of absolute freedom of religious expression that he advised one of his correspondents to refrain from publishing a treatise in defense of deism, lest its criticisms of orthodoxy destroy the checks upon behavior provided by supernaturalist religion. Fearless in his political convictions to the point of willingly risking his life in the struggle for American independence, he nonetheless displayed a marked reticence in exposing himself to public disapprobation by openly defending the deism he privately, albeit ambivalently, endorsed.

Franklin, the first of the mainstream American deists, can thus be characterized as an ambivalent advocate of the religion of nature. Brought up in an era that was still heavily Calvinist in tone and credo, he came of age at a time when the influence of the New Learning and the

British deists was just beginning to be felt in the American colonies. He quickly endorsed the New Learning, but never quite shed all of the early influence of the Calvinist ethos. The resulting dissonance would emerge again and again in his later reflections upon religion as well as ethics. In short, Franklin, like so many of his contemporaries, was a man caught in the transition from one worldview to another. For the most part, he accommodated himself well enough to this unsettling shift. But it was perhaps inevitable that remnants of the earlier worldview he had tried to abandon would remain with him.[3]

This deep-seated ambivalence notwithstanding—or perhaps because of it—early in life Franklin adopted a spirit of toleration in matters religious that inspired subsequent deists and nondeists alike. While in his early thirties, he voiced this open-mindedness in a pair of letters written to his parents, who had expressed concern over reports of their son's infidelity. "You both seem concern'd," he wrote, "lest I have imbib'd some erroneous Opinions." And, he admits, "doubtless I have my Share. . . ." But

> I imagine a Man must have a good deal of Vanity who believes, and a good deal of Boldness who affirms, that all the doctrines he holds, are true, and all he rejects, are false. . . . If I am in the wrong, I should not be displeas'd that another is in the right. If I am in the Right, 'tis my Happiness; and I should rather pity than blame him who is unfortunately in the Wrong.[4]

Franklin remained loyal to these sentiments for the rest of his life. All in all, there are few better encapsulations of the spirit of can deism.

FRANKLIN'S EARLY *DISSERTATION*

Between late 1724 and mid-1726, Franklin served as a journeyman to two London printing houses. He left the colonies for England with five years experience in the printing trade under his belt, and entertained high hopes of launching his own firm, first in London and then back in Philadelphia. As it turned out, his professional ambitions remained unrealized for the time being, largely because the promise of financial patronage by Sir William Keith, governor of Pennsylvania, eventually proved empty. But in spite of this disappointment, Franklin's months in London were not wasted. He refined his knowledge of the printing trade, and was introduced to some of the leading British natural philosophers of his day. More important, it was during this London stint that Franklin wrote and published his *Dissertation on Liberty and Necessity, Pleasure and Pain*. This pamphlet, which appeared in 1725, was his first sustained attempt to come to terms with the New Learning's impact upon theological issues. It was also in many respects the most philosophically sophisticated of all his writings, even though he later repudiated it, referring to it ever afterward as one of his early "errata." The *Dissertation* is a curious document. Although based firmly upon the New Learning's principles, it does not fit comfortably into the deistic framework. Its uncompromising advocacy of Newtonian mechanism resulted in the denial of the possibility of human freedom (or "liberty"), a position not at all in keeping with deism's humanistic defense of free will and rational self-determination. But in spite of this and other nondeistic strands, Franklin's *Dissertation* is more akin to the religion of nature's worldview than not, and it is for this reason that it can be viewed (albeit, admittedly, somewhat arbitrarily) as the opening salvo in American deism's attack upon orthodox Christian belief.

The immediate impetus for the *Dissertation* was William Wollaston's *The Religion of Nature Delineated* (1772). During his stay in London, one of the tasks assigned Franklin was the typesetting of the third edition of Wollaston's book for the printing firm of Samuel Palmer. Given the fact that young Franklin had already read defenses of natural religion while still in Philadelphia, he probably had at least a secondhand acquaintance with Wollaston's thesis before sailing to England. But his prolonged study of *The Religion of Nature Delineated* over the printing press was a revelation for the precocious Franklin. Although deeply impressed by Wollaston's systematic defense of the role of natural philosophy in theology, Franklin also took exception to some of its "reasonings." The *Dissertation* was intended as a corrective to Wollaston's conclusions, the fact that Franklin accepted his method as well as basic principles notwithstanding.

Wollaston, like so many other liberal churchmen of the early eighteenth century, sought to strengthen the case for Christianity by appealing to the New Learning of Bacon, Locke, and Newton. His book is an attempt to show that human reason is capable of ascertaining the existence and, to a certain extent, the nature of God by a judicious examination of the insights of natural philosophy. Like Locke, Wollaston regarded reason as the "great law of our nature," and rejected the existence of innate ideas.[5] Along with Bacon and Newton, he also was impressed by the orderly character of physical reality, by the "grandness of this fabric of the world," and by the "chorus of planets moving periodically, by uniform laws."[6] The causal regularity inherent in physical phenomena, as observed by the senses and reflected upon by reason, convinced Wollaston that there must be an explanation for such apparently designed orderliness, and this in turn pointed to the existence of a divine First Cause. "[T]he motions of the planet and the heavenly bodies . . . must be put into motion, either by one Common mighty Mover, acting upon them immediately, or by causes and laws of His Appointment."[7]

For Wollaston, then, the "just and geometrical arrangement of things" reveals to human reason the necessary existence of a just and geometrical Arranger of things. This much can be ascertained by the natural light of reason. But Wollaston was not, after all, a deist; his defense of natural theology was ultimately intended as an apology for Christian belief. Consequently, after having established the reasonableness of belief in the existence of God, he then went on to argue, in keeping with the central tenets of orthodox Christianity, that humans are free agents, mysteriously immune to the network of immutable and deterministic laws that regulate the activity of physical phenomena, and hence are capable of evil actions for which they are morally accountable. For Wollaston, the consequence of these decisions is that human actions on earth will be rewarded or punished in an afterlife, an assumption that extends the "just and symmetrical arrangement of things" from the physical to the normative, spiritual realm.

Now it is precisely these last two points—that humans are free and perform evil actions which will be punished in an afterlife—to which the young Franklin objected. He concurred with Wollaston's naturalistic deduction of God's existence, but obviously decided that Wollaston had lacked either the courage or the insight to follow his mechanistic first assumptions through to their logical conclusions. Had he done so, Franklin believed, he would have avoided slipping into the inconsistent affirmation of free agency and human ethical responsibility. The *Dissertation* was intended to correct these lapses.

In the first part of his treatise, which deals with the issues of "liberty and necessity," Franklin takes on Wollaston's postulation of human free will. He begins by agreeing with Wollaston on the indisputability of two claims: first, that God as the First Mover exists; second, that this deity is "all-wise, all-good, all-powerful." His reasoning follows the usual course of eighteenth-century thought: the first proposition is deducible from reason's discovery that all objects and events necessarily are the consequences of antecedent causes, and the second is self-evident once one understands what the concept God entails. One can quibble with both of these points, and especially the latter. Surely it is not an entailment that if God exists, he necessarily possesses omni-attributes such as the ones Franklin ascribes to him, or even any at all. But these caveats notwithstanding, such are the axioms upon which Franklin builds the *Dissertation's* case.

Although Franklin concurs with Wollaston's fundamental principles, he quickly uses them to move away from the conclusions defended in *The Religion of Nature Delineated*. If the divine First Cause is omniscient, omnibenevolent, and omnipotent, two conclusions, argued Franklin, necessarily follow. The first is that all events that occur in the natural realm are the results, directly or indirectly, of divine will. The second is that all of these events, set in motion as they are by a supremely good deity, are themselves good, since an omnibenevolent God who is also all-knowing and all-powerful is incapable of willing and bringing about acts that are evil. Thus far there is little here that either an eighteenth-century conventional or a liberal Christian would find offensive. Following the traditional Augustinian distinction, orthodox Christian theology of Franklin's day differentiated between acts *willed by God* and acts *permitted* by God. The former are both necessary and good, because of the divine nature of their source. The latter, however, originate from human acts of will. Consequently, they are merely contingent and always fall short, although in varying degrees, of the good. This is because of the intrinsic finitude (or, in Calvinist terms, "depravity") of human abilities. It follows that actions that are properly designated as morally evil exist in the world, but not as a result of divine will. God allows or permits the possibility of such actions by granting humans the boon of free will, but God in no way can be held accountable for them. Thus the doctrine of God's supreme goodness is maintained without sacrificing an acknowledgment of evil in the world.

Franklin denied this traditional Christian position, arguing that it is contrary to the omnipotence as well as omnibenevolence of the Deity. To claim that there are certain events in the physical realm merely allowed but not directly or indirectly willed by God suggests that the First Cause is wanting in power. When these events include evil human actions that do harm to the agent as well as others, the ascription of limited divine power is compounded by a denial of divine omnibenevolence. As Franklin put it,

> If God permits an Action to be done, it is because he wants either Power or *Inclination* to hinder it; in saying he wants Power, we deny Him to be *almighty*; and if we say He wants *Inclination* or *Will*, it must be, either because He is not God, or the Action is not *evil* (for all Evil is contrary to the Essence of *infinite* Goodness).[8]

Two conclusions emerge from this rather startling line of reasoning. In the first place, it follows that every event that occurs in the natural realm is the result of divine power, determined either remotely or immediately by the direction of divine will. This rule applies to human thoughts and actions as well as to the causal relations that define inanimate bodies, because humans, of course, are as much a part of the natural order as objects. This means, in the case of humans, that every action performed by an individual is necessarily determined by divine will, and hence the notion of free agency is illusory. As Franklin says, "if the Creature is thus limited in his Actions, being able to do only such Things as God would have him to do, and not being able to refuse doing what God would have done; then he can have no such Thing as Liberty, Free Will or Power to do or refrain from an Action."[9] Like every other element in reality, humans are irreducibly bound by the divine will as manifested through the "geometrical" arrangement of natural laws and causal relations. Wollaston's ascription of free agency to humans, then violates the very concept of the God he defends.

This denial of free will in humans is radical enough, but the second conclusion Franklin derives from his argument is even more so. If human activities are the direct or indirect consequences of divine will, and if, moreover, all that God wills is necessarily good, then it follows, first, that "there can be neither Merit or Demerit in Creatures," and, second, that

"Evil doth not exist."[10] Individual humans can do no other than what God wills them to do, and consequently questions of moral responsibility are beside the point. Just as the reprobate cannot justly be condemned for his actions, neither can the saint be praised for hers. Both types of behavior are willed by God, and because God is all-powerful, knowing, and good, the behavior of saint and sinner alike is necessarily good. To the limited human intellect, there is, of course, the appearance of a normative distinction between them. But when regarded *sub specie aeternitatus* such distinctions are specious. As Pope would later affirm in his *Essay on Man* and Voltaire lampoon in *Candide*, "all that is is right."

Having to his satisfaction demolished free agency, moral accountability, and the existence of evil, Franklin is still left with the problem of why each of them appears so palpably real in human experience. In the second part of the *Dissertation*, he addresses himself to this puzzle by examining the concepts of "pleasure and pain."

Franklin begins the section by arguing that humans are sentient creatures, capable of experiencing pleasure and pain. The experience of pain is the origin of the psychological phenomenon of desire, which Franklin defines as the wish to either avoid an anticipated state of pain or to escape from an actual one. The strength of the desire, moreover, is directly proportionate to the strength of the anticipated or actual pain. The experience of pleasure, on the other hand, can be defined as nothing more than the realization of desire's object—in other words, the successful avoidance or alleviation of pain. Just as the intensity of one's desires is determined by the extent of one's experience of pain, so the strength of one's pleasure is also proportionate to the extent to which those desires for the cessation of pain have been fulfilled.

Now, Franklin sees the fact of sentience and its accompanying psychological phenomenon of desire as the source of the illusions of free agency, volition, and evil. Humans, he argues, tend to interpret a mere physical fact—pain—as evil, and its absence—pleasure—as good, when in reality these two experiences are entirely nonnormative in character. Moreover, the desire to avoid pain and enhance pleasure deludes individual humans into supposing that they possess free will, since the desire to avoid pain leads to pain-avoidance behavior. But in fact, counters Franklin, the urge to avoid pain is as much a determined response as is the propensity of a solid object to continue in motion until stopped by another solid body. By virtue of the psychobiological laws that govern human behavior—laws, moreover, ordained by the First Cause—humans *must* experience pain and pleasure, and equally must desire to minimize the one and maximize the other. True, humans "act" to attain a state of pleasure, but such action is not at all synonymous with agency. It is nothing more than the predictable motion the human machine displays when pain exerts a causal influence upon it. The behavior of individual humans, then, is completely in the hands of the God of nature, irrevocably regulated by the physical laws he has ordained.

The ultimate moral Franklin derives from this argument against will is not at all a gloomy one—at least in his estimation. God created a world eminently benevolent, just, and reasonable. Evil does not exist, individuals cannot properly be ethically accountable for their actions, and human behavior is as capable of precise scientific explanation as any other natural phenomenon. Moreover, the justice as well as rationality of the divine plan is further emphasized by a final point: the amount of pleasure experienced by an individual is always counterbalanced and ultimately negated by pleasure. If pleasure is the absence of pain, the fundamental human desire for it will be fulfilled by the death of the individual, which brings in its wake a necessary elimination of pain. This is because pain is a product of physical embodiment, and death, of course, eliminates this necessary condition. Since all humans die, all humans are treated equally by the First Cause in the allocation of pleasure and pain. God plays no favorites and eventually ameliorates the pain of even the harshest of lives. Since pleasure and pain are complementary and hence inseparable, and since all living organisms obey the laws of sensation and must therefore endure pain if they are to enjoy pleasure, "no state of life can be happier than the present."[11]

The *Dissertation*'s first section wreaked havoc upon Wollaston's argument that humans are free agents and hence ethically responsible. The second denied Wollaston's additional claim that evil actually exists and will be punished after death. Most damaging of all was Franklin's arrival at these two conclusions by turning Wollaston's first principles (and, by implication, liberal Christianity's) on their head.

Franklin was all-too-aware that his *Dissertation* would most likely be greeted with less than enthusiastic endorsement. His relentlessly mechanistic analysis of reality and the human condition was too brutal a repu-

diation of the cherished beliefs of Christian and Enlightenment human-
ists alike to gain widespread assent. Franklin acknowledged this in a note
at the end of his *Dissertation*, but did so in a manner ill-calculated to mol-
lify his detractors:

> I am sensible that the Doctrine here advanc'd, if it were to be publish'd,
> would meet with but an indifferent Reception. Mankind naturally and
> generally love to be flatter'd: Whatever soothes our Pride and tends to
> exalt our Species above the rest of the Creation, we are pleas'd with and
> easily believe, when ungrateful Truths shall be with the utmost Indig-
> nation rejected. "What! bring ourselves down to an Equality with
> Beasts of the Field! with the *meanest* part of the Creation! 'Tis insuffer-
> able!" But, (to use a Piece of *common* Sense) our *Geese* are but *Geese* tho'
> we may think 'em Swans; and Truth will be Truth tho' it sometimes
> prove mortifying and distasteful.[12]

It is difficult to know just how seriously Franklin meant his *Dissertation* to be taken. Seen from one perspective, it is a striking *reductio ad
absurdum* of the mechanistic worldview endorsed by the liberal theologians of the day, and could be interpreted as a marvelous parody of the
all-too-earnest attempts by Franklin's contemporaries to categorize and
explain reality in Newtonian terms. Franklin was blessed with an exuberant sense of humor as well as a genuine talent for satire, and it is
entirely possible to see his *Dissertation* as an elaborate practical joke.

On the other hand, there is more reason to think that Franklin was
deadly earnest in his defense of the bleak cosmic machine portrayed in the
Dissertation. His youthful reading had already inclined him toward an
enthusiastic agreement with Newtonian natural philosophy, and even
though his initial zeal would be tempered in later years, his allegiance to
mechanism was never forsaken. Moreover, it is difficult to imagine that a
precocious nineteen-year-old's first significant venture into print would
have been intended as a subtle joke. A prankster Franklin was and would
remain, but he usually approached religious matters with a seriousness that
many of his youthful companions (as he tells us in the *Autobiography*) found
exasperatingly priggish. Finally, as mentioned earlier, Franklin soon
regretted his publication of the *Dissertation*, fearing that its denial of free
will and moral accountability would serve as legitimations for license, and
expended some effort in trying to recover the copies that were printed. It

is true, of course, that Franklin could equally well have come to regret the *Dissertation* if he had intended it as a prank, seeing it as a joke gone sour. But in his references to it in later life, he never gives any indication that his purpose in writing it was anything more than to push the Newtonian worldview to its logical conclusions, regardless of where the enterprise took him.

As a piece of philosophical reasoning, the *Dissertation* is of questionable merit. If one accepts Franklin's premises, the arguments that flow from them are coherent enough. But the problem is that the premises, grounded as they are in a rather rigid mechanism, are themselves dubious. From a metaphysical perspective, it is not at all obvious that God's omnipotence is in any way threatened by the possibility that he "permits" rather than directly "wills" certain events in the natural realm. Moreover, Franklin's denial of the existence of evil as a consequence of God's omnipotence and omnibenevolence possesses the weakness that any attempt at a theogony does: it appears to dissolve by contrived argumentation a nonetheless palpably obvious facet of human experience.

His psychological analysis of sentience is likewise problematic. Even if it is granted that human behavior is ultimately explicable in terms of pain-avoidance and pleasure-enhancement, it does not follow that pleasure is simply the absence of pain, much less that the insensibility of death, the ultimate end of the possibility of pain, is the goal toward which the desire for pleasure is logically directed. To assume that pleasure is nothing more than freedom from pain tends to simplify the concept of pleasure in a way that renders it conceptually arid and psychologically counterintuitive. It posits a mechanistic account of human nature that portrays the individual as a piston-driven automaton, bereft of subjectivity and functional complexity. It may well be that such a psychology is the logical consequence of the mechanistic worldview (although Newton himself would have been horrified at the idea), but it fails to reflect the observable richness of human experience.

For all its questionable philosophy, however, the *Dissertation* does illuminate at least two revealing points about Franklin as a religious thinker. First, it shows how impressed he was by the temperament and direction of Enlightenment New Learning. From first to last, the *Dissertation*'s analysis of both reality and human nature is filtered through the mechanistic assumptions canonized by eighteenth-century natural philosophy. In fact,

Franklin's early fidelity to this mechanistic model is so zealous that his thought at this time more closely resembles the later atheistic materialism of a d'Holbach, Condorcet, or La Mettrie than the softened mechanism of the American deists. Franklin's eventual realization that he had come as perilously close to atheism as he did undoubtedly was one of the factors that prompted him to pull away from the *Dissertation*'s denial of free will and evil.

Second, and more significant within the context of this study, the *Dissertation*'s line of argumentation underscores the element of ambivalence in Franklin's religious thought. On the one hand, Franklin's denial of free agency and moral accountability indicates just how far he had strayed from his "pious" background. It is not only a repudiation of the "Presbyterian way" in which he was raised, but of liberal Christianity's attempts to marry the New Learning with revealed theology. On the other hand, it is too much to say, as one recent commentator does, that Franklin's *Dissertation* "marks a drastic break with his Puritan past."[13] Elements within the treatise smack of the Calvinist background whence he came, even though they are couched in the jargon of eighteenth-century natural philosophy. Most obvious is the resemblance between Calvinism's doctrine of predestination and the *Dissertation*'s denial of free agency on the part of human beings. A less obvious but not unreasonable connection can be drawn between Franklin's insistence that humans are incapable of rising above the laws of sensation that necessarily define and control their behavior, and the traditional Calvinist ascription of utter depravity to humans, which prevents them from overcoming the theologically defined boundaries laid down by original sin. Finally, there is an obvious similarity between the *Dissertation*'s insistence that God is supremely powerful, willing each and every event in the physical realm, and the typically monarchical concept of God preached by Calvinist divines.

The point is not that Franklin deliberately attempted to write a natural philosophy which would accommodate itself to Calvinist doctrine. He obviously retained no conscious allegiance to the Presbyterianism of his boyhood by the time he penned his response to Wollaston. Instead, the claim is that an excavation of Franklin's *Dissertation* exposes two intertwined layers of influence: the predominant one of Newtonian mechanism, and the less recognizable but more ancient one of his

Calvinist background. From such an archaeological perspective, then, the *Dissertation* is an intriguing combination of two different cultures. One culture, the Enlightenment worldview, displays an extremism that shows it to be almost desperately trying to break with its predecessor, the Calvinist tradition. Yet remnants of the earlier worldview nonetheless emerge in the newer one, albeit in subtly shaded guises. In short, the *Dissertation* reveals itself as a document whose ambivalence reflects the intellectual clash in Franklin's own mind.

It might be objected that the case for ambivalence in Franklin's *Dissertation* has been overdone. After all, Continental *philosophes*, who were hardly born and nurtured in a Calvinist setting, were likewise to reject the notion of free agency in their later defenses of radical materialism. Surely (the objection might continue), it is possible to arrive at a cosmological position that shows a vague resemblance to certain features of Calvinist doctrine without actually incorporating Calvinist influences.

This objection is a reasonable one, but it does no serious damage to the claim defended here that Franklin's *Dissertation* can be read as an amalgamation of Enlightenment and Calvinist elements. First, unlike *philosophes* on the Continent such as d'Holbach and La Mettrie, Franklin in fact did come from an ethos in which Calvinism was firmly entrenched, and it is too much to suppose that his subsequent religious thought would reveal no vestiges of this early environment. Second, and more important, Franklin's *Dissertation* cannot be read in isolation from his later religious writings. When measured against them, one discerns a pattern of ambivalence in the 1725 treatise that emerges again and again in his subsequent reflections on religion. As we shall see in later sections, this continuing pattern of ambivalence reveals itself in two ways. First, Franklin quickly retreated from the coldly mechanistic worldview he defended in the *Dissertation*, ameliorating his original position to accommodate—and, indeed, stress—both human agency and moral accountability. Second, even though he retained his belief in the Enlightenment and deistic concept of a supremely rational First Cause who set in motion a clockwork-like universe governed by immutable natural laws, he also allowed for the possibility of "special providences," or direct interventions in the natural scheme of things by an all-powerful deity. As is the case with his early *Dissertation*, Franklin's subsequent thought on nature and nature's God was pulled back and forth between the competing allures of the two cultures that shaped him. As a consequence, it cannot be classified as either typically deistic or typically Calvinist. Instead, it is an amalgamation of elements from both, although in attitude and fundamental principles it leans more toward the religion of reason than toward the theology of Calvin.

FRANKLIN'S "ARTICLES OF BELIEF"

Two features of Franklin's early *Dissertation* especially strike the reader. One is stylistic and the other philosophical. The first is the air of absolute confidence that surrounds Franklin's defense of his arguments. Although the document is at least in part a testament to the essential ambivalence of Franklin's religious thought, its style of presentation gives the distinct impression that the author is completely certain of his position, and that nothing important about either nature or nature's God remains to be said. In addition, from a philosophical perspective, the *Dissertation*'s total deflation of both the meaning and the importance of ethical discourse is almost overwhelming. Evil does not exist, humans do not exercise free will, and the concept of moral accountability is an illusion—period.

Although the *Dissertation* thus appears written in stone, Franklin quickly began to doubt the validity of his own arguments. Suspicions arose, perhaps even as he was finishing his 1725 treatise, that the issues with which it dealt weren't quite as black and white as he had thought. The *Dissertation*, after all, tended to arrive at conclusions that were more distressing than illuminating. The God it defended was distant and unapproachable; the psychology it posited reduced humans to the level of one-dimensional automata; and its manhandling of the problem of good and evil trivialized not only the everyday human experience of value but also the worth and dignity of individual aspirations. Perhaps, contrary to the *Dissertation*'s pristine but lifeless model, reality—divine as well as human—was more complicated than Franklin had initially assumed. Geese are geese even "tho' we may think 'em Swans," but this "Piece of common sense" doesn't rule out the possibility that swans are likewise swans, even though we occasionally mistake them for geese.

By 1728, Franklin had rethought his earlier position and significantly modified it to make room for the swans. Returning to Philadelphia in 1726, he began an on-and-off attendance at various Presbyterian churches, trying to come to grips with his growing dissatisfaction with the *Dissertation*'s mechanistic thesis. He seems to have reexplored the central tenets of Christian orthodoxy in hopes of once again discovering the piety of his youth. But such a return was impossible. Unhappy as he was over his reduction of religion to Newtonian mechanics, he was even more "disgusted" (as he tells us in the *Autobiography*) with the dogmatically sectarian and supernaturalist tenets of Calvinism he encountered in Philadelphia's churches. He realized, as Tom Paine and Thomas Jefferson would later, that he could not in good conscience acquiesce to the creed of any conventional denomination, and that henceforth his theologizing would have to be based upon private reflections and individual seeking rather than on public creeds and statements of belief. In order to systematize his new insights as well as provide himself with a guide for personal worship, he penned in 1728 a memorandum titled "Articles of Belief and Acts of Religion." It is the catechism of a man who has renounced orthodox Christianity as well as dogmatic materialism.

As its title indicates, this new attempt on the part of the mercurial Franklin to make sense of religious issues is divided into two parts. The second, which is intended as a liturgical guide for the private worship of nature's God, need not concern us here. It is in places a strikingly beautiful service, incorporating mellifluous petitions to the God of reason as well as selections from Milton's poetry, but it sheds no additional light upon Franklin's philosophical reformulation of his concept of God. It is the first part of the document, the "Articles of Belief," to which we must turn for that.

Franklin's "Articles of Belief" comprises a number of "First Principles" that summarize his post-*Dissertation* reflections on both the Deity and human nature. These principles are worth quoting at some length.

> I Believe there is one Supreme most perfect Being, Author and Father of the Gods themselves.
>
> For I believe that Man is not the most perfect Being but One, rather that as there are many Degrees of Beings his Inferiors, so there are many Degrees of Beings superior to him.
>
> Also, when I stretch my imagination thro' and beyond our System

of Planets, beyond the visible fix'd Stars themselves, into that Space that is every Way Infinite, and conceive it fill'd with Suns like ours, each with a Chorus of Worlds for ever moving round him, then this little Ball on which we move, seems, even in my narrow Imagination, to be almost Nothing, and my self less than nothing, and of no sort of Consequence.

When I think thus, I imagine it great Vanity in me to suppose that the *Supremely Perfect*, does in the least regard such an inconsiderable Nothing as Man. More especially, since it is impossible for me to have any positive clear Idea of that which is infinite and incomprehensible, I cannot conceive otherwise, than that He, the *infinite Father*, expects or requires no worship or Praise from us, but that he is even INFINITELY ABOVE IT.

But since there is in all Men something like a natural Principle which inclines them to DEVOTION or the Worship of some unseen power;

And since Men are endued with Reason superior to all other Animals that we are in our World acquainted with;

Therefore I think it seems required of me, and my Duty, as a Man, to pay Divine Regards to SOMETHING.

I CONCEIVE then, that the INFINITE has created many Beings or Gods, vastly superior to Man, who can better conceive his Perfections than we, and return him a more rational and glorious Praise. As among Men, the Praise of the Ignorant or of Children, is not regarded by the ingenious Painter or Architect, who is honour'd and pleas'd with the Approbation of Wise men and Artists.

It may be that these created Gods, are immortal, or it may be that after many Ages, they are changed, and Others supply their Places.

Howbeit, I conceive that each of these is exceeding wise, and good, and very powerful; and that Each has made for himself, one glorious Sun, attended with a beautiful and admirable System of Planets.

It is that particular wise and good God, who is the Author and Owner of our System, that I propose for the Object of my Praise and Adoration.

For I conceive that he has in himself some of those Passions he has planted in us, and that, since he has given us Reason whereby we are capable of observing his Wisdom in the Creation, he is not above caring for us, being pleas'd with our Praise, and offended when we slight Him, or neglect his Glory.

I conceive for many Reasons that he is a *good Being*, and as I should be happy to have so wise, good and powerful a Being my Friend, let me consider in what Manner I shall make myself most acceptable to him.

Next to the Praise due to his Wisdom, I believe he is pleased and delights in the Happiness of those he has created; and since without Virtue Man can have no Happiness in this World, I firmly believe he delights to see me Virtuous, because he is pleas'd when he sees me Happy.

And since he has created many Things which seem purely design'd for the Delight of Man, I believe he is not offended when he sees his Children solace themselves in any manner of pleasant Exercises and innocent Delights, and I think no Pleasure innocent that is to Man hurtful.

I *love* him therefore for his Goodness and I *adore* him for his Wisdom.[14]

What a strange and densely compacted statement of belief! In the entire history of American deism, there is no other treatise that can match either its ambiguity or, in my estimation, its depth. These few lines contain a sketch of not only a striking religious perspective but an entire metaphysics as well, and vividly illustrate how far Franklin had wandered in just three years from the rather simplistic worldview of the *Dissertation*. The "Articles of Belief" does not renounce Franklin's fundamental faith in a mechanistic worldview, but it does extend as well as enrich the abstract, sterile model he defended in 1725.

Franklin's credo in the "Articles of Belief" can be reduced to three basic postulates. First, he accepts the existence of an all-perfect Being, the Supremely Infinite, the First Cause of existence itself, which serves as the necessary condition for all of reality. Even though he uses personal pronouns on two occasions in referring to this Supreme Principle, it is clear that Franklin attaches no literal significance to them. The Supremely Infinite that grounds reality is even more distant and inaccessible than the *Dissertation*'s First Cause. It is entirely nonanthropomorphic, "infinite," and therefore rationally "incomprehensible," completely beyond the conceptual reach and affections of puny human striving. Moreover, this First Principle, although all-powerful, does not appear to be omnibenevolent. Franklin carefully avoids using any expression in his credo that would imply otherwise. On the contrary, he suggests that the Supremely Infinite is totally indifferent to human affairs, "infinitely above" the realm of human longing, and consequently "expects or requires no Worship or Praise from us." This indifference to humans on the part of the One Supreme—and perhaps even unawareness of them—is appropriate even if somewhat disconcerting, for by comparison the human race is "almost nothing" and the individual "less than nothing."

The aloof impersonality of Franklin's source of Being is somewhat ameliorated, however, by the second postulate of the "Articles." Franklin tells us that there exists a hierarchy of reality, a great chain of Being, in which humans occupy a middle position. Just as there are beings "inferior" to humans in this hierarchy, so there are also beings that are superior. These latter he describes as "the Gods themselves," each of whom seems to be associated with either a specific "world" or a system of worlds, and who serves as the intermediary between humans and the Supremely Infinite. These higher "Beings or Gods," "vastly superior to Man" as they are, can better conceive of and revere the supreme perfection of the First Principle, and hence are able to bestow upon It "rational and glorious Praise." Humans, incapable of fathoming or loving the Supremely Infinite, properly direct their devotions not to It but to "those created Gods" to whom they can relate to at least some degree. Franklin is unsure whether the divine intermediaries are immortal or temporal, but he does believe that each is "exceeding wise, and good, and very powerful."

Finally, Franklin tells us that, given the inaccessibility of the one Supremely Infinite, he will fix his attention upon the particular wise and good God "who is the Author and Owner of our System." This deity, although vastly superior to humans, is neither inaccessible nor indifferent. As the direct cause of the earth as well as its human inhabitants, this God shares, at least to some extent, in the "Passions" and "Reason" with which he has endowed humanity. Consequently, he reciprocates love, promotes human well-being, and desires that his worshippers enjoy happiness and personal fulfillment. Since virtue is the surest route to happiness available to humans, it follows that the "particular wise and good God" who rules terra firma is most pleased when humans pursue virtuous lives. Given the intimacy of his relationship to and concern for creation, this God is a proper object of human love and adoration, unlike the Supremely Infinite, which at best evokes only a dumbfounded awe.

There is obviously a multitude of ways to interpret such a richly nuanced statement of belief as this. One approach is to take Franklin at his word and read the "Articles of Belief" literally. From this perspective, the model of reality sketched by Franklin is akin to the three-tiered one defended by Plato in the *Timaeus*. In this dialogue, Plato distinguishes between three levels of reality: the undifferentiated One (or Demiurge), from whose erotic creativity emanate the lesser gods as well as the physical and human world over which the lesser gods rule. These intermediate gods of the *Timaeus* are capable of being conceptualized by human reason, but the Demiurge from whose infinite wellsprings they and all else emerge is itself unknowable. It is a matter of debate as to how literally Plato intended his description of reality to be taken, although it is reasonable to presume that the story is best interpreted as an exercise in mythopoesis. Nevertheless, Plato's *Timaeus* can be read in a literal manner as an argument for polytheism; and so, obviously, can Franklin's "Articles of Belief." At least one twentieth-century commentator on Franklin's religion has defended precisely such an approach.[15]

But there is another way to interpret Franklin's curious 1728 credo, one that is less bizarre than the plurality-of-gods thesis and more in keeping with both Enlightenment thought and Franklin's temperament. This interpretation hinges on the assumption that Franklin took the intermediate Gods to whom humans pray to be cultural symbols— metaphorical expressions of the human intuition of the divine.

For all his religious ambivalence, Franklin was too firmly ensconced in the New Learning of the eighteenth century to forsake the concept of deity as an all-powerful First Cause. This is the vision of God he defended in the *Dissertation*, and he retained it in his "Articles of Belief" under the guise of the Supremely Infinite. The abandonment of this source of universal rationality would have destroyed, in Franklin's judgment, the possibility of natural law as well as violated common experiences of uniformity in the phenomenal realm. But Franklin was also aware that such a deity is too impersonal, too far removed from the flesh-and-blood arena of human existence, to serve as either the locus for religious love and adoration or as a psychological inducement to virtue. The extreme conclusion to which he had pushed mechanism in the *Dissertation* had convinced him of that. Consequently, he sought a way to make the divine First Cause more approachable, and settled in the "Articles" on the strategy of humanizing the Supremely Infinite by invoking cultural expressions of it as the proper locus of human worship.

Finite human reason cannot fathom the infinite, incomprehensible nature of the First Cause, but this does not mean that there is no possibility of contact. Symbolic substitutes, which emerge from and help to define historical and cultural contexts, religious traditions, theological speculations, and popular modes of spirituality, are human attempts to think the unthinkable, to grasp the unattainable. The "natural inclination" to devotion in the human soul guarantees that these sometimes faltering efforts to symbolically represent the inconceivable First Principle continuously reappear throughout the ages, despite the fact that the particular metaphors each attempt employs are historically contingent. Consequently, the Gods whom humans worship are both "immortal" and temporal. Moreover, because all such representations are human attempts to give expression to the divine, they are more accessible to the mind and comforting to the heart than the aloof Supremely Infinite, and hence soothe the human spirit as well as encourage virtue. But because these symbolic representations are founded in and motivated by an intuition of the Supremely Infinite's existence, they are not simply fabrications. Like all symbolic constructs, they stand for and shed light upon something other than themselves. They are not accurate descriptions, but neither are they totally illusory.

Franklin's "Articles of Belief," then, can be read as positing the existence of a "God above the gods," an indefinable ground or source of Being that cannot be conceptualized, imaged, or affectively related to by humans except through the intermediation of historically conditioned symbolic representations. This model is reminiscent of Pascal's seventeenth-century distinction between the god of the philosophers and the god of Abraham, Isaac, and Jacob, and strikingly anticipates the existential theology of twentieth-century thinkers such as Karl Jaspers and Paul Tillich.[16]

It is, of course, impossible to say exactly what Franklin actually had in mind in penning his "Articles of Belief." Perhaps even he was not quite sure what he was up to. But the interpretation suggested here has at least a ring of plausibility, especially when weighed against the unlikely alternative that Franklin actually accepted a version of metaphysical polytheism. There are at least three reasons to think that this interpretation of Franklin's credo is an acceptable one.

In the first place, we have already seen Franklin's growing realization that the mechanistic concept of deity defended in the *Dissertation* is religiously suspect because of its impersonality. In addition, we have seen that he was unwilling to forego such a foundation for both nature and nature's laws. Although he came to believe that the physical order was more complex and multifaceted than he had earlier envisioned it, Franklin remained convinced that an almost aesthetically simple pattern of divinely decreed causal relations served as reality's template, and this conviction only underscored his fundamental belief in the existence of an impassible First Cause. Given his certainty that reality is fundamentally defined by a mathematically simple system of natural laws, it is difficult to believe that he would have muddied the cosmic waters by the postulation of a literal plurality of gods. It is much more reasonable to assume that his discussion of Gods in the "Articles of Belief" refers to the culturally defined expressions of the absolute source of Being adopted by various spiritual communities.

Second, this distinction between the god of natural philosophy and the symbolic gods of religious traditions performs an obvious practical function. It enables humans to relate in meaningful ways to the ultimate source of reality, and to derive from such a relationship the obvious psychological benefits that Franklin had implicitly trivialized in his *Dissertation*, without sacrificing the scientific model of a universe governed by immutable natural laws. In addition, the culturally bound symbolizations of the Supremely Infinite as a loving and benevolent deity encouraged virtuous behavior that Franklin, as we shall shortly see, had come to regard as the necessary condition for individual felicity as well as social progress. In short, there is a great deal of utility in metaphorically thinking about the Deity in such a way as to provide an outlet for the innate inclination to devotion in humans and to promote the exercise of virtue. Franklin, like all Enlightenment savants, was a confirmed believer in the eighteenth-century dictum that knowledge is properly evaluated by the degree of its practical benefits, and the utility of a religious model that spoke to the affections as well as to reason had been one of the hard-earned lessons of his *Dissertation*.

Finally, as we shall examine in greater detail later, one of the mainstays of Franklin's religious thought was a deeply engrained respect for spiritual pluralism as well as an often eloquent championship of universal religious tolerance. Obviously part of this attitude can be attributed to the fact that Franklin was dissatisfied with the conventional sectarian creeds of his day;

he realized that none of them had the monopoly on religious truth that they claimed. But it also seems to be the case that his respect for religious diversity stemmed from the belief that there are many routes to the divine, and that all of them, regardless of the particular metaphors and symbols that they employed in their attempts to understand the divine, had something to teach the sincere inquirer. From a cultural perspective, then, it makes complete sense to speak of a plurality of Gods, if one means by that term the multitude of denominational and traditional ways of expressing the intuition of the indefinable and incomprehensible source of Being.

Franklin's "Articles of Belief," then, can be seen as a remarkable compromise between his acceptance of the mechanistic god of the Enlightenment and his appreciation of the fact that a meaningful religious sensibility demands that the ways in which people think about God be psychologically fulfilling. The "Articles" represents, therefore, a watershed in Franklin's lifelong effort to steer a course between orthodox Christian belief and the discoveries of natural philosophy. In his later ruminations upon religion, he would never again return to the exact approach employed in the "Articles," but its influence is obvious. After 1728, he returned to the deism that had captivated him as a teenager, but did so less dogmatically and with a heightened sensitivity to both the ethical and the psychological dimensions of religious belief. It is not surprising that he never in later life recalled his early *Dissertation* without embarrassment and regret.

SPECIAL PROVIDENCES

By 1731, Franklin had worked through his religious ambivalence to the point where he was able to affirm a moderate deism that adhered to the basics of Newtonianism while avoiding the mechanistic reductionism of the *Dissertation*. Shortly after penning his "Articles of Belief," he scribbled a short memorandum to himself sketching the contents of a "Doct. to be Prea[che]d."[17] This outline echoed the "Articles" in its acceptance of "one God Father of the Universe" who is "infinitely good, Powerful and wise," but omitted mention of the earlier document's "Gods" thesis.

Moreover, the "Doct. to be Prea[che]d," in typical deistic fashion, insisted on the primacy of reason and virtue in religious sentiment. Its final three points affirmed that "knowledge and learning is to be cultivated, and Ignorance dissipated," that "none but the Virtuous are wise," and "Man's Perfection is Virtue." These propositions foreshadow what would become a keynote in most of Franklin's subsequent religious musings: the conviction that virtue is the highest form of worship, and that moral/religious perfection has as its necessary condition the exercise of reason.

But even though Franklin settled in his late twenties on the deistic position that he would hold for the rest of his life, he nonetheless clung to at least one theological holdover from his Calvinist background: a belief in the possibility of "special providences." A staple of deism's religion of nature was that the Deity serves as reality's distant First Cause, setting in motion the network of rational and immutable laws that govern and regulate physical phenomena. For most American deists, this tenet was interpreted to mean that the Deity either cannot interfere or freely refrains from interfering with the necessary operations of these laws, lest their immutability and uniformity be violated. Consequently, the Calvinist doctrine of special providences, or the miraculous interference with either historical or natural events by the divine, was rejected. The American deists did not deny that God's providential presence was observable in nature, but insisted that it was identical to the system of physical laws that irrevocably governed the physical realm and served as the basis of natural philosophy.

Franklin, however, disagreed. Although affirming that reality is governed by natural laws, he also argued that the Deity is capable of overturning or even reversing them upon occasion. In a manuscript titled "On the Providence of God in the Government of the World," written in 1732 and intended as a draft of a speech to be delivered to his "Pot Companions" of the Junto Society, Franklin undertook to defend the thesis that God "sometimes interferes by his particular Providence and sets aside the Effects which would otherwise have been produced by [natural] Causes."[18] Such a thesis, Franklin insisted, was consistent "with the common Light of Reason." It relied upon neither scriptural authority nor theological speculation, but instead was demonstrable through an analysis of the concept of God.

It will be recalled that in the 1725 *Dissertation*, Franklin had based his denial of free will and his affirmation of an irreversibly deterministic universe upon the assumption that God necessarily possesses the unlimited attributes of omnipotence and omnibenevolence. It followed, then, that "all that is, is right," and that neither free agency nor evil were either possible or actual. But we have seen that Franklin quickly retreated from these two postulates on the grounds that they violated ordinary experience and militated against the cultivation of virtue. In "On Providence," he retains the belief that God is omnibenevolent and omnipotent, but now affirms that humans possess free will and hence are capable of contemplating and performing acts that do harm to themselves and others. Given this change in his attitude toward the reality of evil, Franklin reversed his earlier position by claiming in "On Providence" that God's nature entails that he is both able and willing to interfere with creation in special circumstances:

> If God does not sometimes interfere by his Providence 'tis either because he cannot, or because he will not; which of these Positions will you choose?
>
> There is a righteous Nation grievously oppress'd by a cruel Tyrant, they earnestly entreat God to deliver them; If you say he cannot, you deny his infinite Power, which at first [you] acknowledg'd; if you say he will not, you most directly deny his infinite Goodness. You are then of necessity oblig'd to allow, that 'tis highly reasonable to believe a Providence because 'tis highly absurd to believe otherwise.[19]

This is quite a reversal of the position defended by Franklin in his *Dissertation*, and it once again underscores his religious ambivalence. He is committed to deism's concept of God as First Cause and sustainer of a rational world order, as well as the notion that God's nature is best discovered through the "common Light of Reason." But at the same time, he is unable to go along with the deistic denial of special providences, fearful that such a conclusion would do violence to the concepts of divine omnipotence and omnibenevolence. It is not implausible to suppose that a good part of the tension obvious in this position stems from Franklin's reawakened appreciation of the ever-present reality of human evil, and such a notion has clear affinities with the Calvinist insistence upon the essential moral depravity of man, as well as the doctrine of divine grace. For all his fidelity to the Enlightenment ideals of individual and social progress, as well as his faith in the possibility of self-improvement, Franklin never endorsed the rather rosy humanism advocated by later American deists. In his eyes, there was a dark underbelly to human nature that demanded the possibility of divine intervention in the affairs of men.

Inconsistent with his deistic sympathies as it was, Franklin never renounced his belief in the possibility of special providences, nor his insistence that the belief was based upon a rational appraisal of divine nature rather than theological authority. As late as 1790, he reaffirmed his position in a letter to Ezra Stiles, president of Yale College.[20] Franklin traveled a long and hard path in his search for a religious perspective. He had started his journey in a "Pious" Presbyterian household, moved to an enthusiasm for deism while still a teenager, passed through the dogmatic stage of the *Dissertation*, and finally arrived in the 1730s at the more moderate form of deism he would endorse for the rest of his life. But even after his religious thought had matured into a rational acceptance of the religion of nature, he was unable to renounce completely his Calvinist background. The ambivalence remained, even if the years somewhat softened its earlier, more blatant, inconsistencies.

CULTIVATING VIRTUE

At about the time that young Benjamin Franklin was converted to the religion of nature by his study of antideistic tracts, he published the "Dogood Papers" in his brother James's paper, the *New-England Courant*.[21] This series of essays, supposedly written by one Silence Dogood, a sharp-eyed but quaint Boston goodwife, contained satiric barbs at both Calvinist orthodoxy and social mores. Its immediate impetus was Cotton Mather's *Essays to Do Good*, a rather smug handbook intended to provide its readers with a set of easily remembered tips for the practice of virtuous (and Christian) behavior.[22] Mistress Dogood is a fictional embodiment of the busybodiness and mean-spiritedness that Franklin saw underlying Mather's sanctimonious moralizing. In attacking what he perceived to be the overweening smugness of Mather's approach, Franklin succeeded in slamming conventional wisdom and outraging a good segment of Boston's citizenry—to such an extent, in fact, that one of his reasons for moving to Philadelphia in 1723 was to escape unpleasant repercussions.

It is appropriate that Franklin's first journalistic adventure should have revolved around the issue of virtue, for it was a subject that intrigued him for the rest of his life. Although the Dogood articles clearly demonstrated his dissatisfaction with Calvinist-inspired moralizing, they also expressed the young Franklin's conviction that questions of good and evil were of grave importance. Although he lost sight of this conviction in the *Dissertation*, the lapse was short-lived. Beginning with his "Articles of Belief and Acts of Religion," Franklin returned to his earlier interest in ethical matters, and eventually arrived at the conclusion that a virtuous life was synonymous with a religious one. This equation was accepted by all the American deists. As we shall see in subsequent chapters, two of them—Thomas Jefferson and Elihu Palmer—devoted a great deal of thought to ethical theory. But it fell to Franklin to concern himself especially with the cultivation of virtue rather than its philosophical analysis.

This interest in the nurturing and practical application of virtue stemmed in part from the very treatise he had so gleefully derided in the "Dogood Papers." Mather's *Essays to Do Good*, although at times insufferably self-righteous, at least had the good sense to stress the practical benefits of virtuous behavior, and it was this lesson that stuck with Franklin. As he confessed years later, his reading of Mather's book "gave me such a turn of thinking, as to have an influence on my conduct through life; for I have always set a greater value on the character of a doer of good, than any other kind of reputation; and if I have been . . . a useful citizen, the public owes the advantage of it to that book."[23]

That Franklin was early on impressed with the importance of being a "doer of good" rather than merely speculating about it, is evidenced in his "Articles of Belief," in which he asserts that "without Virtue Man can have no Happiness in this World." But it was not until the mid-1730s that he began to reflect in earnest upon just what happiness and virtue might be. In a short piece that appeared anonymously in 1735 in the *Pennsylvania Gazette*, Franklin argued that whatever virtue is, it is "not secure, till its Practice [becomes] a Habitude, and [is] free from the Opposition of contrary inclination." By "habitude," Franklin meant the concrete and consistent application of moral injunctions in everyday life. He denied that what designates action as good or evil is merely motivation or "inclination," arguing instead that the ultimate criterion for ethical appraisal is the action itself. As Franklin rhetorically asked, "If a Man does me a Service from a natural benevolent Inclination, does he deserve less of me than another who does me the like Kindness against his Inclination?"[24] For Franklin, the answer was obvious:

> The Truth is, that Temperance, Justice, Charity, &c. are Virtues, whether practis'd with or against our Inclination; and the Man who practises them, merits our Love and Esteem: And Self-denial [or any other motivation] is neither good nor bad, but as 'tis apply'd.[25]

The moral life, then, is rigorously practical in nature, not contemplative, and the dividing line between the good individual and the evil one is not intention so much as actual practice. Moreover, as Franklin had already decided in his "Articles of Belief," the Deity "delights to see [humans] Virtuous." Virtuous behavior, consequently, is the route to both religious sensibility and personal integrity, and it must be practiced in such as way as to become a "habitude." A virtuous person is not one who contemplates the good so much as one who performs it in the course of his life.

But what, then, is virtue? According to Franklin, it is "the Knowledge of our *true Interest*; that is, of what is best to be done in all the Circumstances of Humane Life, in order to arrive at our main End in View, *Happiness*."[26] And what are the "true interests" of humans that, when recognized and pursued, lead to the achievement of happiness? Reason provides us with the answer, responds Franklin. True interests consist in "having a Sound Mind and a Healthy Body, a Sufficiency of the Necessaries and Conveniencies of Life, together with the Favour of God, and the love of Mankind."[27] These are mankind's true interests because they reflect natural needs, which require fulfillment for humans to thrive. In acting to fulfill these needs, the individual accomplishes three goals. First, he satisfies the necessary condition for a rational and healthy existence, free from the burdens of either economic want or psychological distress. Second, he acts in such a way as to promote the well-being of his fellow humans, since the individual's opportunities for an enhanced existence are inseparably bound up with the degree to which society approves of him and admires him. The "Love of Mankind," as Franklin said, is not merely a luxury. It is more significantly a natural need that the individual disdains at great cost to himself. In seeking to earn the esteem of society, then, the virtuous individual serves both himself and others well. Finally, the fulfillment of natural needs by a rational pursuit of one's true interests is pleasing to the Deity, who "delights in the Happiness of those he has created."[28] There are two reasons why God desires that humans achieve their true interests. The first is that God is benevolent, and so from the necessity of his divine nature "is pleased" by the well-being of humans. The second is that such behavior on the part of humans best mirrors divine nature, the imprint of which is stamped upon the human heart as well as upon all of physical reality. The pursuit of true interests is rational—as Franklin says, "none but the Virtuous are Wise"[29]—and thereby reflects divine rationality. This last point is one of the primary reasons why Franklin as well as all the other American deists insisted that the highest, most noble form of worship is the exercise of virtue. What better way to demonstrate one's reverence and adoration of the divine than to strive to emulate its nature?

For Franklin, then, virtue consists in pursuing what is genuinely in our best, "true" interests: the satisfaction of natural needs. In doing so, the individual not only ensures his or her own happiness; he or she also necessarily improves the lot of others, either through example or actual aid, and in the process pays homage to the Deity by cooperating in the rational cosmic scheme designed by him. This analysis of virtue and happiness, it should be noted, is based upon a naturalistic foundation. Franklin derives his notion of true interests from a consideration of natural needs, not from a divine command model or a set of supposedly revealed scriptural injunctions. It is true that the ultimate source of these natural needs of humans is the physical order designed and created by God, but this in no way entails that Franklin's concept of virtue is theocentric. The human pursuit of true interests is pleasing to the Deity because it is virtuous, and not virtuous because it is approved of by God.

As already indicated, Franklin was convinced that "mere speculative Conviction" was not by itself enough to lead to that "uniform Rectitude of Conduct" necessary for both virtue and happiness.[30] What is essential is that the aspirant habituate himself to the practice of virtue such that his ostensible behavior is directed toward the realization of his true interests, even if his inclination pulls him in an opposite direction. To this end, Franklin devised a method for the "art of virtue." He initially experimented with strategies to promote virtuous "habitude" for the purposes of "self-examination" and improvement, but quickly came to the realization that others could profit from his observations. One of Franklin's pet schemes was to write up his method in a booklet to be titled *The Art of Virtue*; he hoped a perusal of it would "be serviceable to people in all religions." He never actually got around to composing the treatise, but he did describe his method for the cultivation of virtue in one of the *Autobiography*'s best-known sections.[31]

Franklin's method revolved around a set of behavioral drills designed to help the practitioner "acquire the *Habitude* . . . of virtues." He settled upon thirteen qualities he considered essential to the good life: temperance, silence, order, resolution, frugality, industry, sincerity, justice, moderation, cleanliness, tranquility, chastity, and humility. Then he devoted a week to single-mindedly practicing each of them, carefully keeping a daily log that recorded wherein and how often he failed to exercise the pertinent virtue. At the end of each thirteen-week cycle, he began again at the top of the list.

In the eyes of many, there is something distasteful about Franklin's method for inculcating virtue. It often strikes one as a set of mechanical calisthenics aimed at behavior modification, a series of artificial maneuvers in which the participant's behavior is carefully tabulated and controlled by a system of negative and positive reinforcements. There is little doubt that such a description aptly fits Franklin's method, but it is one with which he would have had no difficulty. For him, the "art of virtue" was more science than art; its first principles were based upon an empirical consideration of the nature of human behavior. Franklin was well aware that humans are creatures of habit, often settling into modes of predictable behavior out of sheer inertia and laziness. If this is the case, he reasoned, two strategies are necessary to overcome the learned patterns. First, the old habit has to be broken, and this can be done only by actually changing one's behavior in the world, not by merely intending or planning to do so. Second, new, more rewarding patterns must replace the old ones, and become so engrained in one's daily activity that they grow habitual. This, likewise, can only be accomplished by doing, not by contemplating. Such a regimen is necessarily artificial and even strained at the outset. But with perseverance, what was originally unnatural in time becomes natural.

It is certainly possible to call into question Franklin's analysis of virtue as well as his proposed method for making it a habit, but our primary interest in them here is the light they shed upon his religious thought. With his emphasis upon both the utility and the scientific nature of ethics, Franklin falls squarely within the deistic tradition. Moreover, his insistence that virtuous behavior is tantamount to worship of the God of nature is in agreement with mainstream deism. Each of the proponents of natural religion in America focused their attention upon the nature of virtue and its role in the enhancement of human happiness. Franklin was no exception, the ambivalence of his commitment to deism notwithstanding.

But it was precisely his ambivalence in regard to certain deistic principles that led him to concentrate as fully as he did upon strategies by which to habituate individuals to the practice of virtue. Later American deists would unanimously endorse the Lockean assumption that human beings are blank slates, capable of being fashioned by the environment and rational reflection, but essentially "good" by nature. If individuals exhibit such vices as prejudice, greed, or cruelty, it was because their natural propensity to good had been perverted by the poisonous influence of political and ecclesial oppression. Strike off the shackles of ignorance, fear, and superstition, thundered Palmer, and both the individual and society would naturally gravitate toward an attitude of benevolent rationality.

But Franklin, in spite of his Enlightenment-based faith in human progress, was unable to wholeheartedly endorse the optimism characteristic of later American deists. In his youth he had drunk too deeply from the waters of Calvinism to throw over completely the uneasy suspicion that, when it came to the practice of virtue, humans needed a rigorous regimen of disciple and self-inquiry. His entire "art of virtue" revolves around the unstated assumption that there is a quality in humans highly resistant to virtue, or, perhaps, that human will is too weak to cultivate virtue without the application of artificial and rather formidable exercises. There is a hint here of the old Calvinist doctrine of utter depravity of human nature; occasionally peeking through Franklin's otherwise confident program for self-improvement is a glimmer of the Puritan disdain for human ability. Similarly, his insistence on continuous self-measurement in matters ethical is reminiscent of the Calvinist conviction—at times almost obsessive—of the constant need for sinners to examine their consciences for signs of regeneration and election. Franklin explicitly repudiated the gloomy Calvinist ethos of his youth, but we have seen that it nonetheless exerted an influence upon his subsequent advocacy of deism. It is not too much to suggest that his moral reflections are likewise subtly tinted by the darkness of his "pious" background.

FREEDOM OF CONSCIENCE

The ambivalence that allowed certain vestiges of Franklin's Calvinist background to color his general deistic orientation at times led him to endorse religious and ethical perspectives that are occasionally confusing. We have examined several of his writings, from the early *Dissertation* to his later efforts to arrive at an almost mathematical "art of virtue," and have seen that it is difficult to describe Franklin as an outright proponent of deism because of the ambivalence that runs through them. But it is clear that his personal sympathies and first principles lean more toward the religion of nature than supernaturalism. His endorsement of deism was more moderate in tone as well as content than the varieties later defended by Allen, Paine, or Palmer. But for all his reticence in religious matters, Franklin consciously if not completely threw his lot in with Enlightenment rationalism.

While the ambivalence with which Franklin endorsed deism may at times make for some perplexity in attempting to understand his religious orientation, it also served as the foundation for one aspect of his thought that he never forsook: an insistence upon absolute toleration for diverse religious perspectives. Part of the reason for his willingness to live-and-let-live when it came to religious belief stems from Franklin's wholehearted acceptance of the assumption that humans possess a natural right to freedom of conscience. Along with his younger colleague Thomas Jefferson, Franklin believed that neither government nor society had legitimate jurisdiction over a person's religious convictions, and that any attempt to coerce assent to a particular creed was destructive of both individual liberty and rational inquiry. But it is equally the case that Franklin's championship of toleration is a product of his own uncertainty when it came to religious issues.

For all the fame he enjoyed during his lifetime, Franklin remained remarkably humble in his approach to religious beliefs, insisting that no one sect or person—including himself—was warranted in claiming absolute truth. Reason and experience were the ultimate guideposts in reflecting upon the nature of God and human responses to the divine, and the conclusions that both arrived at were always tentative, open to further inquiry and debate. We have seen that as a young man, Franklin declared that "a Man must have a good deal of Vanity who believes . . . that all the doctrines he holds, are true." A bit later, in his "Articles of Belief," he went so far as to suggest that there are many ways of imagining and symbolically portraying the Deity, with the clear implication that no single attempt to represent God can be deemed universally valid. It is likely that his repudiation of the *Dissertation* was prompted by the realization that its dogmatic, catechism-like manner of argumentation closed the doors to future reflection and amendment as much as by his fear that its denial of free will provided a legitimation for license. And at the end of his life, Franklin was still reluctant to defend or deny theological tenets strongly held by others. In a 1790 letter to Ezra Stiles, for example, he refused to speculate upon the question of Jesus' divinity, on the grounds that the issue was unresolvable and that those who accepted it might benefit from it:

> As to Jesus of Nazareth . . . I have, with most of the present dissenters in England, some doubts as to his divinity; though it is a question I do not dogmatize upon, having never studied it, and think it needless to busy myself with it now, when I expect soon an opportunity of knowing the truth with less trouble. I see no harm, however, in its being believed, if that belief has the good consequence, as probably it has, of making his doctrines more respected and better observed; especially as I do not perceive, that the Supreme takes it amiss, by distinguishing the unbelievers in his government of the world with any peculiar marks of his displeasure.[32]

It is impossible to imagine the later generation of militant American deists conceding this much about the possible pragmatic benefits of Christian belief, or even granting that the question allows for honest and rational disagreement. But then the later deists were not as ambivalent in their religious commitments as Franklin.

Tolerant of religious pluralism and moderate in his defense of the religion of nature as he was, one thing that Franklin could not abide and fearlessly spoke against was religious bigotry. As early as 1735, in a *Pennsylvania Gazette* piece titled "Dialogue between Two Presbyterians," Franklin assailed what he took to be the unwarranted dogmatism of Calvinist doctrine. Protestantism, he argued, correctly criticizes the Roman church for its endorsement of papal infallibility. How, then, can Calvinist divines "claim Infallibility for [themselves] or [their] synods in [their] way of Interpreting?"[33] Franklin's point is one with which we are already familiar: humans are by nature fallible in their reasoning and beliefs, and a dogmatic fidelity to written-in-stone doctrine is always suspect. As he characteristically says in the "Dialogue," "Peace, Unity and virtue in any Church are more to be regarded than Orthodoxy."[34]

Franklin was equally opposed to the emotional enthusiasm churned up by sectarian revivalists such as George Whitefield, who was one of the leading figures in the mid-eighteenth century's Great Awakening. Such demagoguery, Franklin feared, spoke to the passions rather than to the reason, and thereby encouraged a blind intolerance on the part of frenzied listeners to religious dissent or inquiry. In addition, those sectarians such as Whitefield who sought sudden conversions through fire-and-brimstone sermons necessarily did so by impressing upon their audiences the utterly fallen and hopeless state of humanity. As Franklin said in recalling Whitefield's style, he thunderously assured his auditors that "they were naturally *half beasts and half devils.*"[35] But all such explicitly antihumanistic denials of the potential of individuals to work their way through to a rational understanding of religious questions were antithetical to Franklin's temperament. As we saw earlier, he was never able to endorse completely the Enlightenment's naively optimistic faith in human goodness, but neither was he willing to agree with Calvinism's scorn of reason. As always, he preferred to take a more moderate course by acknowledging human fallibility while applauding humanity's promise.

Who, then, as we asked at the beginning of this chapter, is the *real* Franklin when it comes to religious issues? He was a man who cherished freedom of thought and inquiry, an individual who recognized that there are many paths to God, and who personally felt most comfortable with the one laid out by the Enlightenment tradition. As such, he was one of America's earliest proponents of deism, albeit a deism that was often shot through with a certain degree of ambivalence. Franklin was neither as strong in his convictions as the deists who would succeed him, nor as militant in his defense of what he saw as the truth. But when weighed against the background of Franklin's overall accomplishments, these two factors may be viewed as strengths rather than weaknesses.

NOTES

1. Benjamin Franklin, *Autobiography*, in *The Writings of Benjamin Franklin*, vol. 1, ed. Albert Henry Smyth (New York: Macmillan, 1905–1907), pp. 295, 324. Biographical treatments of Franklin are numerous. Two of the best are Carl van Doren, *Benjamin Franklin* (New York: Viking, 1938), and Walter Isaacson, *Benjamin Franklin: An American Life* (New York: Simon & Schuster, 2004). Leo Lemay's multivolumed work in progress, *The Life of Benjamin Franklin* (Philadelphia: University of Pennsylvania Press, 2005–), is the definitive biography.

2. Franklin, *Autobiography*, p. 295.

3. For more on the worldview clash in which Franklin found himself, see Kerry Walters, *Benjamin Franklin and His Gods* (Chicago: University of Illinois Press, 1999), pp. 17–42.

4. Benjamin Franklin to Josiah and Abiah Franklin, April 13, 1738, in *The Papers of Benjamin Franklin*, vol. 2, ed. Leonard W. Labaree (New Haven: Yale University Press, 1960), p. 203.

5. William Wollaston, *The Religion of Nature Delineated* (London: S. Palmer, 1725), p. 55.

6. Ibid., p. 80.

7. Ibid., p. 78.

8. Benjamin Franklin, *A Dissertation on Liberty and Necessity, Pleasure and Pain*, in Labaree, *The Papers of Benjamin Franklin*, vol. 1, p. 60.

9. Ibid., pp. 61–62.

10. Ibid., pp. 59, 63.

11. Ibid., p. 71.

12. Ibid.

13. Elizabeth Flower and Murray Murphy, *A History of Philosophy in America*, vol. 1 (New York: G. P. Putnam's Sons, 1976), p. 101.

14. Benjamin Franklin, "Articles of Belief and Acts of Religion," in Labaree, *The Papers of Benjamin Franklin*, vol. 1, pp. 102–103.

15. Alfred Owen Aldridge, *Benjamin Franklin and Nature's God* (Durham, NC: Duke University Press, 1967).

16. See Walters, *Benjamin Franklin and His Gods*, pp. 67–95.

17. Benjamin Franklin, "Doct. to Be Prea[che]d," in Labaree, *The Papers of Benjamin Franklin*, vol. 1, p. 213.

18. Benjamin Franklin, "On the Providence of God in the Government of the World," in Labaree, *The Papers of Benjamin Franklin*, vol. 1, pp. 264–69.

19. Ibid., p. 269.

20. Benjamin Franklin to Ezra Stiles, March 9, 1790, in *Benjamin Franklin: Representative Selections*, ed. Chester E. Jorgenson and Frank Luther Mott (New York: Hill & Wang, 1962), pp. 507–509.

21. Benjamin Franklin, "Silence Dogood," nos. 1–14, in Labaree, *The Papers of Benjamin Franklin*, vol. 1, pp. 8–45.

22. The first edition of this work, which appeared in Boston in 1710, was titled *Bonifacius: An Essay upon the Good*. For an excellent treatment of Mather, see Kenneth Silverman, *The Life and Times of Cotton Mather* (New York: Columbia University Press, 1985).

23. Benjamin Franklin to Samuel Mather, November 10, 1779, quoted in Cotton Mather, *Essays to Do Good* (Dover: Samuel Stevens, 1826), pp. 6–7.

24. Benjamin Franklin, "Self-Denial Not the Essence of Virtue," in Labaree, *The Papers of Benjamin Franklin*, vol. 2, p. 20.

25. Ibid.

26. Benjamin Franklin, "A Man of Sense," in Labaree, *The Papers of Benjamin Franklin*, vol. 2, p. 16.

27. Benjamin Franklin, "Proposals and Queries to Be Asked the Junto," in Labaree, *The Papers of Benjamin Franklin*, vol. 1, p. 262.

28. Benjamin Franklin, "Articles of Belief and Acts of Religion," in Labaree, *The Papers of Benjamin Franklin*, vol. 1, p. 103.

29. Benjamin Franklin, "Doct. to Be Prea[che]d," in Labaree, *The Papers of Benjamin Franklin*, vol. 1, p. 213.

30. Franklin, *Autobiography*, in Jorgenson and Mott, *Benjamin Franklin: Representative Selections*, p. 71.

31. Ibid., pp. 71–81.

32. Benjamin Franklin to Ezra Stiles, March 9, 1790, in Jorgenson and Mott, *Benjamin Franklin: Representative Selections*, p. 508.

33. Benjamin Franklin, "Dialogue Between Two Presbyterians," in Labaree, *The Papers of Benjamin Franklin*, vol. 2, p. 33.

34. Ibid.

35. Benjamin Franklin, *Autobiography*, in Jorgenson and Mott, *Benjamin Franklin: Representative Selections*, p. 90.

CHAPTER THREE

THE FRONTIER DEIST
ETHAN ALLEN

Deism, like the Enlightenment ethos from which it sprang, was essentially cosmopolitan in character. Its advocacy of reason, scientific objectivity, and unqualified freedom of conscience reflected a tolerant pluralism, a give-and-take enthusiasm for debate, which is often associated with urban communities accustomed to a wide diversity of thought and lifestyles. Consequently, it is no accident that most of the major American deists either came from pluralistic urban settings or lived significant portions of their lives there. Their exposure to new ideas, different religious perspectives, and a wide spectrum of people only served to reinforce their fidelity to deistic tolerance and to wean them from colonial parochialism. Benjamin Franklin was a city dweller his entire live, both in America and abroad, as was Tom Paine. Freneau and Palmer were New Yorkers by adoption and in spirit. Thomas Jefferson enjoyed a genteel upbringing and education that was subsequently polished by his years in Philadelphia and Paris. Each of these men became American *philosophes* at least in part because fate pushed them into social situations guaranteed to erode their cultural and intellectual insularity. They were not just Virginians, New Yorkers, or Pennsylvanians. They were polished, urbane men of the world, their colonial origins notwithstanding.

But not Ethan Allen. If there was ever an American in the second half of the eighteenth century who resisted the cosmopolitan pull, it was he. Unlike his fellow American deists, Allen was a genuine pioneer, a son of the frontier who disliked and distrusted city folk and city ways with the intensity only a born-and-bred man of the country can feel for the town. He was never happier than when roaming the wilderness or navigating the lakes and rivers of what is northern Vermont. He disdained the pleasantries and conventions of polite society, exulting instead in rough, full-blooded frontier living. He drank like a demon, swore more often (and more inventively) than any other Yankee of his time, and reveled in styling himself an unsophisticated backwoodsman. He did not, in a word, even remotely live up to the eighteenth century's conventional image of a deistically minded *philosophe*, and was terribly proud of the fact. If Allen had a single ambition in life, it was to ignore convention and go his own way.

Allen was a multifaceted, richly complex man, who some considered a genius and others despised as a rogue. In all probability he was both. He was born poor and died rich, but only because of a lifetime of thoroughly shady land speculations. He was an ardent patriot who bravely languished almost three years as a British prisoner of war, but was also more than willing to throw his lot in with the British at war's end when he felt Vermont had been snubbed by the Continental Congress. Despite his nearly total lack of formal schooling, he had a deep love of words and learning, and always considered himself first and foremost a philosopher. He was a proponent of deism who nevertheless denied knowing what the word meant. He was, in short, a virtual embodiment of tensions and downright contradictions, and not at all consistent nor sometimes even very rational in his behavior. But it is precisely for this reason that he comes across as more of a real person than any of the other American deists. For all the difference in time and situation, readers today can see something of themselves in the essentially likable, hell-for-leather Allen. It is much more difficult to empathize with the frostily austere Jefferson, the ferocious Paine, or the visionary Palmer. We admire these men, but we like Allen.

Amazingly, it was this unschooled frontiersman, this backwoods despiser of drawing room conversation, who published the first book-length defense of deism written by a native-born American: *Reason the Only Oracle of Man* (or *Oracles of Reason*, as it is more commonly known). This ponderous tome, published in 1784, is neither a literary masterpiece nor a philosophical tour de force. Allen's prose is cumbersome, his grammar and spelling are idiosyncratic, and his philosophical defense of natural religion and criticism of Christianity are for the most part derived from the works of British deists such as Collins and Tindal. But his was the first American pen to defend, in a systematic and unabashed manner, the basic tenets of rational religion. The other American deists unquestionably were more cultured and better read than Allen. But he was the movement's pioneer, its frontiersman.

THE STRONG MAN

Ethan Allen, whom the Reverend Nathan Perkins some fifty years later would excoriate as "one of the wickedest men that ever walked this guilty globe,"[1] entered the world in an innocent enough way in January 1738. He was the son of a relatively prosperous Litchfield, Connecticut, farmer. Most of the Allen children were given Old Testament names, presumably in the hopes that they would live up to them. Ethan certainly did. In Hebrew, his name means "strong."

Almost nothing is known about Ethan's early years except that in 1740 his father relocated the family to a frontier community in northwestern Connecticut. It is a safe bet, however, that Ethan spent most of his childhood and youth in farm work—a type of labor he hated and avoided as an adult—and received no formal schooling until he was fourteen. At that point he was sent to study in a neighboring town under the Reverend Jonathan Lee, who was charged by Ethan's father with preparing the boy for admission to Yale College. Lee's tutelage was short-lived, however. Ethan's father died in 1755, thereby putting an end to the Yale dream. As the eldest son, Ethan returned to his father's farm and assumed leadership of the family.

Except for a two-week hiatus in 1757, when he served with the local militia during the French and Indian War, Ethan remained on the family farm until he was twenty-five. The holding prospered under his supervision, but Ethan was eager to be on his own. Consequently, in mid-1763, he married and relocated to Salisbury, Connecticut, where he entered into business with a couple of his brothers. It was there that he met Thomas Young, a physician who lived just across the New York line. It is arguable that Allen's yearlong acquaintance with Young was the most important factor in his development as a deist.

Although Allen never had the opportunity for formal schooling, he early on fell under the spell of what he liked to call "matters of the mind."

He grew up on Plutarch's *Lives* and the Bible, the only two books owned by his family, and could quote long passages from both throughout his life. But it was not until he met Young that his natural inquisitiveness focused upon the issue of religion.

Young was a freethinker, a self-proclaimed disciple of Enlightenment luminaries such as Newton and Locke as well as British deists such as Collins. Under his tutelage, Ethan was introduced to the religion of nature and the Enlightenment worldview. Even before his friendship with Young, Ethan had made no secret of his skepticism about orthodox Christian doctrine. But the year's worth of discussions with Young provided him with an alternative to the traditional religious worldview he had begun to doubt. As Ira Allen, one of Ethan's brothers, put it years later, "After an acquaintance with Dr. Thomas Young, a deist, my brother embraced the same sentiments."[2]

Allen's friendship with Young is important for another reason. The two young men decided to pool their collective wisdom and write a book that would expose supernaturalism's follies and defend natural religion. Although the available evidence is ambiguous, a pact seems to have been made whereby the proposed manuscript would become the exclusive property of whichever of the two survived the other. Young apparently contributed much of the argumentation drawn from the British deists, while Allen concentrated on attacking Christian scripture. Half of the manuscript was probably finished when Young moved away from the area in late 1764, thereby ending the collaboration. He took the manuscript with him. Some twenty years later, Allen would retrieve it from Young's widow, finish it, and present it to the world as *Reason the Only Oracle of Man*.

Shortly after his collaboration with Young, Allen left Connecticut for the New Hampshire Grants, a stretch of wilderness composing what is now the state of Vermont, but then claimed by both New Hampshire and New York. Ownership of the territory had been under dispute for some twenty years before Allen arrived there. Although the land most likely rightfully belonged to New York, the royal governor of New Hampshire, Benning Wentworth, had been cheerfully treating it as his own since 1749, selling huge grants of it to anyone willing and able to purchase them. Hundreds of farmers as well as land speculators from Connecticut—including Allen, who was always on the lookout for a quick

profit—bought land in the Grants area from Wentworth, only to discover afterward that New York refused to acknowledge their deeds of
sale. Tensions between Yankee and Yorker settlers escalated, with Allen
one of the most outspoken critics of Yorker "aggression." The tension
eventually culminated in the formation in 1770 of the Green Mountain
Boys, a militia organized to protect the "rights" of Grants settlers from
the encroachments of New York. Allen was elected the militia's colonel
commandant and, until the outbreak of the War of Independence five
years later, roamed up and down the Grants territory expelling Yorker
settlers and generally harassing and embarrassing New York officials.

Allen was an immensely popular figure, revered as a patriotic champion by the fledgling Republic of Vermont (which declared its independence in 1771), despite—or perhaps because of—his willingness to play the
swaggering, colorful soldier of fortune. His ardent defense of Yankee
rights so endeared him to his fellow Vermonters that they were perfectly
willing to tolerate the open secret of his religious infidelity. As one of
them wrote of Colonel Allen in 1771, "it is said that he denies the Being
of a God and Denies that there is an Infernal spirit existing."[3] It may have
been that folks on the frontier were more tolerant of heterodox religious
views than their more proper brethren on the Eastern shores. Or perhaps
the Grant settlers, accustomed as they were to Ethan's hard drinking, his
marvelous talent for swearing, and his general carousing, looked upon his
infidelity as just another manifestation of his radical individualism. Whatever the reason, Allen's unabashed disbelief in Christian dogma seems to
have gotten him into no trouble until the end of his life, when his popularity had diminished and he had published *Oracles of Reason*.

Allen and his Green Mountain Boys may have been the darlings of
Vermonters, but so far as Governor Tryon of New York was concerned,
they were "abominable wretches, rioters, and traitors." Accordingly, in
late 1771 Tryon offered a reward of twenty pounds for Allen's capture,
and in early 1774 raised the bounty to one hundred pounds. But the
increasing likelihood of outright conflict in the Grants territory was pre-
empted in April 1775 by the eruption of hostilities between the American colonies and Britain. Allen and his homespun militia quickly threw
in their lot with the patriots, and on May 10, 1775, acting under orders
of dubious authority from the government of Connecticut, the Green
Mountain Boys captured the strategically located Fort Ticonderoga on

Lake George. In typical bombastic style—but, given his religious convictions, rather incongruously—Allen proclaimed at the decisive moment that he had seized the fort "in the name of the great Jehovah, and the Continental Congress."[4] Ticonderoga's surrender was an important tactical and psychological victory for the rebellious colonies, but it was not an especially memorable military triumph. Allen and his men essentially walked into the crumbling and poorly manned fort and took it without firing a shot. But Allen, always blessed with a vivid imagination and a generous estimation of his own worth, took the campaign as a portent of greater military victories to come. Four months after Ticonderoga, he set out to fulfill his destiny as a warrior by leading a foolish attack against British-held Montreal. The attack failed miserably and Allen was captured. Washington and other top officers in the Continental Army were rather relieved at this turn of events. In their estimation, Allen was too much of a glory-seeking maverick to be a good officer, and his capture, although unfortunate, at least prevented him from doing further damage to the American military cause.

Allen sat out the next three years as a prisoner of war. He eventually was released through a prisoner exchange in 1778, received the brevet rank of colonel from the Continental Congress, and then was politely but firmly ignored for the rest of the war. General Washington had been willing enough to negotiate for Allen's release, but had no intention of giving him a command. Allen was too unpredictable as a man, and hence unreliable as an officer. Quite probably, too, the aristocratic Washington was offended by the reports that undoubtedly reached him of Allen's frontier rowdiness. The man simply was not a gentleman.

Like most egoists, Allen was particularly sensitive to what he took to be social or personal slights, and he was stung by Washington's refusal to entrust him, the past leader of the famous Green Mountain Boys, with a command. The bitterness of this personal affront was increased by what Allen took to be the cavalier way in which the self-styled Republic of Vermont was being treated by the Continental Congress.

Vermont had regularly petitioned Congress since the Declaration of Independence for recognition as a separate state. Allen himself, in fact, had presented Vermont's case to Congress in late 1778, but had been snubbed, at least in his own estimation, by the delegates present. Congress refused to act upon Vermont's petition for an obvious reason: given the wartime need for a united front against the British, it could not afford to antagonize New York by recognizing Vermont as an independent constituency. Allen, however, either could not or would not see the difficult position Congress was in, and interpreted its reluctance to act as a sign of snobbish Eastern contempt for western frontiers. Beginning in the summer of 1780, Allen and his brothers Ira and Levi entered into an extensive correspondence with General Haldimand, commander of the British forces in Canada. The ostensible reason for the correspondence was to negotiate a prisoner exchange. But in fact, the Allen brothers were sounding out Haldimand about the possibility of Vermont's being taken back into the British empire. It is not clear whether Ethan and his brothers seriously contemplated selling out to the British. Some have argued that their overture was a ploy designed to frighten Congress into recognizing Vermont's independence from New York. At any rate, nothing came of the negotiations. It was apparent that Vermonters would not go along with a reconciliation with Britain, and before long it became equally obvious that the war would soon be over, with England the loser. Vermont eventually was accepted into the American union as a separate state in 1791, after Allen's death. But neither his aboveboard pleas to Congress nor his shady negotiations with Haldimand had much, if anything, to do with the decision.

There was one clear outcome of Ethan's dealing with the British, although certainly not the one he had expected or hoped for. When word of his private negotiations with Haldimand leaked, Allen's star set once and for all. Vermonters had been willing in the past to tolerate his religious infidelity as well as his swaggering, but treason was another matter entirely. By 1783, Allen was relegated by popular opinion to the role of private and politically impotent citizen.

Allen took his forced retirement from public life in stride. As he told a friend in early 1782, "I have put aside my studies for too long,"[5] and he intended to take advantage of his free time to return to them. He retrieved the old manuscript that he and Thomas Young had worked on from the latter's widow and, after pasting and polishing, published the work in 1784. Allen had written other books, including an immensely popular autobiography and several political tracts. But this book *Reason the Only Oracle of Man* was quite different from his previous works—so different, in fact, that charges of plagiarism besieged him from the very start. Questions of authorship aside, however, the *Oracles* was the first systematic defense of natural religion written by an American—and an unschooled, frontier-rough American at that.

Just how influential was the book? The most likely guess is that it was one of those treatises that served as a red flag to some and a rallying banner to others, but which few people, critic or defender, actually read. There are at least two reasons why the *Oracles* did not enjoy a wide readership. First, it was a hard book to get through, written as it is in a repetitious, awkward, and sometimes torturous prose. Second, few copies of the original edition ever saw the light of day. Although Anthony Haswell, Allen's (rather reluctant) Bennington printer, ran off fifteen hundred copies, no more than two hundred were actually sold. The rest, stored in Haswell's attic, were destroyed in a fire a few years later. The faithful attributed the fire to divine wrath; deists said it was arson committed by bigots; and the uninterested middle-of-the-roaders shrugged and wrote off the conflagration as an accident.

But the couple of hundred copies of *Oracles* that had been sold passed from hand to hand, and if not always read were certainly talked about. The clergy helped to keep popular interest in the book alive by repeatedly condemning it in pulpit and broadside. A typical example of this unintended publicity is Timothy Dwight's self-righteous (and doggerel) dismissal of its author in his *Triumph of Infidelity:*

> In vain thro realms of nonsense ran
> The great clodhopping oracle of man.
> Yet faithful were his toils; What could he more?
> In Satan's cause he bustled, bruised and swore;
> And what the due reward, from me shall know,
> For gentlemen of equal worth below.[6]

Allen was unperturbed by such clerical attacks; as he pointed out to an acquaintance, he had expected the clergy to denounce the book because it was "fatal to their Ministerial Damnation Salvation system their merchandise thereof."[7] But he was confident that his defense of natural religion would survive the petty stings of orthodox critics. Although he modestly described the book as "the untutored logic and sallies of a mind nursed principally in the Mountainous wilds of

America,"[8] Allen was immensely proud of his accomplishment. As it turned out, he had reason to be.

Four years after the *Oracles* was published, Allen died—appropriately, after an all-night drinking spree. Orthodox clergy and the country predictably took his passing as an opportunity to reflect on the abominations of infidelity. Yale College's Ezra Stiles, an otherwise tolerant, compassionate man, wrote in his journal: "Died in Vermont the profane and impious Gen. Ethan Allen. And in Hell lift up his eyes, being in Torments." Timothy Dwight, a future president of Yale, condemned Allen as a man "impatient of restraints of government or religion, and not always submissive to those of common decency." The Reverend Uzal Ogden pitied Allen as "an ignorant and profane deist who died with a mind replete with horror." And, as already mentioned, the Reverend Nathan Perkins described him as "one of the wickedest men that ever walked this guilty globe."[9] But when all was said and done, the inscription carved upon Ethan's gravestone is both more temperate and accurate than such priestly denunciations:

> The Corporeal Part of Ethan
> Allen Rests Beneath this Stone . . .
> His spirit tried the
> Mercies of his God
> In Whom he firmly Trusted.[10]

A RELIGIOUS MAVERICK

The full title of Allen's deistic treatise is *Reason the Only Oracle of Man; or, a Compenduous [sic] System of Natural Religion*. In point of fact, however, there is nothing compendious about it. *Oracles* was a veritable encyclopedia of rational religion, with each entry treated in a fulsome way. A critique of revealed religion, an examination of proofs for the existence of God, discussions of divine nature, analyses of natural law and reason, reflections upon ethical and social issues—all these topics and more were covered by Allen in his book. Unhappily, they were all too often handled in a cumbersome, awkward prose. *Oracles*, in short, is a badly written book. Although at times a limpid or even eloquent passage strikes the reader's eye, the treatise as a whole is overlong, redundant, and stylistically torturous. Allen himself seems to have been aware of its imperfections and, in the preface, apologetically attributes them to his hit-or-miss frontier education:

> In my youth I was much disposed to contemplation, and at commencement in manhood, I committed to manuscript such sentiments or arguments as appeared most consonant to reason, lest through the debility of memory my improvement should have been less gradual: This method of scribbling I practised for many years, from which I experienced great advantages in the progression of learning and knowledge, the more so as I was deficient in education, and had to acquire the knowledge of grammar and language, as well as the art of reasoning, principally from a studious application to it, which after all I am sensible, lays me under disadvantages, particularly in matters of composition.[11]

Like so many of Allen's self-descriptions, this one should be read with a somewhat skeptical eye. On the one hand, there's no reason to doubt that he was genuinely uncomfortable with his lack of formal schooling, and felt the need to apologize for the grammatical coarseness of his prose. But it is also a fact that Allen was his own best press agent, and carefully cultivated the image of the rough-edged insightful frontier philosopher. And, indeed, he was. But he also was not above indulging in rather transparent displays of false modesty in the hope of highlighting the novelty of his homespun thought.

Even more disingenuous than his apology for his style is the following disclaimer, also found in the preface to *Oracles:* "I am generally denominated a Deist, the reality of which I never disputed, being conscious I am no Christian, except mere infant baptism makes me one; and as to being a Deist, I know not strictly speaking, whether I am one or not, for I have never read their writings."[12] This is a most curious admission of ignorance, coming as it does from the author of a book that gained notoriety throughout the American Republic for its unabashed espousal of deism. What sense can be made of it?

It is likely that Allen had at least two purposes in mind when he denied knowing anything about deism. It is probable that at least some of what he claimed as his own in the book was written by Thomas Young. Allen's disclaimer, then, may have been intended to distance himself from

Young in order to discourage readers from associating the two and raising embarrassing questions about its authorship. More revealingly, his prefatory refusal to be defined within the deistic tradition underscores just how much of a maverick Allen really was. He insisted on going his own way both personally and politically, and this fierce need for independence was likewise reflected in "matters of the mind." The arguments that comprised the *Oracles* had to be *his*, not someone else's. It was *his* philosophy, not Collins's, Blount's, or Toland's—much less Thomas Young's—which he defended. If, by chance, individuals who called themselves deists just happened to agree with Allen's views on religion, that was their affair. But the bottom line was that he felt the need to resist aligning himself with any school of thought, even one with which he was sympathetic because he had to go it alone. Given the depth of this fierce individualism, as well as Allen's talent for mythologizing himself, it is quite likely that he really believed his own disclaimer. But if so, he was the only one who did. Even before the *Oracles* saw the light of day, Allen was regarded by all those who knew him, as well as by those who only knew of him, as a most profane and irredeemable deist.

BLEMISH-FREE REASON

Allen was a born fighter, and it didn't matter to him whether the battle involved matters political or intellectual. Consequently, it is not surprising that he comes out swinging in the opening pages of *Oracles*. The desire for knowledge, he says, has engaged the attention of mankind throughout the ages and extended the sway of art and science in all directions. But despite this progress, it is a sad fact that "the bulk of mankind . . . are still carried down the torrent of superstition, and entertain very unworthy apprehensions of the BEING, PERFECTIONS, CREATION and PROVIDENCE of God, and their duty to him." This alarming state of affairs in turn lays an indispensable obligation on the philosophic friends of human nature, "to endeavour to reclaim mankind from their ignorance and delusion, by enlightening their minds in those great and sublime truths concerning God and his providence, and their obligations to moral rectitude, which in this world and that which is to come, cannot fail to affect their happiness and well being."[13]

How can humankind disabuse itself of the impediments to truth that ignorance and delusion impose? Allen answers: through a rational analysis of religious claims that is unafraid to follow the debate wherever it goes. And Ethan Allen was just the man to initiate the debate.

His gambit was that of all the dogmas of revealed religion in general and Christianity in particular, none are more "derogatory to nature of man, and the rank and character of being which he holds in the universe" than the doctrine of the depravity of human reason. The idea that human reason is utterly corrupted by virtue of the original Fall was one of the central tenets of Calvinist Christianity. All colonial Christian denominations subscribed to it to one extent or another. The doctrine's implications were obvious. First and foremost, the depravity of reason meant that human well-being and salvation are utterly in the hands of an omnipotent God. If the rational faculties are inherently tainted, humans can never trust to their own devices in matters of spirit. Instead, they must rely exclusively upon divine grace, which provides a peace that passes understanding—or at least the minimal degree of understanding of which humans are capable. Scriptural revelation and ecclesial authority, therefore, become the only trustworthy guides in a soul's journey to God.

Allen asserted that the doctrine of the complete depravity of human reason spelled doom to the possibility, much less progress, of the arts and sciences. If the tool by which nature is measured suffers from irremediable flaws, the readings it provides likewise will be flawed. The aspirations of the Enlightenment, the ideals of the New Learning, must thus be dismissed as illusory. Again, all that humans have left to fall back on is blind faith in the veracity of scriptural revelation and church tradition.

Like all deists, Allen objected to this disregard for reason's claims. According to him, the arguments invoked by Calvinists in defense of the doctrine of utter depravity are self-refuting: "admitting the depravity of reason, the consequence would unavoidably follow, that as far as it may be supposed to have taken place in the minds of [theologians], they could be no judges of it, in consequence of their supposed depravity." But theologians in fact do judge their arguments to be sound, and do so on the grounds that they rationally follow from scriptural revelation as well as natural philosophy. Consequently, they are in the strange position of invoking reason to defend the depravity of reason. As Allen dryly concludes,

Those who invalidate reason, ought seriously to consider, whether they argue against reason with or without reason; if with reason, then they establish the principle, that they are laboring to dethrone; but if they argue without reason (which, in order to be consistent with themselves, they must do), they are out of the reach of rational conviction, nor do they deserve a rational argument.[14]

This denial of the doctrine of reason's depravity does not imply that all humans are equally and fully rational. Allen is quick to acknowledge that "there are degrees in the knowledge of rational beings, and also in their capacities to acquire it." Not every person, he says, is capable of the exalted reasoning of a Locke or a Newton. Moreover, accidents of birth to one side, it is equally undeniable that "a blow on the head, or fracture of the pericranium, as also palsies and many other casualties that await our sensorium" can lessen and in some cases completely destroy the exercise of reason. But neither being born with a lesser degree of reason than others, nor losing the power of reason through accident or illness, marks rationality as being depraved. Regardless of its strength and duration in specific humans, reason itself is "free from any blemish or depravity."[15]

Why precisely is reason, in any of its gradations, without blemish? For Allen, human rationality is a direct reflection of divine omniscience: "The most inconsiderable human beings, who can discern any truth at all, bear a resemblance or likeness to God." There is not, of course, an identity between divine and human reason; human reason is eternal but finite, while God's is both eternal and infinite. Still, the participation of the race in the divine reason that permeates reality is so strong that it provides humans with a faculty with which to attain reliable knowledge of themselves and the world: "Though human reason cannot understand every thing, yet in such things, which it does not understand, its knowledge which is acquired by reasoning, is as true and certain, as the divine knowledge may be supposed to be."[16] It is not, therefore, reason that is depraved; instead, it is Calvinist doctrine, "started and taught by depraved creatures," the "greatest weakness and folly imaginable," which is at fault. For Allen, endorsement of such an antihumanistic dogma "comes nearer a proof of the doctrine of a total depravity, than any arguments which have ever been advanced in support of it."[17]

FAITH AND MIRACLES

In denying the Calvinist doctrine of reason's depravity, Allen went far in separating himself from colonial Protestantism. His reflections upon the nature of faith likewise reveal his distance from eighteenth-century orthodoxy. He rejected the traditional Christian notion of faith by rewriting it to conform to his own empiricist orientation. It was a strategy that would be adopted later on by Tom Paine and Elihu Palmer, Allen's deistic descendants.

The Christian concept of faith, as Anthony Kenny has pointed out,[18] usually refers to one or both of two distinct but related beliefs: an assent to specific doctrines revealed by God, and a trust in and living commitment to the saving grace of God. In the first case, the individual doctrines assented to are "above reason": they cannot be discovered nor understood rationally, and hence are "revealed" by God through Scripture or tradition. In the second case, the belief in God's love can come about only as the result of an intensely personal experience of grace that is emotive rather than rational, evocative instead of discursive. In either instance, the person of faith presumes the absence of rational justification. Given Calvinism's insistence upon reason's depravity, revelation and personal experiences of grace were the only two avenues by which humans could acquire reliable information about themselves and God.

Allen sets this traditional interpretation of faith on its head by claiming that the propositions of faith are nothing more than the conclusions of inductive chains of reasoning.

> Faith is the last result of the understanding, or the same which we call the conclusion, it is the consequence of a greater or less[er] deduction of reasoning from certain premises previously laid down; it is the same as believing or judging of any matter of fact, or assenting to or dissenting from the truth of any doctrine, system or position; so that to form a judgment or come to a determination in one's own mind, or to believe, or to have faith, is in reality the same thing, and is synonymously applied both to writing and speaking.[19]

This redefinition of faith as an inductive or deductive inference in turn served as the foundation for Allen's deistic critique of both Christian scripture and doctrine. If a proposition of faith is simply "the consequence of a greater or less[er] deduction of reasoning," it follows that any theological tenet that violates established canons of logic and observation is immediately suspect. This, of course, implies that Christianity's central claim, the divinity of Jesus, is unworthy of serious consideration. As worked out by early Christian councils, the doctrine insists that Jesus is a "hypostatical union" of divine and human nature. But surely, Allen argues, such a belief is self-contradictory, and hence incapable of serving as the conclusion of a sound inferential chain. "But wherein does [the hypostatical claim] consist? Does it unite the two natures so as to include the human nature in the essence of God? If it does not it does not deify the person of Christ; for the essence of God is that which makes him to be what he is." On the other hand, "if the hypostatical union includes human nature in the divine, then there would be an addition of the human nature to the essence of God, in which case the divine nature would be no longer perfectly simple, but compounded." In either case, Allen concludes, "it is a contradiction to call it a union."[20] Consequently, he rejects the orthodox doctrine of "perfect God and perfect man" as a contradiction. As such, it cannot be accepted by a person of faith—with "faith" here, of course, referring to Allen's reformulation of the traditional meaning of the word.

Similarly, the doctrine of miracles reveals itself to be unworthy of rational attention. If miracles exist, they are ruptures in the otherwise uniform fabric of natural law. The rub is that their acceptance obliges the believer to concede that God, the architect of natural order, is less than omniscient and omnipotent: "Any supposed miraculous alteration of nature, must imply mutability in the wisdom of God."[21] But a mutable God, in Allen's estimation, is no god at all; that is one of the reasons why he rejected as contradictory the doctrine of the Incarnation. The orthodox endorsement of miracles, therefore, creates a quandary that destroys the very possibility of rational belief in God. The reality of miracles either entails that God is mutable, thereby denying the essential attributes of omnipotence and omniscience, or it entails a reformulated but contradictory notion of God as susceptible to error. Neither alternative, says Allen, is acceptable.

But the doctrine of miracles does not simply render belief in the God of Christianity problematic. It also, insists Allen, embroils the believer in the throes of confusion and despair by implying that reality is chaotic and unpredictable. Miracles do not "expound or explain" the natural scheme of things. Instead, they "perplex and confound us, in our logical and doctrinal speculations. . . . Such supposed miraculous changes in nature, would to us be mysterious, and altogether unintelligible. . . ." In other words, the doctrine of miracles, if taken seriously, not only violates rational inferences derived from natural religion and philosophy, but also cuts the psychological ground from under humans, and is therefore downright destructive of well-being. It is no surprise, then, that Allen concludes that belief in miracles "cannot be edifying or instructive to us."[22] The very fact that they are ubiquitously endorsed by orthodoxy is an indication of how the dogma of reason's depravity has perniciously blinded otherwise sensible persons. To deny the lessons of experience and the dictates of reason is to do more than fall victim to logical absurdities. It is also irrationally to accept tenets that are antithetical to human progress and happiness.

ALLEN'S COSMOLOGICAL ARGUMENT

Thus far, Allen has rejected orthodox Christianity's worldview on several grounds. He has argued that human reason is a necessary as well as sufficient means of understanding reality, that scriptural accounts of miracles are suspect because they blemish the concept of God, and that faith, properly understood, is a conclusion derived from either deductive or inductive logic ("a greater or less[er] deduction of reasoning"), not a mysterious and intrinsically incomprehensible revelation. But in making these claims, Allen obviously has begged two questions: What is the nature of reality, such that reason and experience are capable of understanding it? and, What is the nature of the deity, such that the divine mutability implied by the doctrine of miracles does violence to the concept of God? For Allen, as for all eighteenth-century deists, these two questions are indissolubly related, and inquiry into one illuminates the other. An examination of nature points to the existence of God. Moreover, a fuller understanding of the physical realm sheds light upon the deity's essential attributes.

It is a curious fact that few American deists concerned themselves overmuch with formal proofs of God's existence. There are at least two explanations for this. First, despite their orthodox opponents' mechanical condemnation of them as atheists, the deists tended to assume God's existence as a self-evident presupposition of natural philosophy as well as religion. Second, and more fundamentally, the American deists were too empiricist in their methodological orientation to place a great deal of trust in traditional a priori arguments for God's existence. True, they recognized the value of deductive reasoning, but only as an auxiliary to inductive analyses of empirical data. Consequently, when demonstrations of God's existence were attempted by the deists, they normally focused upon appeals to experience—such as, for example, the argument from design.

Allen, however, was more concerned with demonstrating God's existence than most of his fellow deists, and went to some pains in *Oracles* to spell out an argument he believed establishes divine reality. Moreover, the argument he defends is not the one from design usually appealed to by other deists. Instead, it is a version of the cosmological argument from causation—or "dependency," as Allen puts it. Although the argument is not an a priori one, it is more abstract in character than one would expect from a deist. It could well be that it was one of Thomas Young's contributions. But regardless of its authorship, Allen thought enough of it to include it in the final version of *Oracles*.

Allen's starting point is what he takes to be a common human experience: the perception of uniformity in nature, suggesting the ubiquitous dominion in the phenomenal realm of causation or dependency. Natural phenomena, regardless of how occasionally unexpected they may be, are neither spontaneous nor gratuitous. Reflection and cautious observation reveal that all events in the world are the effects of antecedent ones, which themselves, of course, in turn must be the effects of still prior causes. The discoveries of natural philosophy enable us, at least to a certain point, to chart this cosmic pattern of causal relations, and nowhere is the general principle of causation or dependency observed not to hold. This leads Allen to posit that "we are authorised from reason to conclude that the vast system of causes and effects are thus necessarily connected."[23]

But once it is realized that any event in the natural realm is dependent for its emergence upon a prior, causal one, and that moreover all of physical reality is nothing more than a vast assemblage of interconnecting causal relationships, the question of the origin or dependency of the entire assemblage naturally arises. It cannot simply have sprung into existence, says Allen. Such an assumption would violate the inferred continuity of causation, and the notion of a spontaneous, uncaused natural event (in this case, the entire set of natural events) is repugnant to reason. "Nothing from nothing and there remains nothing, but something from nothing is contradictory and impossible."[24] Allen therefore concludes that reason demands that an "independent cause" be posited, a power that is itself sui generis and separate from (but generative of) the natural succession of causes.

> For a succession of causes, considered collectively, can be nothing more than effects of the independent cause, and as much dependent upon it, as those dependent causes are upon one another; so that we may with certainty conclude that the system of nature, which we call by the name of natural causes, is as much dependent on a self-existent cause, as an individual of the species in the order of generation is dependent on its progenitors for existence. [25]

This independent and self-existent cause, remarks Allen, is "a ruling power, or . . . GOD, which ideas are synonymous."[26]

The sense of dependency, then, gleaned from experience and rationally formulated into the major premise in an argument from causation, provides "the first glimpse of a Deity."[27] But in fact it does more than that. It also provides the necessary starting point for an understanding of the essential attributes of God as well as the natural order. Knowledge of God's existence, in and of itself, can only take us so far. As Allen says, "although a sense of dependency discloses to our minds the certainty of a Supreme Being, yet it does not point out to us the object, nature or perfection of that being."[28] But realization that the God which exists is also the cause of the natural order enables us, through analogous reasoning, to infer more specific characteristics of each.

Observation of natural events leads to the inductive conclusion that phenomena are regular, harmoniously interconnected with one another, and immutable. Within the deistic tradition, this is just to say that the succession of events that compromises the natural order is rational. In the language of natural philosophy, this can be expressed by saying that natural events unfailingly conform to uniform law, thereby making science possible. But, continues Allen, the natural realm is the causal consequence, as demonstrated earlier, of an independent and self-existent First Cause. Since the attributes of an effect must reflect, even if only dimly, the attributes of its cause, the implication is that the Supreme Architect likewise is endowed with the qualities of regularity, harmony, and immutability. But inasmuch as God as First Cause is also self-existent, sui generis, God must also be omnipotent. Consequently, "the ruling power or God" is impassibly harmonious, regular, and immutable, which is just to say that the Deity is supremely rational.

Regardless of the strengths or weaknesses of this argument, Allen believes it has established two points. First, that God exists; second, that the attributes of the natural realm are analogues of divine ones. He expresses the necessarily intertwined relation of natural philosophy and natural religion by remarking that "as far as we understand nature, we are become acquainted with the character of God; for the knowledge of nature is the revelation of God."[29] Given his insistence upon the immutability and rationality of both the Deity and natural laws, it is now clear why he argued earlier that the doctrine of miracles does violence to the idea of God. Moreover, given that both reality and God are essentially rational, it is also clear why Allen argues that human reason is capable of coming to an understanding of both. His analysis also supplements his earlier logical argument against the depravity of reason with a metaphysical one. Human rationality is a natural phenomenon dependent, like all natural phenomena, upon the First Cause. As such, it reflects the rational nature of that First Cause and hence cannot be depraved, although it clearly is finite. Finally, if nature is God's revelation, and if human reason is a sufficient means of deciphering that revelation, it only follows that the Christian notion of faith must be rewritten to mean simply the mental act by which humans infer generalizations from nature's testimony.

THE ETERNAL RULE OF FITNESS

The book of nature teaches that the First Cause is supremely rational as well as immutable, and has implanted vestiges of these qualities in the system of natural law that regulates physical phenomena. But reflection upon this system also reveals that God is good, precisely because natural laws are promotive of the felicity and progress of the human race.

That God is good and benevolently imparts a degree of this quality to creation is obvious, claims Allen, if one regards the "natural fitness" of events, objects, and relations. By "natural fitness" he seems to mean the apparent design that undergirds and regulates natural phenomena. Creation is lawlike, and hence trustworthy. Even if natural events occasionally appear indifferent or outrightly hostile to human welfare, reason teaches that the overall structure of reality is benevolent. Humans dwell in a natural matrix that is nonwhimsical, nonchaotic, and, in principle at least, partially controllable. True, there are obstacles to be faced in the conquest of nature, but God has provided humans with the necessary tool—reason—with which to overcome them. The First Cause, in short, has set in motion a system of natural actions and reactions that cohere with one another to form a rational, uniform pattern; and such a network, concludes Allen, necessarily reveals a providential desire that humans should flourish. Scrutiny of the natural order, then, discloses it to be such as to maximize the prospects of individual happiness, social improvement, and scientific progress. And this in turn points to the supreme benevolence of the Deity.

The underlying pattern of benevolent design discernible by human reason also provides the starting point for an understanding of how to live a happy, fulfilled existence. According to Allen, the providential network of design also reflects a "moral law" for the regulation of human behavior. This law, he says, "is engraven on our hearts by the hand of the creator, is unchangeable and of universal and eternal obligation." It is not, he continues, "a human invention, nor an arbitrary political institution, it is in its nature eternal and of universal obligation." Although human attempts to codify this moral law may vary in different contexts and at different times, it itself is eternal, "subject to no change from any difference of place, or time." In short, "it extends variably to all ages and nations, like the sovereign dominion of that being, who is the author of it."[30]

All of this sounds reasonable enough in an abstract sort of way, but the rub is that Allen never quite explains what he means by this moral law, unchangeable and universal, which is engraved on the hearts of humans. The closest he comes to a description of it is in the following ambiguous passage:

> The promulgation of this supreme [moral] law to creatures, is co-extensive and co-existent with reason, and binding on all intelligent beings in the universe; and is that eternal rule of fitness, as applicable to God, by which the creator of all things conducts his infinitude of providence, and by which he governs the moral system of being, according to the absolute perfection of his nature.[31]

This passage has two implications that, when read against the backdrop of Allen's natural philosophy, help to make sense of what he means by the moral law. First, whatever the moral law is, humans become aware of it (when they do) through the exercise of reason. Allen has no use for a Jeffersonian moral faculty that serves as the nonrational source of moral intuitions. Instead, moral knowing is "coextensive and co-existent" with rational knowing, which clearly suggests that humans are virtuous (or at least cognizant of virtue) just insofar as they are rational. Second, the moral law is tied into that providential "natural fitness" or "eternal rule of fitness" that Allen sees as synonymous with natural design. But what precisely is the relationship between the two?

Given the direction of Allen's thought, the argument he seems to be struggling to formulate is something like the following. God's providential design in the natural order ensures that the latter's operations function together to form a coherent and rational whole. The interlocking nature of the network of relations that comprises the cosmic mechanism is such that chance spontaneous occurrences, much less miraculous interventions, are outside the realm of logical possibility. Put another way, they are "unnatural" because they are indeterminate. They do not "fit" into the natural order because they violate its essential rationality.

Similarly, human actions that fail to reflect the intrinsic rationality and benevolence definitive of the natural order fail to "fit" the divinely ordained template. But there is an important distinction between "unnatural" human actions and "unnatural" physical events. The latter are outside the realm of logical possibility. The former are not. Although humans, as integral parts of the natural order, are bound by the dictates of physical laws, they are also, claims Allen, creatures "endowed with sensation and reflection . . . , together with the power of agency."[32] Consequently, humans are perfectly capable of performing actions that are neither rational nor benevolent. When they do, two consequences ensue. First, they harm themselves, directly or indirectly, by willfully transgressing the natural order of things. Second, their actions are harmful to others as well as to themselves, because they set in motion events that disrupt the "natural fitness" of human relations to the divinely ordained standards of reason and benevolence.

The upshot is that the "moral law" of which Allen speaks is an analogue to "natural law." The latter is a principle directly based upon the divine attribute of reason, which regulates the relationships between physical events. The former is a principle, directly based upon the divine attributes of reason and benevolence, which regulates the relationships between humans. A violation of the natural law would be a cosmic irrationality, and is impossible. A violation of the moral law is possible, given the agency of human beings, but is equally irrational and hence destructive.

It follows for Allen that vice and virtue are, respectively, deviations from, and conformity to, the moral law. Human vice, which violates moral natural fitness and is destructive of human well-being, is an exclusively individual choice. It is not, contrary to the Christian story, the result of inherited original sin, nor is it the consequence of human depravity. Similarly, human virtue is the consequence of human choice, not a result of mysterious divine grace. Put another way, humans are virtuous when they perform in rational ways, and evil when they act irrationally.

> Virtue, did not derive its nature merely from the omnipotent will of God, but also from the eternal truth and moral fitness of things; which was the eternal reason, why they were eternally approved by God, and immutably established by him, to be what they are; and so far as our duty is connected with those eternal measures of moral fitness, or we are able to act upon them, we give such actions, or habits, the name of virtue or morality. But when we in writing or conversation say, that virtue is grounded on the divine will, we should at the same time

include in the complex idea of it, that the divine will, which constituted virtue, was eternally and infinitely reasonable.[33]

Given this identification of rationality and virtue, it is not surprising that Allen insists that natural philosophy is "the original of moral obligation and accountability."[34] To understand the "eternal rule of fitness" imbuing reality is to understand what actions are necessary for the attainment of individual virtue and social justice.

ASSESSMENT

There is scarcely an argument in Allen's *Oracles of Reason* that cannot be subjected to severe criticism. Nor is there anything very surprising about this. For all his native intelligence and commitment to the deistic worldview—his disingenuous prefatory disclaimer notwithstanding—metaphysical waters are both deep and dangerous, and Allen, the self-educated frontiersman, was often out of his depth. Whether the arguments he defended were actually his or Thomas Young's, it is clear that Allen dealt with them in a philosophically awkward way.

Consider, for example, his causal argument for the existence of God. It is one thing to posit that every physical event is the product of an antecedent cause (although, as Hume pointed out, such a postulation may well be more of a psychological assumption than a logical entailment).[35] But it is quite another to infer from this postulation that the entire set of physical events itself must be the effect of an antecedent cause. As Bertrand Russell (among others) has pointed out, such a move could be based upon an appeal to the fallacy of composition—the erroneous assumption that a set must possess the attributes of its members. It is obvious, for example, that it is nonsensical to presume that the set of all red things is itself red, or the set of all sensations itself sensate. Similarly, the criticism runs, it is illegitimate to presume that the set of all causal relations (or creation) is itself the effect of a cause—or, to put it in Allen's terminology, that the perception of dependency in particular physical events entails that the entire set of particular dependencies is dependent upon a First Cause. Regardless of whether Russell is justified in his criticism of causal arguments for the existence of God, it is clear that criticisms such as his cannot be ignored.

Still, it may be a bit unfair to blame Allen for failing to anticipate a twentieth-century caveat to his eighteenth-century argument. He is, after all, in good historical company, inasmuch as none of the causal argument's traditional proponents seemed aware of the possibility that it might involve a fallacy of composition. But it is less easy to exonerate Allen from the charge that his ethical theory is both confused and confusing.

This is a particularly telling criticism, since Allen, no less than any other deist, was intimately concerned with questions of value and morality. A common theme throughout the entire deistic tradition is insistence that the most proper way to worship the Deity is through virtuous behavior. Consequently, deism's analysis of the tenets of natural religion is inseparable from its reflections upon the nature and origins of morality. Allen himself obviously was aware of the close connection between these two inquiries, as evidenced by his somewhat clumsy efforts to show that good and evil can be understood in terms of the category of natural fitness. But he was unable to demonstrate with clarity precisely how that relationship should be understood.

The general thrust of Allen's argument is that virtuous behavior and happiness result from living in accordance with the divine/natural attributes of reason and benevolence. But there are two obvious problems with such a suggestion. The first is that it is difficult to justify the qualitative leap from "is" to "ought" that serves as the basis of Allen's moral philosophy. Even if physical reality does exhibit reason (in the sense of immutability and regularity) as well as providential (benevolent) design, it is unclear how these two descriptions also serve as normative standards for human conduct. Moreover, Allen's virtual identification of moral thinking and rational thinking raises perhaps insuperable problems concerning human accountability. Under his scheme, for example, are only rational people capable of virtue, and completely rational people of complete virtue? There is a disconcerting elitism embedded in the identification of reason and virtue that ill accords with the deistic tradition of republicanism. It is precisely such elitism, in fact, that would lead Thomas Jefferson to deny the identity, and argue instead for the existence of a nonrational moral faculty in humans that provides them with intuitions of good and evil, regardless of their level of rationality.

Ethan Allen, then, does not belong in the intellectual first rank of American deism. His prose and his arguments are frequently clumsy, and sometimes, it must be admitted, incomprehensible. But for all that, his is an indispensable chapter in the history of American deism. Crude as Allen's philosophizing may have been, the issues with which he dealt blazed a trail for the work of subsequent, more sophisticated champions of natural religion. His criticisms of scriptural tradition, for example, would be taken up and expanded by Paine. His unsuccessful attempt to formulate a naturalistic ethic would inspire Elihu Palmer's later efforts. And all future American deists would gain inspiration from Allen's courage in exposing himself to the vituperation and slander of orthodox opponents. Ethan Allen was neither the best nor the brightest of American deists, but he was, in the richest sense of the word, the movement's pioneer. He was the first to chart the new frontier, and he pointed the way for others. Such an accomplishment is neither small nor mean.

NOTES

1. Quoted in Charles A. Jellison, *Ethan Allen: Frontier Rebel* (Syracuse, NY: Syracuse University Press, 1969), p. 332. No original source cited. Other useful biographies of Allen include Michael Bellsiles, *Revolutionary Outlaws: Ethan Allen and the Struggle for Independence on the Early American Frontier* (Charlottesville: University of Virginia Press, 1995); Henry Hall, *Ethan Allen* (New York: D. Appleton & Co., 1892); Stewart H. Holbrook, *Ethan Allen* (New York: Macmillan, 1944); and John Pell, *Ethan Allen* (Boston: Houghton Mifflin, 1929).

2. Ibid., p. 16.

3. Ibid., p. 59.

4. Ethan Allen, A *Narrative of Col. Ethan Allen's Captivity* (Walpole, NH: Thomas & Thomas, 1807), p. 19.

5. Jellison, *Ethan Allen: Frontier Rebel*, p. 304.

6. Timothy Dwight, *Triumph of Infidelity: A Poem* (New York, 1788), pp. 23–24. Dwight's influence as a champion of Christian orthodoxy and scourge of infidelity was immense. See John R. Fitzmier, *New England's Moral Legislator: Timothy Dwight, 1752–1817* (Bloomington: Indiana University Press, 1998).

7. Jellison, *Ethan Allen: Frontier Rebel*, p. 311.

8. Ibid.

9. Ibid., p. 331.

10. Ibid., p. 332.

11. Ethan Allen, *Reason the Only Oracle of Man; or, a Compenduous System of Natural Religion* (Bennington, VT: Haswell & Russell, 1784), pp. v–vi. For discussions of Allen's *Reason*, see George Pomeroy Anderson, "Who Wrote 'Ethan Allen's Bible'?" *New England Quarterly* 10 (1937): 685–96. Dana Doten, "Ethan Allen's Original Something," *New England Quarterly* 11 (1938): 361–66; Clarence Gohdes, "Ethan Allen and His Magnum Opus," *Open Court* 43 (1929): 148; and B.T. Schantz, "Ethan Allen's Religious Ideas," *Journal of Religion* 18 (1938): 183–217.

12. Ibid., p. vii.

13. Ibid., p. 24.

14. Ibid., pp. 177–78, 180.

15. Ibid., pp. 182, 183.

16. Ibid., p. 183.

17. Ibid., p. 185.

18. Anthony Kenny, *Faith and Reason* (New York: Columbia University Press, 1983).

19. Ethan Allen, *Reason the Only Oracle of Man*, p. 331.

20. Ibid., pp. 354–55.

21. Ibid., p. 267.

22. Ibid., p. 269.

23. Ibid., p. 29.

24. Ibid., p. 34.

25. Ibid., p. 29.

26. Ibid., p. 26.

27. Ibid.

28. Ibid., p. 28.

29. Ibid., p. 30.

30. Ibid., pp. 190, 191.

31. Ibid., p. 191.

32. Ibid., p. 186.

33. Ibid., p. 190.

34. Ibid., p. 186.

35. David Hume, *A Treatise on Human Nature*, bk. I. pt. 3, secs. 1–4.

CHAPTER FOUR

THE ICONOCLASTIC DEIST

THOMAS PAINE

It may seem a bit arbitrary to refer to any one of the American deists as "iconoclastic." Each of them, after all, was a breaker of idols. Each gained notoriety for assailing the cherished beliefs of Christianity as well as much of the eighteenth century's received ethical and political wisdom. Each of them, finally, suffered to one extent or another from a predictable backlash of vilification from the orthodox camp. Even the relatively temperate Benjamin Franklin was no exception. Why, then, single out Thomas Paine?

There are two reasons for doing so. The first is that Paine, more than any of his fellow American deists, delighted in savaging the sacred cows of supernaturalist religion. In a steady barrage of pamphlets, articles, and speeches, he assailed the doctrines and dogmas of Christianity, mincing no words, pulling no punches, and giving as good as he received. Paine was a natural polemicist who genuinely enjoyed sparring with his Christian opponents. Part of his delight in intellectual gymnastics undoubtedly stemmed from his love of the limelight. Even his friends and admirers noted his almost obsessive need to be in the public eye. But it would be churlish as well as inaccurate to assume that Paine's hard-hitting and sometimes tastelessly vituperative assaults upon Christianity were motivated solely by self-interest. As much as he craved notoriety, he also genuinely seems to have believed in what he was doing. For Paine, Christianity was one of the primary obstacles to the inauguration of the Age of Reason in which individuals would thrive, societies flourish, and freedom and material prosperity reign. In attacking it and its doctrines, then, he was waging war against the centuries-old shackles of superstition, fear, and ignorance that prevented the human spirit from soaring. He was a man who enjoyed popularity, but he was also a man with a cause.

But there is another reason for singling out Paine as the iconoclastic deist. He came to be seen as the embodiment, the archetype, of the free-thinking, brimstone-reeking infidel. No other American deist so captured the popular imagination—not even Elihu Palmer, although he certainly gave Paine a run for his money. Eighteenth-century sympathizers with deism adopted Paine as their champion, seeing in him the fiery prophet whose intellectual hammer would bring down the walls of supernaturalist bondage and ignorance. Palmer spoke for them when he effusively lauded Paine as "probably the most useful man that ever existed upon the face of the earth." Paine's detractors overstated the case in the opposite direction, condemning him as evil and debauchery incarnate. To their eyes, he was a "detested reptile," a "lilly-livered sinical [*sic*] rogue," a "drunken atheist." In short, few people, during his time or since, remained indifferent to Paine. They either worshipfully applauded him as the first saint in a new world order of reason and harmony, or contemptuously dismissed him, as Theodore Roosevelt put it a century after Paine's death, as "a filthy little atheist." But regardless of which side of the debate they stood on, people then and now think of Paine when they think of American deism. For them, he is *the* American deist, *the* iconoclast.

Given the infamy that surrounds his name on the one hand, and, on the other, his elevation to almost mythological status in the pantheon of American freethinkers, it is not surprising that a great many confusions and misconceptions about Paine have acquired canonical status during the last two centuries. Contrary to his critics, he was neither a drunkard nor a libertine, although he does seem to have had a lifelong taste for strong brandy. Nor was he an enemy to religion, much less a "filthy little atheist." His primary deistic work, *The Age of Reason*, was in fact written partly to offer an alternative to the official atheism of the French Revolution, as well as to recall humanity to the "original" religion of nature. But neither was Paine a self-denying martyr to the cause of freedom of conscience, a pure and noble spirit who deliberately spent himself upon the altar of reason. Although he suffered for his convictions, no person was ever more averse to martyrdom and self-sacrifice than Tom Paine. He was, in short, neither saint nor sinner, savior nor devil. Instead, he was something arguably rarer: a man of conviction and eloquence who dared to speak his mind and refused to back down when challenged.

A MAN OF COMMON SENSE

Nothing in Paine's youth and early middle years would have triggered the suspicion that one day he would occupy a prominent place in the history of American letters. He was born in January 1737 in the English country town of Thetford-on-Norfolk, the son of Joseph and Frances Pain (Thomas only added the final "e" to his surname when he immigrated to America in 1774). His father, a none-too-successful corsetiere, was a Quaker, and his mother an Anglican. Young Tom was baptized and confirmed in the Church of England, but apparently attended Quaker meetings more often than Anglican services. He never formally joined the Society of Friends, but throughout his life he spoke positively of its relative absence of religious dogma. He was much less impressed with Anglicanism. In his later years, he reminisced that his apostasy from Christianity began at the tender age of eight while listening to an Anglican divine expatiate on the Redemption. The sermon, he relates, impressed upon him the latent cruelty in orthodox Christianity.[1] This anecdote probably should be read with a grain of salt. On occasion, when it suited his purposes, Paine melodramatically embellished his past. But it is significant that his earliest exposure to formal religious thought was a study in contrasts. This early experience of sectarian discord seeded his later conviction that even within the ranks of professing Christians there was no general consensus as to which doctrines were true and which false.

Like his contemporary Ethan Allen, Paine had little formal education. His father managed to send him to a local grammar school for some eight years, but financial hardship brought an end to his schooling in 1750, whereupon he entered his father's corset shop as an apprentice. As a result, Paine never quite mastered the niceties of English grammar, a shortcoming his later orthodox critics never tired of pointing out. But unlike the even less schooled Allen, Paine had a natural eloquence and easy style that more than made up for whatever he may have lacked in the way of grammatical finesse. In addition, he appears to have possessed astounding retentive powers and (like Allen) committed entire passages of the Bible to memory. This stood him in good stead, as we shall see, when he came to write the first part of *The Age of Reason* in 1793.

Young Paine appears to have heartily disliked the corset trade. He ran away at the age of sixteen to sign on as a seaman with one Captain Death, the master of the privateer *The Terrible*. His father managed to catch up with him before *The Terrible* set sail, and Tom endured the paternal trade for another three years. But in 1756, at the outbreak of the Seven Years' War, he once again ran away to sea, this time joining the crew of the privateer *King of Prussia*. He served for about a year and, at the age of twenty, found himself back in England, laboring at the despised trade of corset making under a London master.

Both professionally and personally, the next twenty years of his life were one long period of bleak failure. From London he relocated to Dover and then Sandwich, where he set up his own corset business and married. But Paine, never an acute businessman, soon went bankrupt and moved yet again, this time to Margate. His wife died (possibly in childbirth) less than a year into their marriage. Paine threw over his trade to enlist in His Majesty's service as an excise officer, charged with the collection of taxes on domestic commodities. But once again he was dogged by failure. After less than five years in the service, he was dismissed for approving a consignment of goods he later admitted he had not inspected. Although readmitted to the excise service a year later, he was not given another post until 1768.

In the meantime, the peripatetic Paine returned to London and then Kensington, at both of which he taught elementary school. After receiving his new excise assignment, he moved to the Sussex coast, remarried, was once again dismissed from government service, opened a tobacco and household goods shop which, like all his business ventures, quickly failed, and separated permanently from his second wife. By 1774, the year he sailed to America, Paine was by any and all accounts a failure, seemingly unable to sustain either professional or personal relationships. As he later laconically remarked, "Trade I do not understand." He might have added that the demands of marriage likewise mystified him.

But for all their ostensible bleakness, these years were important formative ones for Paine the thinker. During them he served his apprenticeship to his true calling as intellectual, polemicist, and amateur natural philosopher. Although Paine never was an avid reader, he had a naturally inquisitive mind and eagerly sought information about the subjects that interested him. Upon his move to London in 1757 after sailing with the *King of Prussia*, he began to pursue the scientific studies that would fascinate him for the rest of his life. As he later reminisced, "As soon as I was able I purchased a pair of globes, and attended the philosophical lectures of Martin and Ferguson, and became afterwards acquainted with Dr. Bevis, of the society called the Royal Society, then living in the Temple, and an excellent astronomer."[2] In spite of his wanderings and the employment difficulties he would face, Paine appears to have kept up his youthful investigations into the mysteries of natural philosophy.

Moreover, it was during these years that politics became an abiding passion for him. In his earlier years, he tells us, "I had no disposition for what is called politics. It presented to my mind no other idea than is contained in the word jockeyship."[3] But his experiences in the excise service convinced him that the word had richer, more profound meanings, and by the summer of 1772 he entered the political (and polemical arena) for the first time with a pamphlet that appealed to Parliament to raise the wages of its excise officers. His main argument was that the lack of decent wages encouraged otherwise conscientious excise men to succumb to bribery. Paine printed some four thousand copies of this pamphlet—at his own expense, it should be noted—and spent the winter of 1772–1773 in London hawking them. This first foray into political agitation did not meet with success. Parliament remained unconvinced. Paine's agitation cost him his position with the excise office, and the cost of printing his pamphlet saddled him with a huge debt. But the experience initiated him into a new realm, the world of political debate. Moreover, his return to London also enabled him to renew and enlarge his scientific and literary circle of acquaintances. He met Oliver Goldsmith, attended more Royal Society lectures, and, most important, was introduced to Benjamin Franklin, agent for the American colonies and already a luminary of natural science. It was Franklin who persuaded the thirty-seven-year-old Paine to strike out afresh in the New World. Armed with a letter of recommendation from Franklin, Tom Paine arrived in Philadelphia in late November 1774.

Evidently Paine's earlier venture into authorship had persuaded him of the advantages of journalism over corset making. Upon landing in Philadelphia, he almost immediately began writing for a new monthly called the *Pennsylvania Magazine*. His first article for it was a tribute to his new home. In it, Paine lauded the opportunities of the New World as well as its benevolent climate. The *Pennsylvania Magazine's* printer, Robert Aitken, was so impressed by this inaugural piece that he made Paine managing editor. By January 1775 Paine had more than doubled the subscriptions of the fledgling periodical and contributed several more pieces under a variety of pseudonyms. Aitken wished to avoid controversial religious or political issues, but Paine managed to slip in a few articles and poems of his (most of the latter, alas, quite bad) that hinted at his growing radicalism. Among the poems was a paean to political freedom that transparently challenged British authority in the colonies. It bellicosely concluded:

> From the east to the west blows the trumpet to arms,
>   Thro' the land let the sound of it flee,
> Let the far and the near—all unite with a cheer,
>   In defense of our *Liberty Tree*.[4]

In addition, Paine composed less lyrical (but equally bellicose) pieces, which included a condemnation of the Quakers for their pacifism, a technical article explaining how to make saltpeter for ammunition, and an impassioned attack upon the Pennsylvania Assembly for instructing its delegates to the First Continental Congress to vote against a motion for national independence.[5] As it turned out, these and similar pieces were but overtures to the main event. In February of 1776, Paine dropped the bombshell that has since been credited as being the catalyst for the Second Continental Congress's ratification of the Declaration of Independence. That bombshell was *Common Sense*.

Common Sense pulled no punches. Written in the pithy style that was to become Paine's trademark, it called for an immediate rupture with Great Britain; a continent, said Paine, could not remain tied to an island. There were more than just political reasons for severing the connection, he asserted. It was America's moral destiny to serve as an exemplar of liberty and equality to the rest of the world.

Although the first edition of *Common Sense* was published anonymously, the identity of its author soon became known as edition followed edition. Its success was astounding. Fifty-six editions, totaling some 150,000 copies, were sold in its first years. Almost overnight, Paine moved from the status of being a middle-aged failure to that of being a national (and, indeed, international) celebrity. The swiftness of his rise must have bewildered even him.

Paine quickly followed up his initial triumph with the *Crisis* series. Written to stir up and sustain the colonial war effort, the first article in the series began with the famous lines, "These are the times that try men's souls. The summer soldier and the sunshine patriot will, in this crisis, shrink from the services of their country; but he that stands it *now*, deserves the love and thanks of man and woman." Fifteen other *Crisis* articles would appear throughout the war years, and their impact was as great as *Common Sense*'s had been.

But Paine was not content to sit on the sidelines as merely an intellectual defender of the revolution. Like many Enlightenment thinkers, he was convinced that the value of human existence, as well as of ideas, was measured in terms of utility. Consequently, he threw himself into active politics. In April 1777 he became involved with the Continental Congress's committee on foreign affairs. In late 1779 he was appointed clerk of the Pennsylvania Assembly. In addition to devoting himself full-time to his official duties and polemical calling, Paine willingly sacrificed his own financial resources for the revolutionary cause, donating huge sums of money for the relief of Washington's army. He was also instrumental in persuading France in 1781 to contribute much-needed financial support to the war effort. At war's end, Paine was exhausted physically as well as financially. A grateful but financially troubled Republic partly compensated him with a tract of land and a small amount of cash. But his greatest reward was the successful culmination of the war. As he said in the last of the *Crisis* pieces, published in April 1783, "The times that tried men's souls is over—and the greatest and completest revolution the world ever knew, gloriously and happily accomplished."[6]

For the next few years, Paine returned to the less busy life of a private citizen. He resumed his scientific studies and devoted most of his energies to what became a pet project: the designing of an iron bridge. He also continued to write on political and social issues for the newspapers. But by 1787 the sedate life of a private intellectual had begun to wear on his restless spirit, and he sailed to Europe.

For the next two years he divided his time between Britain and France. He eventually built his iron bridge in England, although its construction came close to ruining him financially. But the revolution that erupted in France so fired his republican ardor that he once again deserted his scientific studies to plunge into political waters. He became a militant champion of the French cause, seeing in it a continuation of the world revolution to which the American struggle had given birth. His involvement in the second wave of the world revolution led to the publication of *The Rights of Man* (1791–1792). Ostensibly a reply to Edmund Burke's *Reflections on the Revolution in France*, which harshly condemned the recent events on the Continent, Paine's book was a philosophical defense of republicanism based upon the theory of natural rights. In it, he argued that it is the duty of government to protect those natural rights that the individual, left to himself, cannot ensure. These rights, equally possessed by all persons, include liberty, property, security, and freedom from intellectual and social oppression. The only form of government capable of protecting them is republicanism, and Paine saw the French Revolution of 1789 as the initial thrust in a European-wide movement toward republican liberty that would eventually topple all forms of nonrepresentative authority. "I do not believe that Monarchy and Aristocracy will continue seven years longer in any of the enlightened countries in Europe," he wrote. "If better reasons can be shewn for them than against them, they will stand; if the contrary, they will not. Mankind are not now to be told they shall not think or they shall not read."[7]

Predictably, Paine's *Rights of Man* was a bestseller in England. But just as predictably, it outraged the British authorities, who promptly suppressed its publication and convicted its author of treason in December 1792. Fortunately for Paine, he was in France when the sentence was handed down. Along with a few other American patriots, he had been made a French citizen by the National Assembly in mid-1792, and so could now add a third country to his list of homes. He was elected to the assembly, even though he could not speak French, and became a close associate of the revolutionary vanguard. But his pleas for the banishment rather than execution of Louis XVI, coupled with a wave of xenophobia, soured the Jacobin wing of the assembly, and by the end of 1793 Tom

Paine's newly adopted country had turned on him. He was stripped of his French citizenship as well as his parliamentary immunity, and incarcerated in the Luxembourg prison.

Although Paine later insisted that he feared for his life during his imprisonment, his eleven-month stint in the Luxembourg at least provided him with the leisure to write the book that would earn him a place in the front ranks of American deism: *The Age of Reason*. Part I appeared in 1794; part II in 1796; and part III in 1807. It is the first part that is of most interest. In it, Paine pointedly criticizes Christian doctrine and offers as an alternative his vision of a religion of nature and reason. It was written, he tells us, without the aid of notes or a Bible. The scriptural passages he cites and discusses are quoted from memory. The final two parts, written after his release from the Luxembourg, are devoted to a close (and at times tedious) analysis of the Old and New Testaments. Paine composed these sections, he tells us, to answer those critics who charged that part I had distorted Scripture. According to him, a close perusal of the Bible strengthened rather than weakened his original case. "[My critics] will now find that I have furnished myself with a Bible and Testament; and I can say also that I have found them to be much worse books than I had conceived. If I have erred in any thing in the former part of *The Age of Reason*, it has been by speaking better of some parts of those books than they have deserved."[8]

Paine's *Age of Reason* can be read as a theological extension of his republican convictions. Just as political authority has no justification for interfering with natural rights of liberty and property, so ecclesial authority is equally unwarranted in interdicting freedom of conscience. Each individual has the natural right and indeed obligation to think through his or her own religious beliefs, and the ultimate test of such reflection is reason, not supernaturalist creeds or dogma. Reason and conscience, then, are the sole guides in matters religious, and to believe otherwise is to embroil oneself and others in absurdities that give rise to ignorance and moral perversion. This general orientation is succinctly expressed by Paine in the credo that opens *The Age of Reason*.

I believe in one God, and no more; and I hope for happiness beyond this life.

I believe in the equality of man; and I believe that religious duties consist in doing justice, loving mercy, and endeavoring to make our fellow-creatures happy.

I do not believe in the creed professed by the Jewish church, by the Roman church, by the Greek church, by the Turkish church, by the Protestant church, nor by any church that I know of. My own mind is my own church.

All national institutions of churches, whether Jewish, Christian or Turkish appear to me no other than human inventions, set up to terrify and enslave mankind, and monopolize power and profit.

I do not mean by this declaration to condemn those who believe otherwise; they have the same right to their belief as I have to mine. But it is necessary to the happiness of man, that he be mentally faithful to himself. Infidelity does not consist in believing, or in disbelieving; it consists in professing to believe what he does not believe.[9]

For Paine, the sentiments expressed in these lines were both temperate and reasonable. After all, it seemed to him an "exceeding probability that a revolution in the system of government"—such as had occurred in America and France—"would be followed by a revolution in the system of religion," a revolution that would enable humans to "return to the pure, unmixed and unadulterated belief of one God, and no more."[10] The militant atheism of the French Jacobins frightened him. He correctly saw such disbelief as inevitably sliding toward excess and, indeed, atrocities, and he hoped that *The Age of Reason*'s defense of deism would stem its influence. But he was sadly disappointed. The book was unable to prevent the Terror, and what Paine saw as its reasonable defense of natural religion was rejected with horror and loathing by the orthodox Christian community.

Paine languished in the Luxembourg prison until 1794, ill fed and suffering from a "malignant fever," which at times he feared would carry him off. James Monroe, the recently appointed American minister to the French Republic, was instrumental in his release. Monroe rather disingenuously protested against Paine's incarceration on the grounds that he was a citizen of the United States. Legally dubious as Monroe's claim was, it worked. Paine was not only released by the French authorities but also rather incongruously restored to his seat in the National Assembly.

Paine stayed on in France for another seven years. During this time he lived a financially precarious existence, barely managing to eke out a living through journalistic fees as well as financial contributions from generous friends. But he continued to champion deism as the only religion worthy of a free and rational man, and helped found the Society of Theophilanthropists, a fraternal order dedicated to the discussion and dissemination of natural religion.

In October 1802 Paine returned to the United States. It must have been something of a shock for him to discover that he was no longer a hero to either the average American or the two leading political factions. The American publication of his *Rights of Man*, which contained a laudatory preface by Jefferson, had outraged the Federalists and convinced the Republicans that Paine was too controversial a character to publicly defend. His *Age of Reason* had infuriated America's orthodox establishment, which saw Paine as a loathsome infidel instead of a patriotic champion of liberty. Realizing that his star had set, Paine lived the last seven years of his life in relative retirement, confining his activities to occasional journalism and participation in the deistic movement launched by Elihu Palmer. When he died in early June 1809, he was refused burial in consecrated ground and was laid to rest at his New Rochelle farm, which a once-grateful America had given him in partial payment for his efforts in the War of Independence. Nor did the rather pathetic wanderings of Tom Paine end there. In 1819 William Cobbett, intending to erect a monument to the author of *The Rights of Man*, had Paine's body exhumed and shipped to England, the place of his birth. The monument was never erected, and when Cobbett died some sixteen years later, Paine's bones and coffin were purchased by a London dealer in secondhand furniture. At that point, in 1844, the mortal remains of Thomas Paine disappear from history's stage. Their ultimate fate is still unknown.

It is difficult to think of any American literatus who cut a more tragic figure than Paine. So long as he contented himself with political defenses of American independence, he was the darling of the young Republic. But the moment he stepped over the line of respectability in religious matters to extend his championship of liberty from the political to the theological arena, his fall from grace was swift and brutal. Reviled as an atheist (which he was not), detested and feared by established political leaders as a hotheaded revolutionist (which he was), and contemptuously dismissed as a drunkard and libertine (a charge that contains a grain of truth—but only that!), Paine was subjected both during his life and afterward to a campaign of vilification fueled more by prejudice than fact. He was not the most profound of the American deists in either his biblical criticism or his defense of natural religion. That honor falls to Thomas Jefferson and Elihu Palmer. But he was a man who valued truth above conventional and safe wisdom, and was able to express his reflections with an eloquence and piquancy that has immortalized certain of his more memorable phrases. He may not have been, as Palmer asserted, "the most useful man who ever existed upon the face of the earth." But who, after all, deserves such a tribute? Instead, he was a courageous and stalwart champion of freedom of conscience and human dignity. And that, surely, is tribute enough for anyone.

CHRISTIANITY AND MENTAL LYING

In his *Age of Reason*, Paine's strategy is to reveal the weaknesses of supernaturalist religion in general and Christianity in particular, and to defend as a superior alternative the religion of nature and reason. The first stage of his attack centers around two separate but related charges. Supernaturalism, he claims, is irrational. It mandates belief in propositions and perspectives that no reflective person can accept without ignoring the dictates of reason. Even more damagingly, the irrationalities that supernaturalism defends inevitably lead to a debasement of human dignity and the promulgation of immorality. Deception, which Paine assumes is the predominant characteristic of what he scornfully refers to as "priestcraft," serves no good purpose. It embroils the laity and clergy alike in falsehood that may generate a certain degree of immediate psychological comfort, but that in the long run is destructive. As Paine says in the book's opening pages,

> It is impossible to calculate the moral mischief, if I may so express it, that mental lying has produced in society. When a man has so far corrupted and prostituted the chastity of his mind, as to subscribe his pro-

fessional belief to things he does not believe, he has prepared himself for the commission of every other crime. He takes up the trade of a priest for the sake of gain, and, in order to qualify himself for that trade, he begins with a perjury. Can we conceive anything more destructive to morality than this?[11]

The harshness of this indictment is overwhelming. Other American deists, most notably Elihu Palmer, periodically indulged themselves in anticlerical invective. But none of them asserted as baldly as Paine that the clergy deliberately sought to deceive the public for purposes of self-aggrandizement. Paine's charge of clerical dishonesty, overheated as it is, rests upon his conviction that the central tenets of Christianity are too absurd to be creditable in the eyes of the very individuals who espouse them. Given such a conviction, only two options remain: either one assumes that clerics themselves are ignorant and hence deceived by their own rhetoric, or one assumes there is a deliberate attempt on their part to promulgate beliefs that they know to be false. Faced with the alternative of clerical stupidity or mendacity, Paine opted for the latter as the more likely of the two. Christianity, then, is a worldview too irrational for even professed champions to accept. Consequently, their promulgation of it is a conspiracy of "mental lying" geared toward the corruption of their parishioners' ability to think for themselves. Such a corruption, in turn, only serves to solidify the hegemony of ecclesial authority and the empowerment of its priests. It is arguable that this sweeping condemnation better fit the character of French Catholicism than American Protestantism, but Paine failed to make such a distinction. For him, priestcraft is priestcraft, regardless of the sectarian guise under which it hides.

As Paine sees it, the ultimate foundation upon which supernaturalism's worldview rests is its assumption that God has directly communicated a message to believers, a "special mission" that bestows on the human mind what unaided reason is unable to fathom. This special communication, immediately transmitted from God to humans, is called revelation. Each "church," Christian, Jewish, or Muslim, claims its own divine revelation. "The Jews say that their Word of God was given by God to Moses face to face; the Christians say, that their Word of God came by divine inspiration; and the Turks say, that their Word of God (the Koran) was brought by an angel from heaven." The problem is that "each of the churches accuses the other of unbelief." This is only predictable, since each insists upon the exclusive truth of its own revelatory foundation. But, says Paine, "for my part, I disbelieve them all."[12] Paine does not presume to deny that God possesses the power to communicate directly to humans if he so pleases. The rub, however, is that supernaturalist sects have forgotten or deliberately ignored the way they themselves define revelation—that is, as an *immediate* message from God to humans. Revelatory messages, even if they did at one time occur, are properly speaking revelations only to the person to whom they are directly transmitted. Once the original communication is recorded in oral or written tradition and passed on to others, it ceases, Paine says, to be revelation. Instead, it is mere hearsay, secondhand testimony.

> Revelation is necessarily limited to the first communication. After this, it is only an account of something which that person says was a revelation made to him; and though he may find himself obliged to believe it, it cannot be incumbent on me to believe it in the same manner, for it was not a revelation made to *me*, and I have only his word for it that it was made to *him*.[13]

Supposed revelatory messages that have been passed down from generation to generation as authoritative communications are, then, but "hearsay upon hearsay." No rational person would accept such testimony as strong evidence in a court of law. Similarly, there is no good reason to accept it as evidence for the truth of supernaturalism's claims.

This criticism of revelation is strong enough, Paine believed, to show that sacred Scripture lacks the authority that believers bestow upon it. But its unreliability becomes even more clear when the specific claims of Holy Writ are individually examined. A close textual analysis reveals that Scripture, whether Muslim, Jewish, or Christian, offers unreliable and vague evidence for the conclusions it presents. This lack of persuasive evidence for supernaturalist claims is especially apparent, argues Paine, in the Christian tradition.

The New Testament pretends to be a record of the life and teachings of Jesus Christ. But the book's claim to be a reliable biographical rendering is spurious. None of its parts were actually written by Jesus himself. Each of them, in fact, was composed only after his death, and even then they do not present a complete or consistent account of either his life or his intentions. The four Gospels were written by persons unknown, subsequent translations of them have adulterated their original texts, and the stories they relate are "detached anecdotes" that bewilder at best and insult reason at worst. Nor are the epistles contained in the New Testament authoritative. "The forgery of letters has been such a common practice in the world, that the probability is at least equal, whether they are genuine or forged." Finally, John's so-called Revelation is a book of "enigmas" that no rational person can read with either pleasure or conviction.[14] So much, then, for the book upon which Christianity rests its case. Reason dismisses its claim to be an authoritative revelation of God to humans, because revelation ends where hearsay begins. Analysis shows that when examined from a purely textual perspective, the New Testament is anecdotal, inconsistent, of dubious authorship, and written long after the events it purports to describe. As such, it violates every canon of evidence accepted by humankind. There is no good reason, Paine concludes, to accept its accounts as authoritative. In fact, reason demands just the contrary.

As was the case with all deists, Paine singled out the doctrine of miracles as the most obvious example of doctrinal absurdity and scriptural unreliability. In his estimation, "Of all the modes of evidence that ever were invented to obtain belief to any system or opinion to which the name of religion has been given, that of miracle, however successful the imposition may have been, is the most inconsistent."[15] There are three reasons for this charge. First, says Paine, the appeal to miracles reveals a "lameness or weakness in the doctrine that is preached."[16] A miracle is supposed to be a supernatural rupture in the system of natural laws that regulates natural phenomena. As such, it cannot be rationally understood, because the uniform system of nature necessarily serves as a point of reference for all knowledge claims, and miracles eschew that foundation. Consequently, to appeal to a miraculous intervention to "explain" a phenomenon is to cite no explanation at all. It is merely an expedient, but quite irrational, attempt to account for a dogmatic belief. Miraculous "explanations," then, are lame efforts to explain the unknown by an appeal to the inexplicable.

Second, the dogmatic postulation of miraculous interventions in the system of natural law degrades the Almighty to the "character of a showman" who plays "tricks to amuse and the people stare and wonder."[17] The belief that the Deity at times interferes with his own established handiwork casts suspicion on the doctrine of divine omnipotence. The implication is that God erred in his original blueprint and must play an ad hoc role of celestial handyman. But this suggests that the Supreme Architect is less than fully powerful; he would be error-prone, and such an assumption demeans the dignity and majesty of God. It reduces the awesome Creator of the universe to the status of a fumbling magician.

Finally, God's nature to one side, the weight of evidence is against the possibility of miracles when alternative explanations are considered. In an argument reminiscent of David Hume's, Paine asks: "Is it more probable that nature should go out of her course, or that a man should tell a lie?" For him, the answer is obvious. "We have never seen, in our time, nature go out of her course; but we have good reason to believe that millions of lies have been told in the same time; it is, therefore, at least millions to one, that the reporter of a miracle tells a lie."[18]

The upshot is that one of the primary foundations upon which Christianity bases its creed is unworthy of rational belief. The incarnation and the resurrection, the twin doctrines around which Christian faith revolves, are as egregious as the Old Testament accounts of the dividing of the Red Sea or the transformation of Lot's wife into a pillar of salt. Such beliefs, contrary to the assertions of the Christian church, do not strengthen religious sensibility so much as parody and hence sully it. "Instead, therefore, of admitting the recitals of miracles as evidence of any system of religion being true, they ought to be considered as symptoms of its being fabulous. It is necessary to the full and upright character of truth that it rejects the crutch; and it is consistent with the character of fable to seek the aid that truth rejects. Thus much for . . . Miracle."[19]

The irrationality of Christian doctrines such as revelation and miracles is reason enough for its rejection, but the logical case against Christianity is normatively underscored when one considers that its absurdities give rise to immorality. Recall that Paine earlier insisted that the Christian system gives birth to incalculable "moral mischief." This is because it espouses "mental lying," which prostitutes and corrupts the chastity of reason. The mental lying Paine refers to here is an example of what we today might call "doublethink." At one and the same time, Christianity mandates acceptance of contrary beliefs such as natural law and miraculous intervention, reason and revelation, free inquiry and dogmatic authority. But the only way such doublethink contradictions can be psychologically maintained is if the believer blindly refuses to brook dissent and criticism. This stubborn grasp of irreconcilable tenets, Paine argues, destroys freedom of conscience and encourages intolerance and persecution. As he says in one of *The Age of Reason*'s most memorable passages:

> The most detestable wickedness, the most horrid cruelties, and the greatest miseries, that have afflicted the human race, have had their origin in this thing called revelation, or revealed religion. It has been the most dishonourable belief against the character of the divinity, the most destructive to morality, and the peace and happiness of man, that ever was propagated since man began to exist. It is better, far better, that we admitted, if it were possible, a thousand devils to roam at large, and to preach publicly the doctrine of devils, if there were any such, than that we permitted one such imposter and monster as Moses, Joshua, Samuel, and the Bible prophets, to come with the pretended word of God in his mouth, and have credit among us.[20]

In addition to the intolerance spawned by Christianity's dogmatic insistence upon irrational beliefs, the worldview's "detestable wickedness" is also, in Paine's estimation, attested to by a variety of scriptural "moral" injunctions. These are "irregularly and thinly scattered" throughout the New Testament and are completely unsystematic in tone. They fall into two camps. Some, such as the maxim that has come to be known as the Golden Rule, are truly edifying but are simply "the natural dictates of conscience," and hence not at all unique to Christian thought. But other normative maxims are less instructive. They recommend behavior that, says Paine, is "mean and ridiculous" because they demean human dignity.

One of these mean and ridiculous injunctions is Jesus' command that "If a man smite thee on the right cheek, turn to him the other also." According to Paine, such a recommendation "assassinates" the "dignity of forebearance," "sinking man into a spaniel."[21] Closely associated with it is the New Testament command to love one's enemies. It is, remarks Paine, a "dogma of feigned morality, and has besides no meaning."

It is incumbent on man, as a moralist, that he does not revenge an injury; and it is equally good in a political sense, for there is no end to retaliation; each retaliates on the other and calls it justice: but to love in proportion to the injury, if it could be done, would be to offer a premium for a crime. Besides, the word *enemies* is too vague and general to be used in a moral maxim, which ought always to be clear and defined.[22]

Paine takes most offense, then, at those normative injunctions in Christianity that prescribe, in his estimation, a demeaning acquiescence. Such meekness ill behooves people concerned with the eradication of social and political evils. It not only does nothing to deter future occurrences of hurtful behavior; it actually encourages them through reward. Even more perniciously, institutional Christianity fails to heed its own moral advice, as becomes apparent when the history of the Church is scrutinized. "Those who preach this doctrine of loving their enemies, are in general the greatest persecutors, and they act consistently by so doing; for the doctrine is hypocritical, and it is natural that hypocrisy should act the reverse of what it preaches."[23]

This charge of hypocrisy brings Paine full circle in his denunciation of Christianity, returning him to his original point that the "mental lying" practiced by priestcraft corrupts the mind and breeds moral mischief. From first to last, his appraisal of Christian supernatural belief is harshly negative. Had he ended his case here, *The Age of Reason* would have horrified late eighteenth-century believers, but in all likelihood would have been a short-lived scandal, eventually dismissed as the sometimes clever but ultimately directionless ramblings of a village atheist. But iconoclast that he was, Paine recognized the insufficiency of merely wielding the hammer of destruction. He realized that the demolition of Christian pretensions had to be complemented by a judiciously defended vision of an alternative religious sensibility. Again, Paine was no atheist, and he had no desire to promote disbelief in God per se, but only in the God of Christianity. His objections to supernatural religion reduce to the charge that it mandates belief in tenets for which there is no evidence or rational support. But it was one of his cardinal rules that "a thing which everybody is required to believe, requires that proof and evidence of it should be equal to all, and universal."[24] Using this tenet as his fundamental working assumption, Paine went on to defend a religion of nature and reason that he was convinced lived up to this standard.

PUTTING THEOLOGY RIGHT

Enlightenment thinkers both in America and on the Continent were highly skeptical of metaphysical speculation. Bacon had spelled out the risks involved in entangling human thought in abstract syllogisms. Locke showed that all legitimate knowledge is necessarily grounded in empirical data, unencumbered by innate, a priori ideas. Newton clinched the point by successfully mapping nature's laws without recourse to "feigned" hypotheses. The accomplishments of these three men convinced Enlightenment savants that a clear distinction had to be drawn between fanciful opinion and empirical knowledge, between merely "invented" theory and theory based firmly upon the apperception of natural law. To collapse the two ran the risk of accepting as fact what is merely interpretation.

Paine accepted this distinction without reservation. His lifelong involvement with scientific and engineering problems persuaded him of two things: first, that reality is lawlike in its operations; and second, that human reason is capable of discovering and understanding such laws, thereby enabling humans to discriminate between unfounded superstition and legitimate belief. The methodological implications of Paine's basic orientation is obvious: if one wishes to understand reality, one must start with the raw data of experience, stripped of theoretical presuppositions and personal biases. Otherwise, one's descriptions are contrived rather than objective, and one's explanations speculative instead of empirical.

This simple procedural rule is one that Christian theology, in Paine's judgment, ignores. Instead of examining the available evidence, supernatural religion interjects an a priori model into the picture that serves to separate humans from reality. This model blocks an accurate understanding of natural law and God, opening the door to the elaboration of a theology that clouds reason and distorts reality, both divine and mundane. But such a fanciful system is not true theology. Instead, says Paine, "it is a compound made up chiefly of man-ism with but little deism, and is as near to atheism as twilight is to darkness. . . . It has put the whole orbit of reason into shade. The effect . . . has been that of turning everything upside down, and representing it in reverse."[25]

If the knowledge of God has been turned upside down by Christianity's refusal to base its claims upon observable fact, then the obvious way to set theology right again is to ground it firmly in a reflective observation of actual phenomena. The study of humanity demands that one examine human works: analogously, the study of God demands an investigation of divine work. God's handiwork is not a timeworn set of canonized books. Instead, it is nature itself. Consequently, the most appropriate avenue to true knowledge of God is the scientific investigation of nature. "That which is now called natural philosophy, embracing the whole circle of science, of which astronomy occupies the chief place, is the study of the works of God, and of the power and wisdom of God in his works, and is the true theology."[26]

Paine acknowledged that a critic might respond by insisting that science itself is "man-ish," a human invention that has forgotten its human origins, and that consequently the "true theology" of deism is but one more imaginative "contrivance." After all, natural philosophy goes far beyond mere descriptions of physical phenomena. It also infers generalizations from such descriptions, and claims that these generalizations are in turn expressions of natural laws. Surely, the critic could conclude, such generalizations are themselves interpretations, and all interpretations are human inventions. Why, then, are deism's interpretations preferable to nondeistic ones?

Paine answers this objection by distinguishing between natural "principles" or laws, and the application of them. He admits that applied science is a human contrivance, subject to debate and revision. But he contends that the basis of such applications—the system of natural law that is deducible from an investigation of reality—is not. "Every science," he says, "has for its basis a system of principles as fixed and unalterable as those by which the universe is regulated and governed. Man cannot make principles, he can only discover them."[27]

Take, for example, astronomy, which Paine claimed occupied "the chief place" in the "circle of sciences." It is true that the almanacs that predict eclipses and other stellar phenomena are calculated and written by human beings. They are attempts to symbolize and predict a certain type of physical phenomenon, and as such qualify as human "inventions." But the very fact that almanacs are able to predict with mathematical exactitude the future occurrence of astronomical events indicates, according to Paine, that while the almanac itself is a human contrivance, the principles upon which it is based are not. "It would . . . be ignorance," he says, or something worse, to say that the scientific principles, by the aid of which man is enabled to calculate and foreknow when an eclipse will take place, are a human invention. Man cannot invent any thing that is eternal and immutable; and the scientific principles he employs for this purpose must, and are, of necessity, as eternal and immutable as the laws by which the heavenly bodies move, or they could not be used as they are to ascertain the time when, and the manner how, an eclipse will take place.[28]

But, it might be objected, the scientific principles that enable humans to ascertain the time and manner of stellar events are mathematical, encompassing trigonometry and geometry. Surely, however, "it may be said, that man can make or draw a triangle, and therefore a triangle"—and the entire realm of mathematics known as geometry—"is a human invention."

Not so, responds Paine. To take this objection seriously is once again to confuse the application of a principle with the principle itself. A triangle, when drawn with the aid of a straight-edge, is "no other than the image of the principle: it is a delineation to the eye, and from thence to the mind, of a principle that would otherwise be imperceptible." But the triangle in no way depends upon the drawing for its definition, much less for its existence. Both of these are mathematical in character, and hence independent of human applications.

> The triangle does not make the principle, any more than a candle taken into a room that was dark, makes the chairs and tables that before were invisible. All the properties of a triangle exist independently of the figure, and existed before any triangle was drawn or thought of by man. Man had no more to do in the formation of these properties or principles, than he had to do in making the laws by which the heavenly bodies move.[29]

The drawn triangle, then, or any other contrived representation of a mathematical principle, is admittedly but a human invention for the delineation and manipulation of an immutable and eternal law. It is, in other words, a tool, analogous to the engineer's lever. But even though humans concretize natural principles in order to grasp and utilize them, this in no way implies that the principles themselves are likewise contrived. The principle by which a lever acts or a triangle is mathematically defined differs from the actual mechanical instrument or the drawing.

The action and the drawing, human contrivances that they are, underscore the eternal principles that lie behind them. The "effect" of the lever, no less than the visualized triangle, "is no other than the principle itself rendered perceptible to the senses."[30]

The human sciences, then, which serve as the basis of "true" theology, are not contrived by human imagination. Even their interpretive applications point to an underlying law that humans only discover and do not create. And the ultimate source from which the natural philosopher draws his discoveries is nature. "It is the structure of the universe that has taught this knowledge to man. That structure is an ever-existing exhibition of every principle upon which every part of mathematical science is founded."[31]

But why does Paine claim that scientific principle, discovered and not invented, is the basis of "true" theology? How is it, as he declared earlier, that natural philosophy "is the study of the works of God, and of the power and wisdom of God in his works?"

Paine's answer to this question is that the system of natural laws that are deducible from a scrutiny of physical phenomena are "written" in a "universal language," independent of "human speech or human language." Such a system, he seems to be suggesting, far transcends the limits of human reason or creativity. "It cannot be forged; it cannot be counterfeited; it cannot be lost; it cannot be altered; it cannot be suppressed. It does not depend upon the will of man whether it shall be published or not; it publishes itself from one end of the earth to the other."[32] Experience teaches that human abilities are radically finite, as well as that everything that is has a cause external to itself. We know that humans are capable of causing-to-be any number of inventions, material as well as conceptual. Moreover, the nature of creations reflects the nature of their creators. Since humans are finite, temporal, and error-prone, their creations necessarily convey the qualities of finitude, temporality, and provisionality. Consequently, we also know that no human is capable of creating an immutable, uniform, and universal law, much less a cosmic system of such laws. We cannot "speak," as Paine puts it, in such a "universal language." It follows, then, that we are justified in inferring that reality, like everything else which exists, has a cause external to itself. Moreover, the nature of this cause is reflected in its works. Since reality exhibits immutability, eternality, and universality, these qualities likewise must be present in its creator. And this shows the creator to be divine. Paine expresses the point succinctly:

> Everything we behold carries in itself the internal evidence that it did not make itself. Every man is an evidence to himself, that he did not make himself; neither could his father make himself, nor his grandfather, nor any of his race; neither could any tree, plant, or animal make itself; and it is the conviction arising from this evidence, that carries us on, as it were, by necessity, to the belief of a first cause eternally existing, of a nature totally different to any material existence we know of, and by the power of which all things exist; and this first cause, man calls God.[33]

Natural science is the true foundation of true theology, then, because it irresistibly points to the existence of a First Cause who set in motion the system of secondary causations that define reality. The scientific scrutiny of physical phenomena, in other words, reveals the necessary existence of a divine principle.

A few years after he wrote this argument for the existence of God, Paine offered a second, modified version of it. It is spelled out in an address titled "The Existence of God," which Paine delivered as the inaugural lecture at the first meeting of the Parisian Society of Theophilanthropists in January 1797.

Paine offers this second argument, he tells us, in order to respond to those natural philosophers who "instead of looking through the works of creation to the Creator himself. . . , stop short and employ the knowledge they acquire to create doubts of His existence." Their fall into atheism is the result of their assumption that all observable events in nature can be chalked up to the "innate properties of matter."[34] But this is a conclusion that cannot be rationally defended if one considers the phenomenon of "motion."

It is true, Paine concedes, that matter possesses certain innate properties such as those of mass, extension, and "state," by which Paine means the possibility of decomposition and recomposition. Thus far he and the atheists agree. But the point of departure for Paine is the atheistic insistence that motion is a fourth intrinsic quality of matter. Paine admits that motion—by which he seems to mean "locomotion"—is an observable natural phenomenon, but denies that it is a property innate to matter. "The universe is composed of matter, and, as a system, is sustained by motion. Motion is not a property of matter, and without this motion, the solar system could not exist. Were motion a property of matter, that undiscovered and undiscoverable thing called perpetual motion would establish itself."[35] Since perpetual motion is both an actual impossibility and a logical absurdity, the origin of motion must be looked for apart from matter in motion.

But how to account for it? Gravitation, in spite of the claims of some, is not its source, but only another manifestation of it. The power that holds the solar system together, which sustains the heavenly bodies in their relational motion to one another—that, in short, ensures the "perpetual preservation" of the system as a whole—is itself not a property of matter. Instead, it is a function of the universe's overall structure. This function, in turn, can only be accounted for by an appeal to a source that is external to both matter and the relations that hold between material bodies in motion. "When, therefore, we discover a circumstance of such immense importance that without it the universe could not exist, and for which neither matter, nor all the properties can account, we are by necessity forced into the rational belief of the existence of a cause superior to matter, and that cause man calls GOD."[36]

These two arguments for God's existence take slightly different approaches, although each claims to demonstrate divine existence from reflection upon the phenomenon of causation. In the first, Paine's point is that since nothing in the physical order can cause itself to be, the entire set of physical objects—reality—likewise is incapable of causing itself to be. The first argument, then, focuses upon the origin of reality. But Paine's approach in the later address "The Existence of God" concerns itself not so much with reality's origin as with its endurance. It argues that the network of material bodies and physical relations, or motions, cannot sustain itself through a set of intrinsic properties. Consequently, the network's continued existence must be preserved, or "caused" to continue, by an external divine source.

Regardless of whether these two cosmological arguments are ultimately satisfactory, Paine uses them to underscore his insistence that "true" theology is natural science. This in turn suggests two additional conclusions. First, God *does* reveal himself, although not through the supposed sacred writ of supernaturalist Christianity. Instead, God reveals himself through nature. As Paine says, "the word of God is the creation we behold."[37] Second, "it is only by the exercise of reason, that man can discover God."[38] Mysterious illuminations, miraculous interventions, faith: none of these traditional Christian tenets are required for a knowledge of God. They obfuscate rather than clarify, interposing between human reason and the book of nature an almost impenetrable fog of superstition and confusion. As Paine concludes,

> Instead then of studying theology, as it is now done, out of the Bible and Testament, the meanings of which books are always controverted, and the authenticity of which is disproved, it is necessary that we refer to the Bible of creation. The principles we discover there are eternal, and of divine origin: they are the foundation of all the science that exists in the world, and must be the foundation of theology.[39]

The truly religious person, then, will devoutly turn to nature and the discoveries of past natural philosophers in the attempt to understand God. "The Almighty is the great mechanic of the creation, the first philosopher, and original teacher of all science. Let us then learn to reverence our master, and not forget the labours of our ancestors."[40]

But just how far does human knowledge of the divine extend? Paine's optimistic insistence that God's true revelation is creation suggests that knowledge of God is directly proportionate to knowledge of creation. If, as Paine says, "we can know God only through his works," then, at least in principle, such knowledge is unlimited.

> Could a man be placed in a situation, and endowed with power of vision to behold at one view, and to contemplate deliberately, the structure of the universe, to mark the movements of the several planets, the cause of their varying appearances, the unerring order in which they revolve, even to the remotest comet, their connection and dependence on each other, and to know the system of laws established by the Creator, that governs and regulates the whole; he would then conceive, far beyond what any church theology can teach him, the power, the wisdom, the vastness, the munificence of the Creator.[41]

In actuality, however, such a cosmic perspective is beyond the powers of human reason. Individuals always know in a context and from a specific perspective. Consequently, Paine admits that human knowledge of the Deity, although in principle perfectible, is in practice "confused" because knowledge of the divine handiwork is necessarily limited.

Still, Paine insists that a lack of comprehensive understanding of God's works does not mean that nothing significant can be said about God's nature. This is because humans have fathomed the principles by which the natural order operates, even if a complete cataloging of reality's minutiae is impossible. These principles, of course, are natural laws. Our knowledge of how they define and regulate observable phenomena can be used as paradigms by which to infer, even if we can't be directly acquainted with, the nature of the whole as well as God.

> Though man cannot arrive, at least in this life, at the actual scene I have described, he can demonstrate it, because he has knowledge of the principles upon which the creation is constructed. We know that the greatest works can be represented in model, and that the universe can be represented by the same means. The same principles by which we measure an inch or an acre of ground will measure to millions in extent. A circle of an inch diameter has the same geometrical properties as a circle that would circumscribe the universe. The same properties of a triangle that will demonstrate upon paper the course of a ship, will do it on the ocean; and, when applied to what are called the heavenly bodies, will ascertain to a minute the time of an eclipse, though those bodies are millions of miles distant from us.[42]

Deduction from the first principles of reality—natural laws—therefore provides humans with a systematic blueprint of nature and nature's ways. The immutability and universality of these natural laws lead to the reasonable conclusion that no aspect of reality is impervious to them, even if the awesome quantity of available physical data staggers the human mind. Moreover, since knowledge of God is proportionate to knowledge of God's revelation, it can be surmised that the general nature of the Divine Architect, as an entity immutable as well as supremely rational, is also demonstrable. Humans are incapable of knowledge of either God or reality as a whole through direct acquaintance, but the essence of both can be ascertained through logical demonstration. It shows that both natural law and God exist, and also provides the human intellect with a general, albeit imprecise, model of the natures of both. Given this perspective, it is not surprising that Paine tells us in *The Age of Reason* that the nineteenth

Psalm, which proclaims that "the heavens declare the glory of God; and the firmament sheweth his handiwork," is his favorite. To his mind the sentiment it expresses is the heart of deism's true theology.

VIRTUE PROPORTIONATE TO REASON

The natural religion of deism, for Paine, is "the only religion that has not been invented, and that has in it every evidence of divine originality." Given both its simplicity and purity, he continues, "it must have been the first [religion] and will probably be the last that man believes." The supernaturalism Christianity espouses is by contrast a centuries-old accretion of superstition, false doctrine, and other forms of "mental lying," all of which are calculated by churchmen to befuddle the reason and intimidate the spirit. Historically, says Paine, both political and ecclesial authorities have profited from the intimidation, ignorance, and moral cowardice Christianity promotes. But deism's call for individuals to heed the dictates of conscience and reason "does not answer the purpose of despotic governments."[43] Instead, it encourages genuine religious as well as moral sensibility by building its case upon natural law and the light of reason, both of which are equally accessible to everyone, and by defending a doctrine of God unblemished by fantastic doctrinal inventions. True, Christianity likewise proclaims a deity, but one which is so offensive to reason that "a man, by hearing all this nonsense lumped and preached together, confounds the God of the Creation with the imagined god of the Christians, and lives as if there were none."[44] But moral bankruptcy bred from the atheism of despair is not an inevitability. "Were a man impressed as fully and strongly as he ought to be with the belief of a God," asserts Paine, "his moral life would be regulated by the force of belief; he would stand in awe of God, and of himself, and would not do the thing that could not be concealed from either."[45] Deism, in Paine's judgment, defends a concept of God capable of "fully and strongly" impressing itself as such an incentive to virtue.

In keeping with other eighteenth-century deists, Paine believes that a life of virtue is the highest form of adoration a human can offer to the Deity. But unlike most of his deistic compatriots, he is rather vague about what constitutes a virtuous existence. Franklin, Jefferson, and Palmer each went to great efforts to spell out their respective ethical theories. Paine, however, never did so. Consequently, one can only speculate about what he means in claiming that belief in the God of deism promotes morality.

In all likelihood, what Paine has in mind is the thesis that virtue is proportionate to reason—the more rational a human is, the more drawn he or she is to benevolence, compassion, tolerance, and so on. Deism promotes human virtue, then, because it endorses the unencumbered exercise of reason and thereby discourages mental lying. To cultivate the one and avoid the other is to live in a godly way, accommodating one's will to the natural order ordained by the Divine Mechanic. It is, in other words, to live in accordance with natural principle, to conform one's existence to the natural scheme of things. Such conformity not only does honor to God by holding him up as the supreme standard of behavior; it also promotes individual felicity and social well-being. Deceptions, irrationalisms, intellectual coercion, and social intolerance are never in the true interest of mankind. They retard science, shatter self-discipline, and stifle creative inquiry. They breed ignorance and self-loathing, which in turn are the midwives of wickedness. To be the "mere slave of terror," says Paine, is ultimately to lead a life in which "our belief would have no merit, and our best actions no virtue."[46] But the religion of nature strikes off the chains of terror, first by exposing superstition, and second by revealing to humans that knowledge about reality, God, and virtue is well within their reach. All that is required is an unafraid and unimpeded exercise of reason. If governments and ecclesial hierarchies have blocked free inquiry in the past, thereby nurturing poisonous environments that give rise to ignorance and wickedness, there is no necessity that they continue to do so in the future. The American and French revolutions as well as the concomitant growth of republican sentiment offer tangible evidence in support of such a contention.

Paine's moral pronouncements, in the final analysis, are really rather unexceptional. He accepts the theory of natural rights and the equality of persons, both of which he defended in his *Rights of Man*, but for the most part explores the political rather than the moral implications of such a perspective. He assumes that rational behavior is ethical behavior, because to act rationally is to act in a godly manner, but he never spells out just what the specifics of such behavior are. As pointed out earlier, he *does* insist in his *Age of Reason* that virtuous/religious duty consists in "doing justice, loving mercy, and endeavoring to make our fellow-creatures happy." But he fails to follow up this claim with reflection upon what precisely constitutes justice, mercy, or happiness.

Unremarkable as his moral reflections are, it cannot be doubted that Paine earnestly believed a virtuous life was the best way in which to serve both humanity and God. In a short essay titled "My Private Thoughts on a Future State," he goes so far as to argue that if an afterlife is possible, it is reserved for those who have endeavored in this life to serve their fellow humans. He does not, he tells us, presume to know what lies in store for us after death. "I do not believe because a man and a woman make a child that it imposes on the Creator the unavoidable obligation of keeping the being so made in eternal existence hereafter. It is in his power to do so or not to do so."[47] But he does think it at least a logical possibility that virtuous behavior may be rewarded after death. He suggests that those individuals who have spent their lives in doing good, "the only way in which we can serve God," will be "happy hereafter." Those who have been "very" wicked may "meet with some punishment." But few people are profoundly good or egregiously wicked. Most fall somewhere in between. And these, he says, who are "too insignificant for notice," will be "dropped entirely."[48] Only an individual with a keen and exacting sense of moral justice could have penned such words.

A MASTERFUL POLEMICIST

For all his notoriety, it is clear that Paine was neither the most profound nor the most systematic of the American deists. The first description best fits Jefferson; the second, Elihu Palmer. Unlike these men, Paine's forte was not rigorous analysis or comprehensive vision. Rather, he excelled in the not-so-genteel art of polemics, which is often willing to sacrifice depth for effect. But it is undeniable that, among polemicists, Paine is in the front rank. He had all the necessary requirements for success: passion, courage, tenacity, and, perhaps most important, the ability to capture his readers' imagination with a finely tuned and memorable phrase.

It is also clear that most of *The Age of Reason* is derivative. Neither its criticisms of Christian doctrine nor its more positive discussions of deism originated with Paine. The same or at least similar arguments can be found in the works of the British deists, the French savants, and even a few eighteenth-century liberal Christians. This fact has prompted one twentieth-century commentator to remark, "there is absolutely nothing new in the book."[49] At first glance, this seems like a fair assessment.

But is it? Even if we grant that Paine's reflections on deism are neither original nor terribly profound, are we justified in concluding that his work contributed "nothing new"? How one answers this question depends, of course, upon what one means by "contribution." If the word is taken to imply a startlingly innovative thesis, a groundbreaking discovery in the realm of ideas, a far-reaching vision that sheds new and unexpected light upon conventional paradigms, then the answer is clear. Paine's defense of deism is not a new contribution.

But surely there is another, less constricted meaning of the word that also deserves consideration. In this sense, a contribution is made when an individual is able to collect and present the arguments of others in such a way as to breathe life into them and thereby render them a potent force in society and in popular thought. This, it may be argued, was Paine's unique contribution to deism. No American deist before him so stirred up public debate over religious issues. Poor Ethan Allen tried to in his *Oracles of Reason*, but few copies of his book ever circulated, and the turgidity of his style probably meant that even fewer were actually read. But Paine's *The Age of Reason* was something quite different. It was readily accessible on the street, and the clarity of its style as well as its outrageously iconoclastic denunciations of supernaturalism propelled it to center stage. In short, there may have been nothing new *in* the book, but there was certainly something new *about* it. It spoke in such strident terms that it simply could not be ignored. It focused public attention on the nature of religious belief in general and Christianity's claims in particular, and in doing so ushered in a twenty-year crusade for deism that would rock the young Republic to its core. Rant and rave against it as they might, orthodox opponents of Paine's book fully recognized it for what it was: the first shot in a war against traditional Christian belief, a war that threatened to leave the American Zion "without an helper." Allen primed the guns for the opening salvo with his *Oracles of Reason*, but it was the iconoclastic spark of Paine's *The Age of Reason* that actually launched the missile. Paine was more correct than even he suspected when he described the final quarter of the eighteenth century in America as a time that "tried men's souls." It is at least in part because of the influence of his unabashed infidelity that this description is fitting.

NOTES

1. Thomas Paine, *The Age of Reason*, pt. 1, in *The Life and Works of Thomas Paine*, vol. 8, ed. William M. Van der Weyde (New Rochelle, NY: Thomas Paine National Historical Association, 1925), p. 71. Hereafter cited *LWTP*. Other biographical treatments include Alfred Owen Aldridge, *Man of Reason: The Life of Thomas Paine* (New York: Lippincott, 1959); Moncure Daniel Conway, *Life of Thomas Paine* (New York: G.P. Putnam's Sons, 1892); David Freeman Hawke, *Paine* (New York: Harper and Row, 1974); and Craig Nelson, *Thomas Paine: Enlightenment, Revolution, and the Birth of Modern Nations* (New York: Penguin, 2007). Studies of Paine's religious views include Robert P. Falk, "Thomas Paine: Deist or Quaker?" *Pennsylvania Magazine of History and Biography* 62 (1938): 52–63 and Franklin K. Prochaska, "Thomas Paine's *The Age of Reason* Revisited," *Journal of the History of Ideas* 33 (1972): 561–76.

2. *LWTP*, vol. 8, p. 69.

3. Ibid.

4. Thomas Paine, "Liberty Tree," in *LWTP*, vol. 10, p. 313.

5. Although Paine took exception to the pacifism of American Friends during the War of Independence, he never lost his early high regard for their religious beliefs and tolerance. When he died in 1809, he left a request in his will to be buried in a Quaker cemetery. The request was denied.

6. Thomas Paine, *The American Crisis*, no. 13, in *LWTP*, vol. 3, p. 237.

7. Thomas Paine, *Rights of Man*, pt. 2, in *LWTP*, vol. 7, p. 56.

8. Thomas Paine, *The Age of Reason*, pt. 2, in *LWTP*, vol. 8, pp. 108–109.

9. Thomas Paine, *The Age of Reason*, pt. 1, in *LWTP*, vol. 8, pp. 4–5.

10. Ibid., pp. 5–6.

11. Ibid., p. 5.

12. Ibid., pp. 6–7.

13. Ibid., pp. 7–8.

14. Ibid., pp. 32, 37.

15. Ibid., pp. 93–94.

16. Ibid, p. 94.

17. Ibid.

18. Ibid., p. 95.

19. Ibid., p. 97.

20. Thomas Paine, *The Age of Reason*, pt. 2, in *LWTP*, vol. 8, p. 12.

21. Ibid., pp. 272–73.

22. Ibid., p. 273.

23. Ibid., p. 274.

24. Thomas Paine, *The Age of Reason*, pt. 1, in *LWTP*, vol. 8, p. 12.

25. Ibid., p. 49.

26. Ibid., p. 50.

27. Ibid., p. 51.

28. Ibid., p. 52.

29. Ibid., p. 53.

30. Ibid., p. 54.

31. Ibid.

32. Ibid., p. 43.

33. Ibid., pp. 44–45.

34. Thomas Paine, "The Existence of God," in *LWTP*, vol. 9, p. 4.

35. Ibid., pp. 5–6.

36. Ibid., pp. 7–8.

37. Thomas Paine, *The Age of Reason*, pt. 1, in *LWTP*, vol. 8, p. 280.

38. Ibid., p. 45.

39. Thomas Paine, *The Age of Reason*, pt. 2, in *LWTP*, vol. 8, p. 280.

40. Ibid., p. 284.

41. Ibid., p. 281.

42. Ibid., pp. 282–83.

43. Ibid., p. 278.

44. Ibid., p. 277.

45. Ibid., p. 279.

46. Ibid., p. 276.

47. Thomas Paine, "My Private Thoughts on a Future State," in *LWTP*, vol. 9, pp. 303–304.

48. Ibid., p. 305.

49. Henry May, *The Enlightenment in America* (New York: Oxford University Press, 1976), p. 174.

CHAPTER FIVE

THE DEISTIC CHRISTIAN

THOMAS JEFFERSON

There is no more profound symbol of the American Enlightenment than Thomas Jefferson (1743–1826).[1] Like all eighteenth-century persons of letters, he defies ready classification. This is because he (and they) deliberately attempted to embrace the entire realm of human learning. There is scarcely a discipline that did not intrigue Jefferson, and the modern reader, born to an age of specialization that assigns a pejorative connotation to the once-noble epithet "dilettante," is left rather dazed at the breadth of his interests. The natural sciences, politics, law, philosophy, ethnology, agriculture, mechanics, music, education, philology, history, architecture: no area of human inquiry was foreign to Jefferson. Moreover, just as he disdained to limit his interests to a narrowly circumscribed field, so he refused to renounce concrete activity in the world for a life of comfortably detached speculation. In typical Enlightenment fashion, he insisted that knowledge is and ought to be useful, and that the true philosopher is one who actively engages in the public arena to promote individual felicity, social justice, and the practical arts.

Along with the catholicity of his interests and the practical bent of his mind, what puts Jefferson at the center of Enlightenment thinkers is his fidelity to the period's twin ideals of reason and tolerance. He was convinced that emancipation from ignorance, superstition, and ossified tradition would eradicate material want as well as social and political oppression. This deep-seated confidence in reason's promise was the guiding force in Jefferson's career as both thinker and statesman. It was also the fundamental principle upon which he based his religious convictions.

Jefferson was a religious man, although not in any orthodox sense of the word. This is a point that many of his contemporaries either missed or chose to ignore. Alexander Hamilton, Jefferson's political nemesis, branded him an "atheist and fanatic." Authors with Federalist sympathies delighted in castigating him as a "French infidel." One of them, signing himself "A Christian Federalist," asked whether "serious and reflecting men" could doubt but that Jefferson's election to national office would expose the Christian religion to "contempt and profanation." During his presidency, clergymen from New England to the Southern states thundered every Sunday against the godlessness of his administration, and Daniel Webster continued the recrimination after Jefferson's retirement from public life by sourly commenting that the sage of Monticello was addicted to French opinions, morals, wine—and irreligion. Nor did the charges of atheism end with Jefferson's death. In 1830 the public library of Philadelphia, a city otherwise noted for its tolerant spirit, primly refused to purchase books about the ex-president because of his supposed infidelity.[2]

Some of the denunciations of Thomas Jefferson, particularly Hamilton's, were without doubt politically motivated. Jefferson himself complained that most of the charges of atheism leveled against him were instances of political calumny. But it is certain that many of them reflected a sincere and horrified belief in Jefferson's infidelity. To the eighteenth-century American mind, denial of the tenets of orthodox Christianity was tantamount to atheism, and Jefferson was too publicly associated with the liberal humanism of the Enlightenment to allow for any doubts about his heterodoxy. Nor did it help that Jefferson, an intensely private individual, refused to respond publicly to his critics, believing "it behooves every man . . . who values liberty of conscience . . . to give no example of concession . . . by answering questions of faith, which the laws have left between God and himself."[3] His aloof silence was taken as an admission of guilt and only reinforced the general assumption that he abjured both God and religion. But prevalent as this suspicion was, it nonetheless missed the mark. Jefferson did forswear religious supernaturalism, but not the deistic God of nature.

JEFFERSON THE EMPIRICIST

As a child of the Enlightenment, Jefferson acknowledged Francis Bacon, Isaac Newton, and John Locke as his philosophical masters. In his estimation, this triumvirate was comprised of "the greatest men that have ever lived; without any exception, [they] having laid the foundation of those superstructures which have been raised in the Physical and Moral Sciences."[4] In hindsight, Jefferson's encomium may be accused of hyperbole, but its sincerity is indisputable. The influence of these three luminaries on his thought is clear as well as fundamental. From them, he imbibed the materialism, empiricism, and insistence upon tolerance and freedom of conscience as inalienable human rights that characterize his worldview in general and his deism in particular. Bacon taught him the value of experimentally testing inductive hypotheses, and convinced him that genuine human knowledge is progressive and utility-laden. Locke reinforced Bacon's empiricist method by providing a philosophical justification for the reliability of sense data, as well as a normative defense of rational inquiry. Newton dramatically illustrated the virtue of the experimental method in his mechanistic natural philosophy, and moreover demonstrated that physical phenomena conform to immutable natural laws. Finally, all three men convinced Jefferson that free inquiry and the give-and-take of ideas in the intellectual marketplace were necessary conditions for the growth of human knowledge and the promotion of social well-being.

Jefferson's worldview, never systematized but regularly discussed in his voluminous correspondence, rested upon two fundamental principles: that the evidence of one's senses is trustworthy, and that such evidence inductively points to an exclusively physical reality. He believed that the subjectivity into which George Berkeley (unwittingly) and David Hume (deliberately) had thrust Locke's empiricism was a cul-de-sac. Contrary to the conclusions of either idealists or skeptics, Jefferson believed that immediate experience disclosed reliable facts about real events in an external world. Adopting a realism similar to that defended by the Scottish commonsense philosophers, he appealed to a "habitual anodyne" reminiscent of Dr. Johnson's famous refutation of Berkeleyan idealism. "I feel," declared Jefferson. "Therefore I exist. I feel bodies which are not myself: there are other existences then. I call them *matter*.

I feel them changing place. This gives me *motion*. Where there is an absence of matter, I call it *void*, or *nothing*, or *immaterial space*." From such immediate nonconceptual experiences, Jefferson felt justified in inferring the presence of a physical reality external to himself. This is because he was convinced that such experiences were epistemically reliable. "On the basis of sensation, of matter and motion, we may erect the fabric of all the certainties we can have or need. . . . A simple sense may indeed be sometimes deceived, but rarely; and never in all our senses together, with their faculty of reasoning. They evidence realities." The conclusion is that legitimate knowledge originates with immediate sensation, sensation is generally reliable, and points in turn to the material nature of existence. Consequently, it follows that "once we quit the basis of sensation, all is in the wind. To talk of *immaterial* existences, is to talk of *nothings*."[5] This is, of course, quite an inferential leap. But it is one with which Jefferson's native commonsense realism was comfortable.

Experience and common sense, then, serve as the twin props of the "superstructures of the sciences." Still, sensation, as Jefferson admitted, is occasionally deceptive. In addition to immediate experience, therefore, reliable knowledge of the physical order depends upon the exercise of the "faculty of reasoning." Reason is that mental operation that reflects upon sense data, comparing and classifying it in order to postulate hypothetical generalizations. The latter, in good Baconian fashion, are then experimentally tested against future observations and accordingly reaffirmed, revised, or rejected. As such, the faculty of reasoning serves as the necessary arbiter between competing explanations of knowledge claims. It is, says Jefferson, an "oracle given by heaven," "every man's . . . own rightful umpire."[6] Without its inductive analysis of sense data, the human sciences, physical as well as normative, would be impossible.

The implications of this empiricist perspective are twofold. The first is that human reason in principle is capable of completely comprehending the physical laws that govern matter in motion. Given enough data to work with, the hitherto mysterious operations of the cosmic machine can be discerned, schematized, and, to a certain extent, manipulated. Such was the clear lesson from Newtonian physics.

The second implication is as fundamental as the first. Jefferson was optimistic about the progressive nature of human knowledge, but he insisted that this confidence was no license for dogmatism or intellectual complacency. On the contrary, it demanded that the natural philosopher realize the merely provisional character of his generalizations, acknowledging that they are always subject to future modifications and even rejection. The laws regulating reality are fixed and immutable, but human formulations of them are tentative. Consequently, toleration of opposing perspectives and theories is an essential attitude in intellectual inquiry. No single school can claim absolute truth. No specific hypothesis enjoys a privileged position in the hall of human learning. This tolerant open-mindedness not only applies to currently competing explanations; as Bacon and Locke had argued, it also demands a skeptical attitude toward traditional wisdom—scientific, normative, or religious—which had become enshrined over the centuries. Reason and experience, not authority, are the standards of adjudication, and if they arrive at results contrary to tradition, so much the worse for tradition. Consequently, free and open inquiry, without fear of persecution or prejudicial recrimination, is a foundation of the superstructures of the sciences. As Jefferson remarked in a 1799 letter outlining the principles by which he lived,

> I am for encouraging the process of science in all its branches; and not for raising a hue and cry against the sacred name of philosophy; for awing the human mind by stories of raw-head & bloody bones to a distrust of its own vision, & to repose implicitly on that of others; to go backwards instead of forwards to look for improvement; to believe that government, religion, morality, & every other science were in the highest perfection in ages of the darkest ignorance, and that nothing can ever be devised more perfect than what was established by our forefathers.[7]

The forward-looking and optimistic humanism conveyed in this declaration captures the heart of Jefferson's vision. It also reflects his confidence that religious sensitivity, freed from the shackles of tradition, will mature hand-in-hand with scientific and ethical progress.

A REAL CHRISTIAN

Given his public reputation for godlessness, it is somewhat surprising to discover Jefferson telling an 1816 correspondent, "*I am a real Christian.*"

This rather defiant confession is even more perplexing when one considers that Jefferson himself never tired of disowning allegiance to any religious denomination. He boasted at various times, for instance, that he was a sect unto himself, that he never allowed himself to dwell upon specific creeds, and that all catechisms were impostures and duperies. In fact, just seven short months after calling himself a "real Christian," Jefferson wrote the following disclaimer to another correspondent: "I have ever thought religion a concern between our god and our consciences, for which we were accountable to him, and not to the priest. I never told my religion, nor scrutinized that of another. I never attempted to make a convert, nor wished to change another's creed."[8]

The key to reconciling these apparently discordant confessions of religious orientation is Jefferson's distinction between two meanings of the word "Christian." On the one hand, the term applies to any individual who admires and seeks to follow the teachings as well as emulate the life of the historical Jesus. On the other, the term is also a name for any individual who belongs to one or another of the various denominations that, collectively, constitute institutional Christianity. Jefferson clearly considered himself a Christian in the first sense, and just as obviously repudiated the second. He admired Jesus the man, but despised Christianity as an ecclesial structure and theological system. His reasons for drawing this distinction between "real" and institutional (or dogmatic) Christians reveals the extent of his indebtedness to the intellectual ideals of Bacon, Locke, and Newton.

In the first place, Jefferson refused to align himself with institutional Christianity because he deplored what he took to be its irrational supernaturalism. His materialist orientation forbade him from taking seriously the possibility of occult, nonphysical causes in the universe that set aside physical law. Hence he rejected the orthodox doctrine of miracles. Similarly, his empiricist model of knowledge disallowed the epistemic legitimacy of nonverifiable and private experiences of divine revelation. Hence he rejected biblical claims of prophecy and, indeed, scriptural authority in general. In short, the belief in supernaturalism that dogmatic Christianity required of its adherents outraged those superstructural foundations of the sciences that were Jefferson's intellectual mainstays. For him, "ideas must be distinct before reason can act upon them," and they are only distinct if they reflect external physical events. Consequently, "no man ever had a distinct idea" of doctrinal tenets such as the trinity, the incarnation, or the resurrection. When confronted by these and similar "unintelligible propositions" of Christian theology, the only "weapon" a rational mind can resort to is "ridicule." "What has no meaning admits no explanation," and it is a waste of time to grant intellectual respectability to such "paralogisms" by taking them seriously.[9]

Although it is too strong to paint the eighteenth-century Jefferson as a positivist (as one commentator has done),[10] it *is* the case that his rejection of supernatural "explanations" stems from a proto-positivist distrust of nonempirical speculation. Like his fellow *philosophes* on either side of the Atlantic, Jefferson was wary of nonverifiable metaphysical claims. Mere logical coherency in metaphysical systems did not impress him any more than it had Bacon. Both men recognized that logically impeccable models of reality could be spun from flimsy or incredible first premises. In addition to internal consistency, then, Jefferson the empiricist required that a theory's first principles be grounded in the real world, and be verifiable through observation and experiment. Perfectly coherent models that displayed no correspondence to publicly verifiable facts were "nothings" or "wind." Such, in his estimation, were the supernaturalist claims of dogmatic Christianity.

Again following the lead of his hero Bacon, Jefferson blamed the abstract and nonempirical fancies of Plato and his followers for the Western mind's disdain of the sensible realm and for its historical infatuation with metaphysical speculation. This Platonic virus, maintained Jefferson, had particularly infected dogmatic Christianity, mutating what once had been the "primitive deism" of Jesus into an "extravagant" theological system "no more worthy, nor capable of explanation than the incoherencies of our own nightly dreams." To discover the original teachings of the man Jesus embedded within the layers of subsequent metaphysical accretions, it was necessary, as Jefferson wrote to John Adams, to "dismiss the Platonists and Plotinists, the Stagyrites and Gamalielites, the Eclectics, the Gnostics and Scholastics, their essences and emanations, their Logos and Demiurgos, Aeons and Daemons male and female, with a long Train Etc. Etc. Etc. or, shall I say at once, of Nonsense."[11]

Institutional Christianity's otherworldly, mysterious Platonism, then, was offensive to a rational mind. Its metaphysics violated the lawlike regularity of the natural order established by Newtonian natural philosophy, just as its revelatory epistemology contradicted the empiricist science of knowledge propounded by Bacon and Locke. Moreover, its lambasting of the canons of reason in the name of faith raised an unhealthy atmosphere of superstitious enthusiasm, fear, and ignorance, in which rational inquiry was not only discouraged but actually condemned by the clergy as blasphemous or heretical. It was in the interest of the priests, after all, to actively promote the "artificial vestments" of Christian dogma. The Church was their "instrument of riches and power."[12] If the "mere Abracadabra of the mountebanks calling themselves the priests of Jesus" could be rationally understood, said Jefferson, it "would not answer their purpose. Their security is in their faculty of shedding darkness, like the scuttle fish, thro' the element in which they move, and making it impenetrable to the eye of a pursuing enemy. And there they will skulk, until some rational creed can occupy the void which the obliteration of their duperies would leave in the minds of our honest and unsuspecting brethren."[13]

These are harsh words, and rather unpleasantly smack of the sometimes vulgar anticlericalism of a Voltaire, Diderot, or d'Holbach. There is no doubt that Jefferson, who with his fellow American deists disliked and distrusted the clergy, was not above baiting men of the cloth. But to give Jefferson his due, his charges of clerical manipulation were prompted by what he took to be the ultimate evil of institutional Christianity: its intolerance of dissenting, nonorthodox perspectives. Jefferson was enough of a student of society to recognize that the Christian establishment's vigilant persecution of heresy was the natural reflex of a powerful structure confronted by challenges to its hegemony. But, contrary to Voltaire's dictum that to understand all is to forgive all, Jefferson condemned ecclesial usurpation of the privileges of conscience as an intolerable (albeit predictable) consequence of "mountebankish Abracadabra."

Jefferson's condemnation of institutional Christianity's intolerance of dissenting religious perspectives rests upon three primary convictions. The first is his Enlightenment-inspired belief that the advance of knowledge in any arena of human inquiry depends upon the possibility of open debate and honest, unintimidated discourse. Like John Stuart Mill after him, Jefferson was confident that an uncensored exchange of opinion between persons of differing perspectives was the necessary crucible for separating the rational from the irrational, the salutary from the super-stitious. Suppression of belief not only stunted individual growth and discovery but also poisoned the collective well from which progressive policies and institutions could come forth.

More specifically, Jefferson condemned religious intolerance and persecution because he believed there was no social justification for man-dating conformity to a uniform set of religious beliefs. Public opinion and legal codes have the right as well as the obligation to prohibit, and when necessary punish, those actions on the part of citizens that harm others or violate their civil liberties. As Jefferson maintained in his *Notes on Virginia*, "the legitimate powers of government extend to such acts . . . as are injurious to others." But expressions of religious belief do not fall into the set of harmful social actions. "It does me no injury," declared Jefferson, "for my neighbour to say there are twenty gods, or no God. It neither picks my pocket nor breaks my leg." True, one sectarian may find the religious views of other sectarians offensive, just as believers may be angered by the rebuttals of atheistic infidels. But the possibility, and even likelihood, of exposure to offensive sentiments is no justifica-tion for legally forbidding their expression. Even if it were, the price for such mandated uniformity would be too great.

> Subject opinion to coercion: whom will you make your inquisitors? Fal-lible men; men governed by bad passions, by private as well as public rea-sons. And why subject it to coercion? To produce uniformity. But is uni-formity of opinion desirable? No more than of face or stature. What has been the effect of coercion? To make one half the world fools, and the other half hypocrites. To support roguery and error all over the earth.[14]

There is no compelling reason, then, to suppose that mandated uni-formity of religious belief is conducive to the health of either the indi-vidual or the state. On the contrary, attempts to stifle religious pluralism stunt the imagination and the spirit of a people. The advantages of plu-ralism in the political realm, Jefferson points out, have been dramatically underscored by the example of the American Revolution. But true social emancipation will be achieved only when "that religious slavery under which a people have been willing to remain, who have lavished their lives and fortunes for the establishment of their civil freedom," likewise has been eradicated.[15]

In addition to his subscription to liberal Enlightenment ideals and his denial that there is a legal justification for the suppression of religious diversity, there is a final reason for Jefferson's condemnation of the intolerance he attributed to dogmatic Christianity: his conviction that religious belief is essentially a private affair, "a concern purely between our god and our consciences, for which we are accountable to him, and not to the priests."

At first reading, such a statement smacks of radical subjectivism, as if Jefferson is arguing that there is no evidence for religious claims and that consequently any privately held conviction is as legitimate as the next. But even though such an inward retreat is certainly characteristic of some religious thinkers—Blaise Pascal and Soren Kierkegaard readily come to mind—it is not Jefferson's position. He in fact did believe that God's existence could be established through the rational scrutiny of physical phenomena. He was too much of a deist to deny this. But, again in keeping with his fidelity to the deistic worldview, he also insisted that the only intellectually honest position one could hold about God's nature is an agnostic one. God's existence is capable of rational demonstration, but his essence is ultimately unknowable and can only be guessed at from observing his creation. Consequently, doctrinal descriptions of the divine nature—such as, for instance, Christian trinitarianism—are purely speculative because completely unverifiable. They represent forays into the "hidden country" of metaphysical fancy.

These Platonic departures from the canons of reason and evidence are never conclusive, much less convincing, even if they occasionally do provide "amusement of leisure hours." Any sect that mandates allegiance to such speculative descriptions, then, demands that its followers abuse reason, their "heavenly oracle," and such an obligation is always unwarranted. A rational religion acknowledges that God exists, but refuses to surmise, much less dogmatize upon, his nature. Jefferson straightforwardly expressed this agnosticism in an 1801 letter to the Reverend Isaac Story.

> The laws of nature have withheld from us the means of physical knowledge of the country of spirits and revelation has, for reasons unknown to us, chosen to leave us in the dark as we were. When I was young I was fond of the speculation which seemed to promise some insight into

that hidden country, but observing at length that they left me in the same ignorance in which they had found me, I have for many years ceased to read or to think concerning them, and have reposed my head on that pillow of ignorance which a benevolent creator has made so soft for us knowing how much we should be forced to use it.[16]

Jefferson was not, then, a Christian in the dogmatic sense of the word. Orthodox Neoplatonic theology, as institutionalized by the various Christian denominations, violated those structural foundations that he deemed necessary conditions of all legitimate knowledge. This violation, in turn, bred superstition and ignorance on the part of the faithful as well as self-interested intolerance and repression from religious authorities.

Yet the curious fact remains that Jefferson insisted upon calling himself a "real Christian." This suggests that he believed there was some way to strip the Platonic accretions from Jesus' original teachings to arrive at their pure, unsullied message. It also implies that Jefferson took that original message to be consistent with his own deistic notion of God. The readiness with which he de-divinized the Christ-figure by painting him as a prophet of natural religion struck many of his contemporaries as a horrifically audacious piece of blasphemy. But for Jefferson, it was the only rational interpretation.

JEFFERSON THE EXEGETE

Each of the American deists read Christian Scripture with a skeptical eye. Sometimes, as with Franklin, the criticism was cautious and minimal. At other times, as with Paine and Palmer, it was savage and relentless, often to the point of rather tiresome hairsplitting. But regardless of the degree of intensity, analysis of the Scriptures was a favorite stratagem of the American champions of rational religion. Their purpose was obvious. The writings that comprise the Old and New Testaments were accepted by orthodox eighteenth-century Christians as the inerrant and literal revelation of God, and thus the final court of appeal in theological disputes. In casting doubt upon Scripture by challenging its authenticity and coherency, the deists sought to undermine the foundation of Christian belief.

Like his fellow deists, Jefferson devoted a good deal of time and energy to biblical studies. But unlike most of them, his analysis of Scripture was based upon an exegetical methodology that was both thoughtful and systematic. Other deists tended to adopt a shotgun approach in their criticisms of Scripture, pouncing at random upon obvious historical inaccuracies or textual inconsistencies and concluding that the entire canon was uninspired and hence fraudulent. Jefferson's more methodological approach reflected his conviction that only a judicious application of reason, aided by the lessons of experience, could separate truth from falsehood. In a move that strikingly anticipated the nineteenth-century "higher criticism" defended by liberal theologians such as David Strauss, Jefferson carefully sifted through scriptural accounts in order to salvage the reasonable wheat from the unreasonable chaff. He steadfastly refused to discount biblical testimony simply because it was regarded as sacred by his orthodox adversaries. Such a blanket condemnation, in his estimation, revealed as great a degree of blind bigotry as that displayed by heresy-seeking Christians. Instead, he sought to "demythologize" Scripture by asking two questions: Is it consistent with reason? Is it in principle verifiable through experience? Those biblical accounts that withstood these inquiries Jefferson accepted as both compatible with deism's rational religion and reflective of the original teachings of the man Jesus. Those that failed to pass the test he dismissed as the interpolations— "mountebankish Abracadabra"—of Neoplatonic metaphysicians. In utilizing his exegetical criteria, Jefferson not only provides a methodology that is a precursor of subsequent biblical hermeneutics but also provides a refreshing alternative to the shrill and often indiscriminate lack of finesse with which so many of his fellow deists interpreted Scripture.

Nowhere is Jefferson's demythologizing approach to Christian Scripture better spelled out than in a letter he wrote to his orphaned nephew Peter Carr while Jefferson was minister to France. This document, composed in 1787, ostensibly aims to provide Carr with a program of study calculated to edify as well as educate. But in the midst of listing books and disciplines that he somewhat overbearingly urges upon his young ward, Jefferson interjects some counsel on how to go about analyzing scriptural testimony in particular and theological claims in general.[17]

True to his most cherished principles, Jefferson first advises Carr to keep an open mind in theological disputes: "divest yourself of all bias in favour of novelty and singularity." Infatuation with the incredible may be a harmless enough eccentricity in some contexts, but succumbing to its temptation in religious matters is perilous. The subject "is too important, and the consequences of error may be too serious." Equally necessary in theological inquiry is the courage to shake off supernaturalist-based fears. There is no fault, much less threat of divine wrath, in honest and sincere questioning of dogma. An individual is answerable not for "the rightness but uprightness" of his intentions. Consequently, Jefferson cautions Carr, one should avoid the pitfalls of enthusiasm on the one hand and intellectual timidity on the other. Instead, "fix reason firmly in her seat, and call to her tribunal every fact, every opinion." No claim is so evident, no belief too sacred, to fall outside reason's jurisdiction.

> Question with boldness even the existence of god. . . . Do not be frightened from this inquiry by any fear of its consequences. If it ends in a belief that there is no god, you will find incitements to virtue in the comfort and pleasantness you feel in its exercise, and the love of others which it will procure you. If you find reason to believe that there is a god, a consciousness that you are acting under his eye, and that he approves you, will be a vast additional incitement.

After instructing Carr in these two general principles of investigation, Jefferson proceeds to more specific advice on how to rationally appraise scriptural testimony. To begin with, he argues, the Bible ought to be read as one would read any other book. Suspend all preconceptions about its divine authorship or inspiration, and subject its content to the same standards of criticism and evaluation proper to the books of other ancient writers. One of two conclusions will become apparent. Either "the [biblical] facts . . . are within the ordinary course of nature" and hence prima facie acceptable "on the authority of the writer, as those of the same kind in Livy or Tacitus," or they are such that they "contradict the laws of nature." If the former, Jefferson tells Carr, "the testimony of the writer weighs in their favour in one scale, and their not being against the laws of nature does not weigh against them." They are not thereby necessarily vindicated, but neither are they immediately disenfranchised by reason or experience. If the latter alternative emerges, however, the putative facts recorded in Scripture "must be examined with more care, and under a variety of faces."

In advising Carr to examine incredible biblical passages "under a variety of faces," Jefferson has in mind a consideration of the possible motives that prompted their original composition, as well as the metaphysical prejudices that encourage their subsequent endorsement by readers. In the case of Sacred Scripture, the most obvious face to be acknowledged is "the pretentions of the writer to inspiration from god." But not even claims to divine inspiration are immune to the standard of reason: "Examine upon what evidence [the writer's] pretensions are founded, and whether that evidence is so strong as that its falsehood would be more improbable than a change of the laws of nature in the case he relates." This appeal to Hume's famous litmus test for deciding on the truth of miraculous accounts gestures at (without actually stating them) Jefferson's own conviction that scripturally based violations of nature are rationally unacceptable.[18] But just in case the allusion is too subtle for his youthful nephew, Jefferson rather transparently underscores the point with a textual illustration.

> For example in the book of Joshua we are told the sun stood still several hours. Were we to read that fact in Livy or Tacitus we should class it with their showers of blood, speaking of statues, beasts, &c., but it is said that the writer of that book [i.e., Scripture] was inspired. Examine therefore candidly what evidence there is of his having been inspired.

It will not do, continues Jefferson, to presume that such a "pretension is entitled to your inquiry, because millions believe it." Reason, not popular consensus, is the only standard of truth.

> You are Astronomer enough to know how contrary it is to the law of nature that a body revolving on its axis, as the earth does, should have stopped, should not by that sudden stoppage have prostrated animals, trees, buildings, and should after a certain time have resumed its revolution, and that without a second prostration. Is this arrest of the earth's motion, or the evidence which affirms it, most within the law of probabilities?

Jefferson concludes his epistolary tutorial in textual criticism by encouraging Carr to apply the method to the New Testament and examine the pretensions of its authors. Their central message, of course, is the divinity of the person Jesus. But if Carr would read their accounts of Jesus with a fresh eye and an open mind, he must keep before him the competing interpretations "of those who say he was begotten by god [as well as] of those who say he was a man." The implication of this advice is that both alternatives should be tested, similar to the way in which the Old Testament story of Joshua halting the sun was tested—that is, against the lessons of experience and the dictates of reason. Jefferson characteristically ends the discussion without letting his nephew know where he stands on the issue of Jesus' divinity. But given Jefferson's earlier invocation of Hume's argument against the possibility of miracles, a discerning Carr could have guessed his uncle's position.

The method of textual analysis Jefferson outlined for his nephew's instruction in 1787 was one he himself put to use on at least three different occasions. In 1804 and again in 1819 and 1820, Jefferson demythologized the New Testament by editing from it any and all passages that violated his two exegetical standards.[19] Accounts of miracles,[20] allusions to the Virgin Birth, Jesus' resurrection and divinity, and metaphysical Platonism (particularly in the Gospel of John) were systematically excised until all that remained in each case was a historical account of the life of Jesus and those passages that contain his philosophical and ethical teachings.

In addition to his editorial demythologizing of the New Testament, Jefferson spent years researching and reflecting upon a book he was destined never to write. The contemplated study was intended as a "euthanasia for Platonic Christianity" that would emphasize the "primitive simplicity of its founder." In it, Jefferson wanted to show that the teachings of Jesus on God and morality were superior to both ancient Judaism and Greek philosophy; that Jesus made no pretensions to divinity himself; and that supernaturalist passages embedded in the New Testament were later glosses added by "schismatizing followers, who have found an interest in sophisticating and perverting the simple doctrines [Jesus] taught, by engrafting on them the mysticisms of a Graecian Sophist [i.e., Plato], frittering them into subtleties, and obscuring them with jargon."[21]

Although Jefferson never actually got around to writing his treatise on the true meaning of Christianity, he did jot down a working outline of its contents sometime in 1803. Copies of this "Syllabus of an Estimate of the merit of the doctrines of Jesus, compared with those of others" were sent to several correspondents, including Joseph Priestley and Benjamin Rush, and Jefferson eventually permitted a British periodical to publish the sketch. He characteristically insisted, however, that his authorship of it remain a secret.[22]

In his "Syllabus," Jefferson lists three doctrines that his demythologizing of the New Testament had convinced him were the original teachings of Jesus. Two of them deal with ethics and will be examined shortly. The third, however, deals with the nature of God. Jefferson's attribution of it to Jesus underscores his belief that the latter's religious orientation, stripped of its later theological perversions, was a form of "primitive deism." According to Jefferson, Jesus "corrected the Deism" (that is, the monotheism) "of the Jews, confirming them in their belief in one only god, and giving them juster notions of his attributes and government."

His investigations into the history of religions had led Jefferson to conclude that ancient Judaism's "deistic" advocacy of monotheism was an advance over the confusing polytheism of other ancient sects. But the characteristics ascribed to the God of Israel disgusted Jefferson. The Hebrew Yahweh, as portrayed in the Old Testament, was whimsically wrathful, jealous, vengeful, and unpredictable in his allegiances as well as his actions. Like one of the members of the Greek or Roman pantheon, this fiery tribal god appeared to be little more than a human personality writ in cosmic letters, with all the predictably disastrous shortcomings. But surely, reasoned Jefferson the deist, the divine creator of a physical order governed by immutable laws must be similar to his creation. How else could he have brought it into being? It is unimaginable that as unpredictable a deity as Yahweh could have planned the pristinely rational cosmos charted by Newton. Consequently, Hebraic "deism," although an improvement over crude polytheism, was still inadequate as a rational theology.

Jesus, however, corrected Jewish monotheism by teaching a more sophisticated concept of God. It was an improvement on at least two counts. First, the Nazarene denied that God was the capricious, unpredictable deity worshipped as Yahweh. Instead, God was benevolent, rational, and immutable, governing his universe in accord with these attributes. Second, evidence of the existence of this deity was discernible in the physical order, because he had imparted vestiges of his divine qualities to his creation. Nature, then, was God's mode of revelation. That such was Jesus' belief is obvious if one demythologizes the opening of the Gospel of John—or at least so Jefferson believed. According to him, the original meaning of the passage is "in the beginning God existed, and reason (or mind) was with God, and that mind was God. This was in the beginning with God. All things were created by it, and without it was made not one thing which was made." Jefferson interpreted this passage as "plainly declaring the doctrine of Jesus that the world was created by the supreme, intelligent being" who imparts exemplars of his divine nature to physical reality. Unfortunately, however, the text "has been perverted by modern Christians to build up a second person of their tritheism by a mistranslation of the word logos. One of its legitimate meanings indeed is 'a word.' But, in that sense, it makes an unmeaning jargon: while the other meaning 'reason,' equally legitimate, explains rationally the eternal pre-existence of God, and his creation of the universe."[23]

Jefferson's interpretation of this scriptural passage is interesting because it reveals both the strengths and the weaknesses of his exegetical method. On the one hand, his reading of John's logos as "reason" rather than "word" *does* help to demystify the text's meaning. It is also an acceptable translation of the original Greek. On the other hand, however, there is absolutely no evidence to support Jefferson's contention that the man Jesus taught the doctrine expressed in the prelude to the fourth Gospel. Even if Jefferson's interpretation of the text is a correct one, it only indicates that early hellenistic Christianity accepted God as the cosmic principle of reason. Jesus of Nazareth may or may not have. In demythologizing scriptural passages such as this one, then, Jefferson ran the risk of sacrificing historical accuracy for textual clarity.

That a usually cautious exegete like Jefferson would defend such a contentious interpretation is revealing, for it points to the pervasiveness of his conviction that the original teachings of Jesus reflected a primitive deism that had been obscured by subsequent theological doctrines. A fundamental tenet of deism, "primitive" or otherwise, is that the God of nature reveals himself in his creation, and that the physical order therefore reflects the divine attributes of order, reason, and immutability. Jefferson himself subscribed to this position, and went on to infer that God's existence could therefore be deduced from an observation of physical reality. As he wrote to John Adams in 1823,

I hold . . . that when we take a view of the universe; the movements of the heavenly bodies, so exactly held in their courses by the balances of centrifugal and centripetal forces; the structure of our earth itself, with its distribution of lands, waters, and atmosphere; animal and vegetable bodies, each perfectly organized whether as insect, man or mammoth; it is impossible, I say, for the human mind not to believe, that there is in all this, design, cause and effect, up to an ultimate cause, a Fabricator of all things from matter and motion.[24]

It is not surprising that Jefferson appealed to arguments from design and causality (both of which are collapsed into one in the preceding passage) to establish the existence of God. Such arguments, after all, were staple articles of belief among eighteenth-century deists. For them, there were too many tokens of intelligence and planning in observable nature to suppose it was merely the product of a sequence of random events. What is unusual, however, is Jefferson's contention that this argument (or at least its ancestor) can be extracted from the logos prelude in the fourth Gospel and attributed to Jesus. But it served as one of the foundations for Jefferson's belief that he, and not "the Platonists, who call themselves Christians and preachers of the gospel," was the real Christian.[25]

AN INNATE MORAL FACULTY

There was another reason why Jefferson so admired the teachings of Jesus that he claimed them for deism: the purity of the Nazarene's ethics and the salutary example of his life. In his "Syllabus," Jefferson held that Jesus' concept of God was superior to the Hebraic concept of Yahweh. Along similar lines, he stated that the Gospels' normative principle of "universal philanthropy, not only to kindred and friends, . . . but to all mankind, gathering all into one family, under the bounds of love, charity, peace, common wants, and common aids," was a qualitative advance over the earlier Mosaic legal code as well as the Greco-Roman ethical tradition. In addition, Jesus' insistence that pure thoughts and intentions were as essential to the ethical life as just actions likewise represented a normative breakthrough. It scrutinized the "heart of man; erected [a] tribunal in the region of his thoughts, and purified the waters at the fountain head."

As with his reconstruction of Jesus' concept of God, it was Jefferson's demythologizing of Scripture that led him to this appraisal of the ethics of primitive Christianity. Although it at times required some rather creative sleuthing, Jefferson was convinced that the "free exercises of reason" enabled the careful reader to discriminate between three different sources of ethical teachings in the New Testament. One tradition was the Mosaic code, which focused upon "idle ceremonies, mummeries and observances [that had] no effect towards producing the social utilities which constitute the essence of virtue." Another, of course, was the later addition of metaphysical "paralogisms and sophisms [that] a schoolboy would be ashamed of." These stemmed, directly or indirectly, from "Plato's own foggy brain, [of which] no writer ancient or modern has [more] bewildered the world . . . in Ethics." But a third source of Scripture's ethical pronouncements, Jefferson deduced, must stem from the actual teachings of Jesus himself.

> We find in the writings of [Jesus'] biographers matter of two distinct descriptions. First a ground work of vulgar ignorance, of things impossible, of superstitions, fanaticisms, and fabrications. Intermixed with these again are sublime ideas of the supreme being, aphorisms and precepts of the purest morality and benevolence, sanctioned by a life of humility, innocence, and simplicity of manners, neglect of riches, absence of worldly ambition and honors, with an eloquence and persuasiveness which have not been surpassed. These could not be inventions of the grovelling authors who relate them. They are far beyond the powers of their feeble minds.

Given the unambiguous difference in tone and contrast between these different texts, ones which render Jesus' sayings "as easily distinguishable as diamonds in a dunghill," "can we be at a loss in separating such material, and ascribing each to its genuine author?" The question is clearly rhetorical. In Jefferson's judgment, the "trivialities and imbecilities" of the one and the "purity and distinction" of the other allow for no doubt.[26]

The diamondlike quality of Jesus' moral principles of universal philanthropy and purity of heart suited well Jefferson's own approach to ethics. Like all deists, Jefferson was convinced that virtue is the highest form of worship, acknowledging and reflecting as it does the essentially benevolent nature of the deity. (It is revealing, for example, that in his private library he classified religion as a division of moral philosophy.) As a child of the Enlightenment, Jefferson had cut his philosophical teeth on the works of the classical moralists, particularly Epicurus and Epictetus. Their doctrines—which he esteemed as "containing everything rational in moral philosophy which Greece and Rome have left us"[27]—early on had persuaded Jefferson that the aim of human existence is the attainment of happiness, and that necessary steps toward this end were restraint of the passions, cultivation of reason, and stoical fortitude—what the ancients called "virtue." As he formulated the point, "happiness is the aim of life, . . . but virtue is the foundation of happiness."[28] This early allegiance to the classical ideal of cultivation of the inner self, then, rendered Jefferson responsive to the scriptural call for a purification of the heart.

But there is a more fundamental reason why he so admired the ethical maxims of Jesus and paid them the ultimate compliment of interpreting them as early expressions of deistic humanism. Much as he was drawn to classical Stoicism and Epicureanism, Jefferson was troubled by their almost exclusive concentration upon the individual. He earlier had rejected the Mosaic code because of its lack of regard for those "social utilities which constitute the essence of virtue." Although he considered the Greco-Roman ethical tradition a qualitative advance over its Hebraic predecessor, he recognized that the former likewise failed to emphasize sufficiently the social dimension of morality. Epicurus, Epictetus, Cicero, and Seneca, each of whom Jefferson admired, focused their attention upon mental disciplines whereby the individual might control his passions in the pursuit of virtue and happiness. But, decided Jefferson,

> in developing our duties to others, they were short and defective. They embraced, indeed, the circles of kindred and friends, and inculcated patriotism, or the love of our country in the aggregate, as a primary obligation; towards our neighbors and countrymen they taught justice, but scarcely viewed them as within the circle of benevolence. Still less have they inculcated peace, charity, love to our fellow men, or embraced with benevolence the whole family of mankind.[29]

The classical moralists, then, tended to focus upon the investigation of "laws for governing ourselves," but abstracted the individual from his broader social context. Jesus went beyond this individualistic approach by preaching universal philanthropy and bequeathing to future generations "a supplement of the duties and charities we owe to others." Consequently, in Jefferson's estimation, Cicero is "enchanting" and Seneca "a fine moralist," but Jesus is "the greatest of all reformers."[30]

In the New Testament, Jesus suggests that individuals should allow themselves to be guided in their "duties and charities" to others by the inner voice of conscience, the "kingdom of God" within all humans. Jefferson the empiricist was particularly impressed by such passages. Following the lead of eighteenth-century intuitionists such as Lord Shaftesbury, Francis Hutcheson, and Lord Kames, he had come to the conclusion that ethical values are directly apprehendable by humans via an innate moral sense or faculty (occasionally referred to by Jefferson as "conscience"). Just as the ultimate foundation of human knowledge is sensory awareness, so the ground of all normative insight is intuition. Our physical faculties serve as the vehicles by which sensuous experience is acquired. Analogously, our normative knowledge is acquired through its own faculty. Moreover, just as our immediate sensory experiences are reliable, reflecting as they do external physical phenomena, so the normative intuitions of the moral faculty are likewise trustworthy, capturing as they do objective values. The one provides raw data for the natural sciences, the other raw data for the human sciences.

In adopting the notion of an innate moral faculty capable of immediate experience of objective values, Jefferson rejected two competing ethical models: rationalism and relativism. To presume that ethical knowledge is rational rather than intuitively immediate, argued Jefferson, would entail that only rational humans can be virtuous. Such a conclusion not only flies in the face of experience but also is an insult to the wisdom and justice of the deity. "He who made us would have been a pitiful bungler, if he had made the rules of our moral conduct a matter of science. For one man of science, there are thousands who are not." Yet those thousands are still capable of virtue, and this is because of their innate moral faculties. As Jefferson piquantly says, "State a moral case to a ploughman and a professor. The former will decide it as well, and often better than the latter, because he has not been led astray by artificial rules." This is not to suggest that reason and science have no role to play in ethical reflection. Moral judgments may call for a rational appraisal of competing claims or clashing obligations. In such situations, the question of how to apply the intuited values are "submitted . . . in some degree, to the guidance of reason." But the heart of ethical awareness and decision lies in the moral sense's immediate apprehension of the good and its impelling of the subject to act in accordance with the intuition. For Jefferson, the bottom line is that "a man owes no duty to which he is not urged by some impulsive feeling," with the proviso that the "impulsive feeling" should be one shared by most people in similar circumstances, not the idiosyncratic response of one individual. Consequently, reason's role, although occasionally necessary, is minimal.[31]

Moreover, the postulation of a moral sense that immediately experiences value entails that morality is not an artificial construct relative to time and place, but is instead a system founded upon objective data—values—discernible by humans. True, the acuity of the moral faculty may differ from person to person; "it is given to all human beings in a stronger or weaker degree, as force of members is given them in a greater or less degree." The fact that some individuals have a more sensitive conscience than others, however, is no more of an argument against an innate moral sense than the fact that some people are dim-sighted or blind is an argument against the ubiquity of vision.[32]

But what about the obvious fact of diversity in cultural norms and mores? Jefferson admits there is a great deal of variation in ethical principles from one society to the next, that "the same actions are deemed virtuous in one country and vicious in another." Still, this is no argument against a natural and universal moral sense that apprehends objective values if one recognizes that diversity of moral judgment is probable and indeed inevitable in a multicultured, pluralistic world. This is because "nature has constituted utility the standard & test of virtue" invoked by all cultures. But, reasons Jefferson, "men living in different countries, under different circumstances, different habits and regimens, may have different utilities." Consequently, "the same act . . . may be useful, and consequently virtuous in one country which is injurious and vicious in another differently circumstanced." Such differences do not thereby imply a relativity of value so much as the contextuality of standards of appraisal.[33]

But it would be a grave misreading to suppose Jefferson is a proponent of ethical utilitarianism. Although he accepts utility as the standard by which different cultures judge behavior, he denies that utility is the basis of ethical principle. Instead, the fundamental principles of virtue, as illuminated by the moral faculty's light of intuition, are remarkably similar to the ideals propounded by Jesus: "nature hath implanted in our breasts a love of others, a sense of duty to them, a moral instinct, in short, which prompts us irresistibly to feel and to succour their distresses." This innate propensity toward empathic union prods humans toward consideration of the welfare of others. Moreover, since it is one of the race's most deep-seated urges, individuals derive pleasure and self-satisfaction from its employment. As Jefferson tersely puts it, "every human mind feels pleasure in doing good to another." In at least a psychological sense, then, virtue is indeed its own reward.[34]

Jefferson's defense of an empathic moral sense broke with several theories of his day purporting to explain the basis of morality. Theologians such as Jonathan Edwards, for example, argued that the love of God underlies and supports morality. But for Jefferson, love of the divine is just one of our ethical obligations, one virtue among many, not the foundation of virtue itself. Otherwise, contrary to experience, all irreligious persons would necessarily be wicked. "If we did a good act merely from the love of God and a belief that it is pleasing to Him," he says, "whence arises the morality of the Atheist? It is idle to say, as some do, that no such being exists."[35] Thus morality is not grounded in religious sentiments. Indeed, in typical deistic fashion, Jefferson insisted upon the contrary: the integrity of one's religion is measured in terms of its salutary effects upon thoughts and actions.

Jefferson likewise denied the position which concludes that morality is based upon self-love or egoism. Holding that "our relations with others [constitute] the boundaries of morality," he maintained that any ethic which grounded itself on individualistic self-interest to the exclusion of serious consideration of the community both violated the spirit of empathic concern and encouraged wickedness. This is because such models bestowed a pernicious pseudo-legitimacy upon selfishness, "the sole antagonist to virtue, leading us constantly by our propensities to self-gratification in violation of our moral duties to others." But, concluded Jefferson, "take from man his selfish propensities, and he can have nothing to seduce him from the practice of virtue. Or subdue those propensities by education, instruction or restraint, and virtue remains without a competitor."[36]

Jefferson's rejection of self-interest as the foundation of morality is significant, underscoring as it does his deep-seated belief that humans are by nature social creatures and accordingly possess innate capacities—love, empathy, generosity, and concern for others—in keeping with this fundamental character. In a terse syllogism, he spelled out the social implications of this theory: "Man was created for social intercourse; but social intercourse cannot be maintained without a sense of justice; then man must have been created with a sense of justice." This sense of justice, of course, is simply the empathic propensity translated into broader, social terms; as Jefferson once wrote to George Washington, "the moral duties which exist between individual and individual in a state of nature, accompany them into a state of society." Justice consists in the realization that individual and societal well-being are dependent upon a respect for certain rights that are neither mere social conventions nor legal stipulations. Instead, these rights are natural freedoms that humans possess by virtue of their very humanity, and are discernible through reflection upon the intuitions provided by the moral faculty. The purpose of society—of a just society, that is—is to maximize the opportunities for these natural rights to flourish. The fulfillment of that goal in turn depends upon two necessary conditions: first, that governmental interference with the lives and actions of its citizenry is minimal, limited to the protection of individuals from unjustified harm; and second, that all members of society empathically respect the freedoms of their fellows. For Jefferson, one of the fundamental principles of social justice was that "no man has a natural right to commit aggression on the equal rights of another."[37] It is this conviction that girded him in his lifelong struggle for freedom of conscience and religious toleration, first in Virginia, then in the Republic as a whole.

Jefferson's theory of morality is really the centerpiece of his entire worldview. Although all the American deists stressed the primacy of ethics in their discussions of the religion of nature, it was Jefferson who was most preoccupied with questions of virtue and justice. In a fundamental way, he saw human virtue as one of the keys to the nature of reality, a clue to the great cipher of existence. Consequently, deeper appreciation of the nature of moral principle prompted human happiness and well-being and fertilized the ground from which the scientific progress would grow.

More specifically, Jefferson believed that judicious reflection upon the nature of morality brought two important points to light. To begin with, as discussed earlier, he was convinced that the original teachings of Jesus revealed themselves as exemplars of moral truth that, if stripped of their subsequent Platonic absurdities, were sufficient foundations for a rational morality. For Jefferson, the sum of Jesus' moral teachings was captured by the scriptural maxim: "Treat others as you would have them treat you" and "Love thy God and thy neighbour as thyself." The influence of these complementary principles is obvious in Jefferson's own designation of empathy and love of others as the twin bases of individual virtue and social justice. As he never tired of repeating, "The essence of virtue is in doing good to others."[38]

But there is another fundamental point driven home by inquiry into the basis and nature of ethics, one that especially suited Jefferson the deist: reflection upon moral principle inevitably sheds light upon nature and nature's God. Jefferson, of course, was a convinced student of the Enlightenment, and held that reality conforms to universal and immutable laws that reflect divine attributes. Such laws define and sustain the moral as well as the physical realm. The latter give expression to the supreme rationality of the Deity, but the former reflect his providential beneficence. The very fact that humans are without exception endowed with an innate moral faculty that, if heeded, is a sufficient guarantor of their happiness, was seen by Jefferson as a token of both the lawlike character of morality and the benevolence of God. As he said, "Nature has written her moral laws . . . on the head and heart of every rational and honest man, . . . where every man may read them for himself. Man has been subjected by his creator to the Moral law of our nature or Conscience as it is sometimes called." This moral law Jefferson elsewhere praises as "the brightest gem with which the human character is studded," because it is a direct reflection of the divine attributes of universal philanthropy and unselfish love.[39]

In short, the lawlike nature of morality reveals the presence of the Supreme Mind just as much as does the nature of human thought explained by Bacon and Locke, or the operations of physical existence charted by Newton. It is this lawlike uniformity, this rational continuity from the physical to the moral realm, that a "real" Christian, as opposed to a "Platonic" one, focuses on and reveres. There is no need for miraculous suspensions of natural law to inspire awe, nor thunderous mandates from a fiery Yahweh to guide human behavior. Instead, a "real" Christian sees the presence of God in the immutable course of natural events, and hears the divine word by harking to the infallible dictates of the moral sense within. Jefferson was confident that the original Jesus had preached such doctrines in his "primitive deism." He felt equally assured that they were sufficient ground for a modern religion of nature, in which "we should all be of one sect, doers of good, and eschewers of evil."

ASSESSING JEFFERSON'S DEISM

In retrospect, Jefferson's deism is best described as firm but moderate. He was not as ambivalent in his endorsement of Enlightenment rationalism as a Benjamin Franklin, who sometimes deliberately and occasionally unwittingly tried to reconcile orthodox Calvinism with New Learning humanism. Nor was Jefferson as stridently contemptuous of the Christian ethos as a Tom Paine or Elihu Palmer. He disliked and opposed credal dogmatism, but stopped short of the militant iconoclasm characteristic of later American deists. Unlike them, he retained an honest admiration for the man Jesus and his original teachings, or at least what Jefferson interpreted as his original teachings. Although he dismissed the "mountebankish Abracadabra" of Platonized, metaphysical Christianity, he insisted that a distinction be drawn between it and the "real" Christianity of "primitive deism." He can be viewed as a deistic Christian, a thinker who endorsed what he took to be the rational heart of Christianity while jettisoning, in good Enlightenment style, its supernaturalist excesses. Reviled as an infidel during his lifetime, he might just as well, from another perspective, have been regarded as an advocate of radical theological reform.

Jefferson was well qualified for the role of religious reformer. Along with Elihu Palmer, he was the most intellectually sophisticated of all the American deists. He was steeped in the natural philosophy of the New Learning as well as Enlightenment political and ethical thought, and few persons in the young Republic were more familiar with the Greco-Roman classics. Moreover, Jefferson was blessed with a remarkable literary style, noteworthy for its masterful combination of expressiveness and restraint.

He had a feel for words, a flair for just the right line by which to get his point across, that rivaled even Tom Paine's. The Declaration of Independence is an obvious example of Jefferson's unique brand of eloquence. His voluminous correspondence, as well as *Notes on Virginia*, his single book, contains hundreds more. He was, in short, one of the finest men of letters the United States has produced, and although he published little, his words both excited the imagination and lodged in the memory. Given his obvious intelligence as well as his limpid style and national prominence, Jefferson was an ideal spokesperson for American deism. He himself seems to have recognized as much. Although he always refused to entangle himself in public debates over deism, his claim to have "never told my own religion, nor scrutinized that of another" is not quite accurate. He dispassionately explained the principles of his deistic Christianity many times in his letters, often written to correspondents whom he must have known would share his reflections with others. Moreover, he rarely let slip an opportunity to criticize Platonic or Calvinist adulterations of Jesus' original teachings. His intense need to protect his privacy was somewhat balanced, then, by his outrage at the intolerance and irrational bigotry of institutional Christianity, and his desire to purify it. He rarely jousted in the open, but was just as effective in spreading the deistic word as many of his co-religionists who publicly engaged the enemy.

Still, Jefferson's attempt to purify Christianity with an infusion of deistic rationalism was not without its weak points. To begin with, his endorsement of commonsense realism, which served as the foundation of his worldview, tended to be too uncritical. His assumption that sensory experience is an epistemically reliable basis of human knowledge ignored, for example, the obvious objection that such a naive empiricism inexorably led to a radical skepticism of the Humean variety. In addition, it is problematic to infer, as Jefferson did, that because the senses experience only physical phenomena, "talk of immaterial existences is talk of nothings." It is one thing to claim that human sensory faculties are capable of experiencing but one class of phenomena. It is quite another to presume that such a class exhausts the range of actual possibilities. This, however, is exactly the position Jefferson defends when he too hastily conflates nonexperiential entities and nonexistence, or "nothings."

Even more problematic is the fact that he himself violates his own commonsense empiricism and physicalism. Neither Jefferson's deity nor the laws of nature about which he spoke so often are physical entities. Physicality cannot be their mode of existence. It seems, then, that loyalty to his own epistemic standards would demand that he dismiss speculation about them as idle talk of nothings. But he clearly does not. Like all deists, he maintained that evidences of divine existence as well as immutable natural law are deducible from the physical realm. Consequently, there is at least one topic for Jefferson in which talk of immaterial existence is *not* talk of nothing. The rub, however, is that he nowhere attempts to defend this obvious exception to his own rule. Indeed, he seems not even to have been aware of the inconsistency.

An even more damaging inconsistency in Jefferson's physicalism is his analysis of moral principle. For Jefferson, values are neither merely subjective inclinations nor cultural inventions. He was confident that they enjoy an objective existence, independent of human psychology as well as social and historical permutations. This suggests that their nature is immutably lawlike, despite the fact that the utilitarian standards by which they are interpreted vary from culture to culture, as Jefferson conceded. But surely the way in which values objectively exist, like the way in which God and natural laws exist, is not physical in character. This is precisely the reason why Jefferson and other ethical intuitionists felt obliged to assume the presence of a "nonsensory" faculty—the moral sense—capable of intuiting them. Once again, then, Jefferson refused to push his physicalism to its logical conclusion, thereby generating fundamental tensions that threaten the coherency of his worldview.

That this tension should have emerged in Jefferson's thought is, in hindsight, not surprising. Deism as a philosophical and religious model is not a variety of physicalism. True, eighteenth- and nineteenth-century deism was heavily influenced by Newtonian mechanism and Lockean sensationalism, but it was not reducible to either. Instead, deism's primary assumption was a pan-rationalistic one which held that physical existence is necessarily imbued by, and reflective of, an underlying, nonphysical principle: reason. Jefferson the deist endorsed this pan-rationalistic premise wholeheartedly, and from it, inferred the existence of God, natural laws, and values. But there is another side to Jefferson's thought, a proto-positivistic one so suspicious of metaphysical speculation, so convinced that the reach of human knowledge is exhausted by sense experience, that it tended at times to collapse into crudely materialistic explanations. This "commonsense" physicalism that was one aspect of Jefferson's thought inevitably clashed with his deistic pan-rationalism. It was a fundamental dissonance he never managed to work out. Hence the pulling in opposite directions often discernible in his thought.

Still, expressions of fidelity to deistic pan-rationalism are more frequent as well as more fervent in Jefferson's writings than his occasional defenses of crude physicalism. Consequently, it is reasonable to see the former rather than the latter as his primary working assumption. Nowhere is his pan-rationalism more evident than in his method of scriptural demythologizing. His chief exegetical principle, as explained to his nephew Peter Carr, was that any biblical text that violates either reason or experience is unacceptable and should be expunged. The presupposition behind this rule is that reality is rationally lawlike, and that descriptions of reality must reflect that quality. In keeping with this presupposition, Jefferson the deist rejected New Testament accounts of miracles performed by Jesus, claiming that they did not strengthen faith or create awe so much as dishonor the deity and abuse the reader's credulity. Consequently, given his conviction that Jesus was an early proponent of the religion of nature, as well as his deep-seated fidelity to pan-rationalism, Jefferson had no choice but to separate scriptural chaff from scriptural wheat, embracing those passages that could be accommodated to deism and rejecting the rest. In the process, he demythologized sacred writ by stripping it of its fantastic elements and focusing instead upon the life and teachings of the man Jesus.

This exegetical method is clearly superior to the blanket condemnations of Scripture given by less discriminating American deists. But it can scarcely be denied that Jefferson's pan-rationalism prompted a certain amount of question-begging in his exegetical studies. It is certainly the case, just as Jefferson discerned, that several different styles as well as levels of discourse can be found in the New Testament, and that they are frequently jumbled together incongruously.

It is also true that those passages dealing with the miraculous and the supernatural can be siphoned off to leave a residue of primarily historical and philosophical passages. Thus far Jefferson is on solid ground and in agreement with contemporary higher criticism. But it is not as obvious as he supposed that the latter class of passages reflect Jesus' original words, actions, and intentions—his "primitive deism," as Jefferson said—while the former are Pauline and Platonic adulterations. He seems to have never considered the possibility that the true situation may have been the reverse—that is, that the historical Jesus both believed in and preached his own divinity, and the philosophical and ethical passages ascribed in him are later addenda. Jefferson ignored this interpretation because he assumed, prior to his exegetical analysis, that Jesus was a good deist. But this question-begging baptism of Jesus in humanistic waters has been denounced, today as well as in Jefferson's time, as anachronistic. Like Jefferson's interpretation of the logos passage in the Gospel of John, it may sacrifice historical accuracy for the sake of textual clarity—and clarity, moreover, defined in terms of the dubious presumption of Jesus' deism.

But even if one admits all this, one is still struck by the force and eloquence with which Jefferson defended his ideal of a deistic Christianity. Its central characteristics are its postulation of a rational and benevolent deity whose attributes imbue creation, its emphasis upon human virtue, and its championing of tolerance in matters of conscience. The sophisticated beauty of Jefferson's arguments for religious freedom are unparalleled in the deistic tradition and, indeed, in American letters as a whole. Their message underscores the deep and abiding humanism that lies at the heart of Jefferson's deism, as well as his hatred for any religious dogmatism that degrades human potential or sullies divine perfection.

Toward the end of his life, Jefferson mused upon his religious convictions in a letter to Benjamin Waterhouse.[40] After rehearsing the merits of Jesus' original "deistic and unitarian" teachings, he went on to compare them with the "demoralizing dogmas" of Calvinism. The latter include the doctrines of trinitarianism, predestination, the inefficacy of good works, the corruption of reason, and the utter depravity of mankind. Jefferson then asked himself and Waterhouse, "Now, which of these is the true and charitable Christian? He who believes and acts on the simple doctrines of Jesus? or the impious dogmatists [such as] Calvin?" Jefferson's answer to his own query is as uncompromising as it is eloquent.

> Verily I say these are the false shepherds foretold as to enter not by the door into the sheepfold, but to climb up some other way. They are mere usurpers of the Christian name, teaching a counter-religion made up of

the deliria of crazy imaginations, as foreign from Christianity as is that of Mahomet. Their blasphemies have driven thinking men into infidelity, who have too hastily rejected the supposed author himself, with the horrors so falsely imputed to him. . . . How much wiser are the Quakers, who, agreeing in the fundamental doctrines of the gospel, schismatize about no mysteries, and, keeping within the pale of common sense, suffer no speculative differences of opinion, any more than of feature, to impair the love of their brethren.

There is no better encapsulation of the spirit of Jefferson's deistic Christianity than this. Tolerance, common sense, the refusal to indulge in idle metaphysical speculations or to dogmatically canonize mere opinion, love of one's fellow humans and God: these tenets, for Jefferson, were the sum and substance of religion.

NOTES

1. Biographies of Jefferson abound, and all of them attest to his stature as a luminary in the American Enlightenment. Dumas Malone's magisterial *Jefferson and His Times* (Boston: Little, Brown, 1948–1981) remains the best treatment of Jefferson the man and thinker. More recent works include Alan Pell Crawford, *Twilight at Monticello: The Final Years of Thomas Jefferson* (New York: Random House, 2009); Joseph J. Ellis, *American Sphinx: The Character of Thomas Jefferson* (New York: Vintage, 1998); and Kevin J. Hayes, *The Road to Monticello: The Life and Mind of Thomas Jefferson* (New York: Oxford University Press, 2008). Charles B. Sanford, *The Religious Life of Thomas Jefferson* (Charlottesville: University of Virginia Press, 1984) is useful for navigating Jefferson's religious thought.

2. Alexander Hamilton to John Jay, May 7, 1800, in *The Works of Alexander Hamilton*, vol. 10, ed. Henry Cabot Ledge (New York, 1904), pp. 372–73; Sanford, *The Religious Life of Thomas Jefferson*, p. 2.

3. Thomas Jefferson to Benjamin Rush, April 21, 1803, in *Jefferson's Extracts from the Gospels*, ed. Dickinson W. Adams (Princeton, NJ: Princeton University Press, 1983), p. 331.

4. Thomas Jefferson to Benjamin Rush, January 16, 1811, in *The Writings of Thomas Jefferson*, vol. 9, ed. Paul Leicester Ford (New York, 1892–1899), pp. 295–96.

5. Thomas Jefferson to John Adams, August 15, 1820, in *The Life and*

Selected Writings of Thomas Jefferson, ed. Adrienne Koch and William Peden (New York: Modern Library, 1944), pp. 700, 701.

6. Thomas Jefferson to Peter Carr, August 10, 1787, in Ford, *The Writings of Thomas Jefferson*, vol. 4, pp. 429–32.

7. Thomas Jefferson to Elbridge Gerry, January 26, 1799, in *The Portable Thomas Jefferson*, ed. Merrill D. Peterson (New York: Penguin, 1988), pp. 478–79.

8. Thomas Jefferson to Margaret Bayard Smith, August 6, 1816, in Adams, *Jefferson's Extracts from the Gospels*, p. 376.

9. Thomas Jefferson to Francis Adrian Van der Kemp, July 30, 1816, in ibid., p. 375.

10. Adrienne Koch, *The Philosophy of Thomas Jefferson* (Gloucester, MA: Peter Smith, 1957).

11. Thomas Jefferson to John Adams, October 12, 1813, in *The Adams-Jefferson Letters*, ed. Lester J. Cappon (Chapel Hill: University of North Carolina Press, 1988), p. 384. The correspondence between Jefferson and John Adams remains the single best source of Jefferson's religious views.

12. Ibid.

13. Thomas Jefferson to Francis Adrian Van der Kemp, July 30, 1816 in Adams, *Jefferson's Extracts from the Gospels*, p. 375.

14. Thomas Jefferson, *Notes on the State of Virginia*, in Peterson, *The Portable Thomas Jefferson*, pp. 210, 211–12.

15. Ibid., p. 210.

16. Thomas Jefferson to the Reverend Isaac Story, December 5, 1801, in Adams, *Jefferson's Extracts from the Gospels*, pp. 325–26.

17. Thomas Jefferson to Peter Carr, August 10, 1787, in Ford, *The Writings of Thomas Jefferson*, vol. 4, pp. 429–32.

18. David Hume, "Of Miracles," in *An Inquiry Concerning Human Understanding*, ch. 10.

19. These two manuscripts are titled, respectively, "The Philosophy of Jesus" and "The Life and Morals of Jesus." Both are reproduced and discussed in Adams.

20. By "miraculous," Jefferson is referring to those scriptural stories that allow for no reasonable naturalistic explanation, such as the account of the loaves and fish feeding the multitude, or the versions of the resurrection. Jefferson at times is willing to retain as nonmiraculous certain of the stories recounting Jesus' "healings," presumably because he interpreted the original maladies as examples of hysteria alleviated by Jesus' strong personality.

21. Thomas Jefferson to John Adams, April 11, 1823, in Adams, *Jefferson's Extracts from the Gospels*, p. 385; Thomas Jefferson, "Syllabus of an Estimate of

the merit of the doctrines of Jesus, compared with those of others," enclosed with Jefferson's letter to Benjamin Rush, April 21, 1803, in Adams, *Jefferson's Extracts from the Gospels*, p. 333.

22. The "Syllabus" eventually appeared (anonymously) in the *Monthly Repository of Theology and General Literature* 11 (October 1816): 573–76.

23. Thomas Jefferson to John Adams, April 11, 1823, in Adams, *Jefferson's Extracts from the Gospels*, p. 412.

24. Ibid., p. 411.

25. Thomas Jefferson to Charles Thomson, January 9, 1816, in ibid., p. 365.

26. Thomas Jefferson to William Short, October 31, 1819, in ibid., p. 388; Thomas Jefferson, "Syllabus," in ibid., p. 334; Thomas Jefferson to William Short, August 4, 1820, in ibid., pp. 395, 396.

27. Thomas Jefferson to William Short, October 31, 1819, in ibid., p. 388.

28. Ibid., p. 390.

29. Thomas Jefferson, "Syllabus," in ibid., p. 332.

30. Thomas Jefferson to William Short, October 31, 1819, in ibid., p. 388.

31. Thomas Jefferson to Peter Carr, August 10, 1787, in Ford, *The Writings of Thomas Jefferson*, vol. 4, p. 430.

32. Ibid.

33. Thomas Jefferson to Thomas Law, June 13, 1814, in Adams, *Jefferson's Extracts from the Gospels*, p. 357.

34. Ibid., p. 356.

35. Ibid., p. 355.

36. Ibid., p. 356.

37. Thomas Jefferson, quoted in John Dewey, *The Living Thoughts of Thomas Jefferson* (New York: Longmans, Green & Co., 1943), pp. 100, 101.

38. Thomas Jefferson to Edward Dowse, April 19, 1803, in *The Writings of Thomas Jefferson*, vol. 10, ed. Albert Ellery Bergh (Washington, DC: Thomas Jefferson Memorial Association, 1907), p. 377.

39. Thomas Jefferson, "Opinion on French Treaties," April 28, 1793, in Ford, *The Writings of Thomas Jefferson*, vol. 6, pp. 220–21; Thomas Jefferson to Thomas Law, June 13, 1814, in Adams, *Jefferson's Extracts from the Gospels*, p. 357.

40. Thomas Jefferson to Benjamin Waterhouse, June 26, 1822, in Adams, *Jefferson's Extracts from the Gospels*, p. 406.

CHAPTER SIX

THE CRUSADER FOR DEISM

ELIHU PALMER

Few educated people today would fail to recognize the names of Franklin, Paine, and Jefferson, or to recall, even if only dimly, that these men were somewhat unorthodox in their religious persuasions. A lesser but still sizable portion of individuals have heard of Ethan Allen and Philip Freneau, although they probably do not associate them with American deism. Allen is remembered as a hero of the American revolution, Freneau as a poet. But almost no one today has heard of Elihu Palmer, much less read him. His name generally fails to evoke even hazy memories.

That historical memory has consigned Palmer to such oblivion is tragic, for no other single individual in the early Republic was as influential as he in disseminating the message of deism. Almost single-handedly, Palmer militantly transformed natural religion from a rather bookish philosophical preoccupation into a popular movement that inflamed the United States for an entire decade. Between 1793 and 1806 he tirelessly stumped from Maine to Georgia, preaching the religion of nature, castigating Christianity, and hurling anathemas at the "double despotism" of church and state. He penned hundreds of newspaper and journal articles, and somehow found the time to write his magnum opus, *The Principles of Nature*, which became the bible of American deism. The popular crusade for rational religion that Palmer spearheaded was the apogee and fulfillment of American deism. After him, religion in the United States was never quite the same.

It was not just the ardor of Palmer's speeches nor his dynamic presence, attested to by even his most ferocious enemies, that made him such a successful crusader for deism. It was also the intellectual depth of his position that attracted the attention of so many people, sympathizers and critics alike. Along with Jefferson, Palmer was the most reflective of all the American deists. He thought things through for himself, disdaining to ape the arguments of earlier freethinkers. He defended a physicalist world-view influenced by Newtonian mechanism, but unlike earlier deistic admirers of Newton such as Franklin and Jefferson, Palmer tried to push the first principles of his physicalism to their logical conclusions. He denied, for example, the existence of a soul that survives the death of the body. Most other deists accepted the doctrine of personal immortality.

Moreover, Palmer grounded value squarely in the psychobiological realm by formulating, in the *Principles*, a systematic naturalistic ethic. Based upon the twin principles of "reciprocal justice" and "universal benevolence," his ethical theory remains one of the finest examples of philosophical analysis in early American letters. And he wrote about all this (and more) in a style that was accessible to the general reading public without condescending to it. Palmer was not simply a masterful advocate of natural religion. He was also an ardent champion of radical reform who called for the complete separation of church and state, the abolition of slavery, an end to the social and legal subjugation of women, an unrestricted freedom of the press, universal education, and the decentralization of political authority. His radical republicanism, which earned him almost as much notoriety as his deism, was in fact a natural outgrowth of his religious convictions. Palmer was convinced that humans are endowed by the Supreme Architect with a semblance of divine reason. Since humans are innately rational creatures, they are capable of controlling their individual passions and collective actions in order to maximize well-being and justice. But a necessary condition for the actualization of a rational society is the eradication of those reactionary institutions that encourage ignorance, superstition, and fear. For Palmer, the church and the state—the "double despotism," as he referred to them time and time again—were the primary impediments to human felicity and social progress. The elimination of them and their oppressive policies would leave the way open for a golden age of rational religion, social and economic equality, political freedom, and universal tolerance. Of this, Palmer had no doubt whatsoever.

A RENEGADE CLERGYMAN

American deism's most fiery and influential champion started life in 1764 as the eighth child of a respectable and very Presbyterian farmer in Connecticut. Not too much is known about the circumstances of Palmer's early life, but his family cannot have been well off. Young Elihu did not matriculate at Dartmouth until he was twenty-one—a relatively late age to begin college studies in those days—and he relied on a college charity to help pay for his education. (Given Palmer's later career as the era's most outspoken critic of Christianity, it is interesting to note that the scholarship he received was earmarked for the training of future missionaries.) Palmer made up for lost time, graduating after only two years with a membership in Phi Beta Kappa and a reputation for personal integrity and literary proficiency. These two traits remained with him for the rest of his life. He coupled immense learning with a character so spotless that even his detractors could uncover no blemish on it.

Palmer's childhood exposure to the gloomy tenets of New England Presbyterianism initially must have struck some kind of responsive chord in him, for immediately after his graduation from Dartmouth he traveled to Pittsfield, Massachusetts, to read theology under the Reverend John Foster. (The good Reverend Foster some years later followed his most famous student into militant apostasy.) But as Palmer read more deeply in Christian doctrine, his childhood faith in its truth began to waver. By the time he accepted a call from the Presbyterian church of Newtown, Long Island, he was already moving away from Calvinism toward a humanistic natural religion. On his way to Newtown, he stopped over in Sheffield, Massachusetts, to preach a Thanksgiving Day sermon. According to John Fellows, a companion and early biographer of Palmer, he delivered a discourse there that fell markedly short of orthodoxy. "Instead of expatiating upon the horrid and awful condition of mankind in consequence of the lapse of Adam and his wife," explains Fellows, Palmer "exhorted his hearers to spend the day joyfully in innocent festivity, and to render themselves as happy as possible." At least some in Palmer's audience were shocked by his departure from the Calvinist doctrine of human depravity; we know, for instance, that afterward "he was lectured by an attorney, a *sound believer*, at whose house he stopped, for giving such liberal advice." Palmer appears not to have taken the chastisement to heart. Before arriving at Newtown, he paused to preach a second heterodox sermon in New York City. This discourse so perturbed Dr. Rodgers, the pastor of the church at which Palmer spoke, that he reproached his young colleague for the liberality of his message. These two episodes at the beginning of Palmer's clerical career prompted Fellows to laconically observe that the young man "was but ill adapted for a Presbyterian pulpit." Just how accurate this dry judgment was revealed itself shortly.[1]

Palmer barely had time to settle into Newtown before his faith as well as his reputation suffered additional setbacks. The immediate cause was the acquaintance he struck up with one Dr. Ledyard, a freethinking and somewhat disreputable physician. Ledyard appears to have been Newtown's village atheist, and he delighted in putting his young clerical friend on the spot by challenging him on the inconsistencies of Scripture and the unrelenting harshness of Calvinist doctrine. After a few months of Ledyard's good-humored taunting, Palmer finally asked for a truce, confessing to the doctor (no doubt after having sworn him to secrecy) that "there was no disagreement in their opinion of revealed religion."[2]

On another occasion, while staying at the home of a physician named Riker who was inoculating him against smallpox, Palmer again let slip an indication of his growing apostasy. As Fellows describes it, the young clergyman one evening "repeated the lines of Dr. Watts which began with 'Lord I am vile, conceived in sin / And born unholy and unclean'; setting forth the doctrine of original sin. Then turning to Mrs. R. he declared that he did not believe a word of it, no, not one word, he repeated with emphasis." The orthodox Mrs. Riker, horrified at her houseguest's audacity, begged him "not to give utterance to such sentiments in public." But Palmer was as little swayed by her well-intentioned rebuke as by the Sheffield lawyer's. Although he refrained from overt expressions of heterodoxy in his Newtown sermons, he also studiously avoided any discussion in them of what he privately scorned as the "peculiar and mysterious doctrines of the Christian religion." Instead, he greeted his increasingly perplexed flock each Sunday with discourses on natural philosophy and morality. But the compromise he tried to strike between Calvinism and humanism was not good enough. His Bible-reared congregation, accustomed to a meatier diet of fire-and-brimstone preaching, soon found itself unable to stomach these nonscriptural lectures. Probably, too, they were suspicious of Palmer's acquaintance with Ledyard, and it is likely that his passionate denial of original sin to Mrs. Riker had leaked out. At any rate, the Newtown congregation sent its young minister packing in early 1789. There seems to have been little, if any, regret on either side over his departure.[3]

After the rupture with his Newtown flock, Palmer relocated to Philadelphia. His move to a cosmopolitan setting was no doubt prompted by the hope that the citizenry there would be more receptive to the message of liberal religion. Although Palmer did not have his own pulpit, he did guest preach at several congregations in the city. But Philadelphia proved to be no more sympathetic to his heterodoxy than Newtown, and invitations to speak at local Presbyterian churches dwindled and ultimately ceased altogether. Palmer was not overly disturbed. As he later admitted, he was "disgusted with preaching from pulpits where the morose, vindictive and uncharitable tenets of Calvinism were generally inculcated and expected by the hearers." Recognizing that his conventional clerical career was over, he disassociated himself from Presbyterianism and in early 1791 joined the recently formed Universal Society of Philadelphia.[4]

The Universal Society, founded by John Fitch of steamboat fame, was a fraternal organization that espoused a rather muddled liberal Christianity. Its membership appears to have endorsed some scriptural accounts of miracles as well as Jesus' divinity, while rejecting typical Calvinist doctrines such as human depravity and predestination. But the Society as a whole good-naturedly accommodated a wide range of religious belief, and Palmer seems to have felt as if he at last had found a safe theological haven. His hopes, however, were unfounded, for his brand of apostasy proved too hot for even the Universalists to handle. In March 1791, shortly after Palmer joined the society, he announced in the Philadelphia newspapers that he would deliver, on the following Sunday, a public discourse proving that Jesus was not divine. Public reaction was swift and predictable. Philadelphia's Christian community was infuriated, and many of its members called for Palmer's indictment and criminal prosecution for blasphemy. Unhappily, Palmer's fellow Universalists, who for the most part were almost as upset about his impending speech as their orthodox counterparts, also became the brunt of public recriminations. Worried about the society's reputation—and, indeed, its very future—the Universalists asked Palmer to cancel his advertised discourse. But Palmer refused to back down, and on the following Sunday punctually arrived at the society's meeting house to deliver the promised address. While he certainly hoped for a large turnout, he got more than he expected. As John Fellows recalled years afterward,

> In consequence of this advertisement, the society of Universalists were in an uproar; and being joined by people of other denominations, instigated probably by their priests, an immense mob assembled at an early hour before the Universalist Church, which Mr. Palmer was unable to enter. In fact, it is stated, that he was in personal danger, and was induced to quit the city somewhat in the style of the ancient apostles upon similar occasions.[5]

Whether in apostolic style or not, Palmer's hasty retreat from Philadelphia on that March morning signaled a watershed in his life. (It was also a watershed of sorts for his fellow Universalists, whom Palmer left behind to brave the fury of an outraged Philadelphia; the really quite inoffensive society of theological misfits was precipitously banned by the enraged citizenry for admitting apostates such as Palmer into its ranks.) In leaving Philadelphia, Palmer also forsook any vestiges of loyalty to Christianity. Dismayed and disgusted by what he saw as the insurmountable bigotry of the orthodox community and disheartened by its vituperative hostility to his liberal viewpoints, he resolved to wash his hands of religion once and for all.

His allegiance to Christianity may have ended with the Philadelphia debacle, but in spite of himself his interest in religious issues steadily increased. Upon fleeing the City of Brotherly Love, Palmer migrated to Pennsylvania's western frontier, determined to make a new start in life. He studied law with one of his brothers for the next couple of years, but supplemented his reading of Grotius and Blackstone with an immersion in the New Learning. Palmer probably had been introduced to the thought of Bacon, Newton, and Locke during his college days, but during his exile in the Pennsylvania wilderness he studied them, as well as the British deists, with newfound interest. By the time he returned to Philadelphia in early 1793 to set up a law practice, he was a convinced deist.

Palmer hadn't been back in the city long before he hurled forth his first overtly deistic challenge to institutional Christianity. A few months after his arrival he delivered a Fourth of July oration, subsequently printed, which once again infuriated Philadelphians. In it, he castigated "king-craft and priest-crafts those mighty enemies to reason and liberty." Arguing that "the pious alliance of church and state" had for too long cast a "veil of darkness" over mankind, he praised the new Republic as an experiment in liberty, equality, and freedom of conscience that would "emancipate the world" from oppressive superstition and "ameliorate the condition of the human race."[6] This assault against the double despotism of church and state was to be the first of many. The unholy alliance of political tyranny and ecclesial oppression became a favorite theme of Palmer's, and one of the major thrusts of his future social reformism was to break the backs of both. In the American context, Palmer may have been tilting at windmills to some extent. Intimate collaboration between church and state was far more common in the Old World than in the New. Even Palmer seems to have recognized this, since he tended to draw primarily upon the European experience for his historical illustrations. But the threat of prosecution for blasphemy with which his aborted 1791 lecture against the divinity of Jesus had been greeted indicated that the Continent had no monopoly on legally sanctioned religious intolerance, and Palmer never missed an opportunity to point this out. It is arguable that his continuous condemnation of church-state allegiances helped to cement the wall-of-separation tradition established in the early Republic.

Palmer's inflammatory Independence Day speech inevitably moved him back into the spotlight of public controversy, which in turn did little to promote his fledgling legal practice. But there was little opportunity for the backlash to do him much harm professionally. Two months after his oration, the great yellow fever epidemic of 1793 swept through the city. Both Palmer and his wife fell ill. She died. Palmer survived, but was permanently and totally blinded. Many Philadelphians sanctimoniously saw Palmer's affliction as terrible and sure retribution from a wrathful God. Benjamin Rush, the city's leading physician, less piously suggested that Palmer lost his sight because he had refused to be bled during his illness. But regardless of its cause, Palmer's blindness destroyed his hopes of a legal career. A less determined individual, blinded and widowed in the space of a few days, might have given up; but not Palmer. As soon as he was back on his feet, he threw himself into his final calling: the popular dissemination of rational religion. After spending a few months in Georgia spreading the deistic word, he eventually settled in New York City, which became his base of operations for the next twelve years. From there, he launched the crusade for natural religion and social reform that, until his premature death in 1806, would make him one of the young Republic's most notorious public figures.

Palmer conducted his campaign for deism with all the evangelical zeal of any early apostle. Other advocates of rational religion by and large concentrated their energies upon defending it philosophically in books and pamphlets. Palmer was keenly aware of the written word's power, but he also appreciated the fact that deism could never acquire a widespread following without enlisting the spoken word as well. In addition, he recognized the strategic importance of consolidating the movement by creating a formal national structure—a church of natural religion, as it were. Consequently, he divided his time and effort between writing, speaking, and organizing. Like his deistic predecessors, he composed dozens of articles in defense of the religion of nature, as well as *The Principles of Nature*. Moreover, he found the time to edit two deistic newspapers, the *Temple of Reason* (1800–1801) and the *Prospect* (1803–1805), both of which enjoyed a wide readership. Unlike the other leading advocates of American deism, Palmer also traveled widely throughout the United States, lecturing extensively in city, town, and countryside to any crowd or gathering that would give him a podium. Moreover, he founded a network of deistical societies, first in New York, then in Baltimore, Newburgh, Philadelphia, and elsewhere; all were devoted to the discussion and propagation of deism, liberal republicanism, and natural philosophy. There were even plans (never realized) for the construction of massive "temples of reason" at which deists could gather and worship the God of nature.

In short, Palmer possessed the leadership qualities—fervor for proselytizing, eloquence, intelligence, and militant courage—needed to transform American deism from the philosophical orientation of a handful of intellectuals into a widespread popular crusade that spoke to the common man and woman. Under his guiding hand, deism in America somewhat ironically took on the character of a national religious revival. It churned up enthusiasm in adherents and intense contempt and alarm in opponents. Had Palmer remained within the Presbyterian fold, he may well have become one of the early Republic's leading evangelists. He had all the requisite talents and energy for such a calling. As it was, however, he turned this zeal against orthodoxy and in support of deism, and came close to beating the Christian establishment at its own game. It is little wonder that no other deist, including even the brutally anti-Christian Tom Paine, inspired so much fright and outrage in the faithful.

CHRISTIAN ABSURDITIES AND DEIST REASON

Palmer's assault upon Christian supernaturalism was the least original feature of his deistic crusade. In criticizing orthodox Christian doctrines, he by and large trod the path laid out by his deistic predecessors on both sides of the Atlantic. The unique attraction of his onslaught was that it came from an ex-clergyman, a renegade minister well schooled in Scripture as well as theology. Earlier rationalistic denunciations of Christian mysteries had been written by laymen, outsiders. But Palmer was a former member of the clerical inner circle. He was a genuine apostate, and such a blatant display of infidelity intrigued the public. Palmer himself was not unaware of the fact that his renunciation of the pulpit drew audiences, and he capitalized on it whenever he could. As he remarks in the preface to his *Principles*,

> The circumstance that the author was once a public speaker in the cause of Christianity, which is here opposed, so far from forming a reasonable objection against the perusal of this work, ought to become an additional motive of attention; for it was by a candid and attentive investigation into the character of revealed religion, that he became convinced that it was neither true nor divine.[7]

Disingenuous as this and similar confessions of his clerical background were, they worked: the public flocked wherever he spoke and devoured his writings. Even the *Principles*, an exercise in solid philosophical reflection, went through four editions during Palmer's lifetime and several more after his death.

Palmer's starting point was the conviction that Western thought is so permeated by the Christian ethos that its doctrines are rarely subjected to rigorous examination. Habituation to them militated against such objective scrutiny. But, he argued, nothing is more important than their investigation, precisely because their influence upon cultural and social institutions is so widespread. Nor was there anything to fear from such an inquiry. As Palmer put it, "If the Christian religion be true, we are essentially interested in a knowledge of this truth; if it be false, our happiness must be increased by a disclosure of those proofs which invalidate its authenticity."[8]

For Palmer, obviously, the latter alternative is the only reasonable one. He argued that Christianity is fundamentally indefensible on two counts: its supernaturalist foundation violates reason and experience, and its ethical maxims are unsystematic and unjust. Palmer's first objection is one with which all American deists agreed. His second was not so unanimously endorsed. Jefferson, for example, was an obvious dissenter.

In keeping with his basic Enlightenment orientation, Palmer's primary objection to supernaturalism, Christian or otherwise, was its appeal to miraculous "explanations." Such accounts of inexplicable breaches in the continuity of nature so violated the otherwise observable uniformity of existence, so "contradict[ed] the testimony of our senses," that their acceptance forced people "to abandon the instructive guide of our own experience, and affirm that the testimony of a few men has more weight than our own positive knowledge." But surely "the human mind is bound to decide according to the greatest portion of evidence." Given the fact that supernaturalist accounts of miracles contradict the testimony of experience as well as the principles of reason, Palmer concluded that the "greatest portion of evidence" was against them. This denial of the miraculous cut at the very heart of Christianity, as he was well aware. "If then, there can be no such thing as a miracle, Christianity, which is built upon this foundation, must be false."[9]

But there is another reason why Palmer rejected the possibility of miracles: their very postulation is "an insult to the dignity" of the Deity, the universe's Supreme Architect. Their violation of the immutability of nature suggests that God is either whimsical or imperfect. If the first, God arbitrarily ruptures the system of natural laws he has set in motion. If the second, he interferes with the natural order because he erred in its original creation and is trying to mend his handiwork. But either alternative ascribes unworthy attributes to the Deity. God is neither arbitrary nor infallible, says Palmer. Contrary to Christian teaching, therefore, the doctrine of miracles does not express the omnipotence and majesty of the divine. Instead, it sullies them by reducing the Divine Architect to either an unpredictable despot or a bungler.

The belief in miraculous occurrences, then, can be justified neither by appeals to reason or experience nor by an analysis of divine nature. Why, then, is it mandated by Christianity? On what basis does the Church rest its case? The answer, of course, is the authority of sacred Scripture, which the Christian community accepts as the revealed word of God, directly transmitted by the Deity to humankind and therefore inerrant.

Palmer sees at least two problems with the belief that scriptural revelation guarantees the truth of miraculous claims. First, even if one grants for the sake of argument that Scripture is a literal transcription of divine revelation and hence possesses the legitimate authority to demand unquestioning belief, this fideistic obligation surely is incumbent only upon the original and direct recipient of God's word. Palmer concurred with Paine's argument in *The Age of Reason* that revealed knowledge by definition can only be an immediate communication from the Deity to a specific individual. Once the original recipient shares the revelation with others, it acquires the evidential status of hearsay. But no reasonable person can be expected to accept secondhand testimony as self-evident, especially when the original putative revelation is as far removed in time and situation as scriptural testimony. Properly speaking, then, neither of the two biblical testaments is a "revelation." Instead, they are at best mere reports of what the original writers *believed* to be revelatory communications, and there is no reason for subsequent readers of Scripture to take their testimony at face value. Even if the biblical authors' sincerity is granted, their air of certainty in no way guarantees the truth of their claims. As Palmer says, in a passage reminiscent of Locke's conclusion in his *Essay Concerning Human Understanding*, "The extent of real attachment which individuals may shew towards any cause, is not conclusive evidence that such a cause is right. It is evidence only, that such persons are deeply interested in it."[10]

In addition to this logical objection to scriptural authority, Palmer offers another, more textual one. The Bible as a text, he argues, is shot through with internal inconsistencies and outright contradictions. Some of the textual problems, he concedes, can be chalked up to the ineptitude of the Bible's several translators, but he argues that this concession only underscores his earlier point about the unreliability of hearsay information. Even allowing for the possibility of imperfect translations, however, a close reading of sacred writ reveals a document that is "in many respects discordant; the historical has no accurate connection; the moral part is distorted, deficient or wicked; the doctrinal parts are either unintelligible, or contrary moral and philosophical truth." Given that "the truth of a book is always to be suspected, in proportion as it deviates from consistency," the Bible fails to meet the standards of rational endorsement. Its obvious textual incoherency invalidates it as a plausible, much less self-evidently indubitable, account of the ways of God.[11]

The obvious response to Palmer's criticisms of biblical veracity is that sacred writ reveals truths which, like the peace of God, surpass all understanding. From a rational perspective, Scripture may appear to contain passages that violate reason and experience, or portray the Deity as imperfect or whimsical. When read in the light of faith, however, such inconsistencies pose no problem. Faith is of a different, higher order than fallible human reason, and is the proper standard by which to penetrate Scripture and understand its claims.

Palmer obviously was not impressed by this objection. He argued that Christianity had needlessly mystified the very notion of faith by defining it as a nonrational assent to propositions that transcend human understanding and experience. For him, this was epistemically unsound, inasmuch as it ignored the evidential base upon which all reliable knowledge necessarily rests. Faith in the proper sense of the word is not a mysterious and hard-earned acceptance of transcendental truth. Instead, Palmer argued, it is merely "assent of the mind to the truth of a proposition supported by evidence. If the evidence adduced is sufficient to convince the mind, credence is the necessary result; if the evidence be insufficient, belief becomes impossible." This reduction of the concept of faith to simple induction obviously is too facile a move on Palmer's part to be taken seriously. But it just as obviously reveals the depth of his Enlightenment-based conviction that Christianity's supernaturalism has needlessly obfuscated straightforward empirical epistemic categories. Given this belief, it is not surprising that he concluded his naturalistic reformulation by sarcastically asking, "Why then is the principle of faith considered a virtue?"[12]

In addition to his condemnation of supernaturalist first principles such as revelation, faith, and miracles, Palmer also attacked the Christian worldview from a normative perspective. Ethically speaking, it is "distorted, deficient, or wicked." He did not deny that Christian scripture advocated "some good moral maxims," especially those praising the ideals of love and compassion. But these virtues, argued Palmer, were not unique to Christian thought. They had been routinely defended by pagan philosophers antedating Jesus—and defended more systematically than in the Bible. Normative passages in Scripture are "thinly interspersed," with no attempt on the part of the original authors to weave them into "any thing like a pure *system* of genuine morality." Moreover, they with few exceptions are "inaccurate and incomplete, trifling, and often without utility."[13]

Orthodoxy's lack of systematic normative analysis was troubling enough to a philosophical temperament such as Palmer's. But even worse, from his perspective, was the fact that certain of Christianity's central ethical beliefs revealed themselves upon examination to be unjust as well as promotive of human irresponsibility and wickedness. The doctrine of original sin, which Palmer attributed to Paul, violates every "standard of distributive justice" accepted by reason. It "makes the intelligent beings who are now in existence accountable for the errors and vices of a man who lived six thousand years ago," thereby instilling a sense of normative helplessness that breeds pàssivity and fatalism. But surely, argued Palmer, "every man is accountable for himself" and can be neither condemned nor praised for the actions of another. To suggest otherwise, as Christianity does, is to erode the very foundations of moral responsibility.[14]

Similarly, the orthodox doctrine of eternal damnation is an obstacle to moral responsibility. How can an individual justly be damned for all eternity, asks Palmer, when he or she is incapable of performing any action that would properly deserve such a radical response? Human beings are necessarily finite creatures, and each of their acts, virtuous or wicked, is likewise finite. Consequently, infinite (or eternal) damnation for wickedness is disproportionate. Like the doctrine of original sin, it violates the standard of distributive justice.[15]

Even the doctrine of the atonement, which to the orthodox Christian mind stands out as the supreme example of divine love and compassion, is harshly condemned by Palmer as neither instructive nor salutary.

> In plain terms, to destroy one evil [the fallen nature of humanity], another must be committed [the sacrificial death of Jesus]. To teach mankind virtue, they are to be presented with the example of murder; to render them happy, it is necessary to exhibit innocence in distress; to provide for them the joys of Heaven, wretchedness is to be made their portion on earth. . . . In fine, to procure for intelligent beings, the happiness suited to their nature, cruelty and vindictive malice must be exhibited for their contemplation. This doctrine presented in its true colours, contains neither justice nor utility.[16]

Christian staples such as the doctrines of atonement, eternal damnation, and original sin erode human happiness and lessen the likelihood of responsible, virtuous behavior on the part of individuals. But even more damningly, the Church's espousal of them, like its promulgation of the doctrine of miracles, insults the Deity's character. At best, they imply that he is unjust; at worst, that he is malevolent. Such a concept of God, maintains Palmer, is blasphemous as well as illogical. It paints the Divine Principle in such immoral colors as to render God "the bane of moral virtue." Yet this is precisely the type of deity that Holy Writ describes and Christianity accepts. At times the Deity portrayed in Scripture mandates charity and compassion; at others, he condones and sometimes even commands murder and destruction. In some instances God punishes mendacity, but at other times orders his prophets to deceive the people with false tidings. Jesus entreats his followers to love their enemies, but also cautions that discipleship entails forsaking one's family. The son of God rebukes Peter for attacking the Roman guard, but declares that he himself comes with a sword. He promises liberation from shame and degradation, yet demands certain courses of actions—such as turning the other cheek—whose passivity sacrifices "the dignity of our character," "invite[s] fresh injuries," and disgraces "the manly part of our nature."[17] Such a God, in short, manifests all the inconsistencies and passions that reason condemns in humans. He is "ever at variance with himself, and in him no genuine confidence can be reposed. Can any one then be happy who trusts a being of this description? To one who has, in fact, no uniformity of conduct, no system of action, and no immutability of procedure? No!"[18] In fact, Palmer goes on to say, "It would be more consistent

with the true interest of man, that he should be destitute of all theological ideas, than that he should yield to the reception of such incoherent and unjust opinions of the divine character. Atheism is far
preferable to that theology which includes folly, cruelty, and ferocious
fanaticism."[19]

But if all this is the case, why does Christianity continue to espouse
such an ethically corrupt notion of God? The explanation, Palmer insists,
is simple. The most effective way for the Church to consolidate its hegemony is to insure that the faithful remain dependent upon its "inspired"
guidance. To this end, institutional Christianity adopts two strategies.
First, it teaches that humans without exception are, to use Jonathan
Edwards's phrase, "sinners in the hands of an angry God," thereby cowing
frightened laymen into submitting to ecclesial authority as their only
chance for salvation. Second, the Church recognizes the advantages of
keeping its followers ignorant and confused about the nature of the Deity;
it thereby maintains its own position as the sanctioned interpreter of
God's ways. The ignorance and fear cultivated by institutional Christianity breeds gullibility, and the latter in turn encourages an "attachment
to the marvelous" that predisposes the masses to a blind acceptance of
irrational theological solutions to basic questions about nature, virtue and
God.[20]

But if these strategies of dissimulation are convenient for the
Church, they are deadly to the human spirit. Ignorance and fear enslave
humanity in the chains of superstition. They breed docility in the face of
authority and intolerance of dissenting perspectives. To make matters
even worse, political authority more often than not endorses and supports this ecclesial usurpation of private conscience, recognizing that its
interests are also served if the Church succeeds in numbing the populace
into stupidity and frightening it into meek submission.

Palmer's diagnosis is a gloomy one, but it is not pessimistic. He was
too much a child of the Enlightenment to entertain doubts about the
inevitability of reason's ultimate triumph over superstition and ignorance.
If human nature is malleable enough to be perverted by corrupt institutions, he reasoned, it is also sufficiently malleable to be salvaged. Irrationality, credulity, and gullibility are unnecessary weaknesses stamped
upon the race by ecclesial and political authorities, and can be eradicated.

If the passions of man and the impulses of his nature have frequently produced a moral eccentricity in his conduct, it is certain that a corrupt government and a corrupt religion have rendered him habitually wicked, have perverted all the conceptions of the mind upon moral and political subjects. . . . [Human felicity and virtue] will never succeed extensively till the civil and religious tyranny under which they groan shall be completely annihilated. . . . If civil and ecclesiastical despotism were destroyed, knowledge would become universal, and its progress inconceivably accelerated.[21]

REJECTING ATHEISM

So much, then, for an orthodox Christianity founded upon supernaturalism. It promoted immorality, ignorance, and injustice, insulted the Deity, and stunted humanity. As Palmer said, it was better to be an atheist than a Christian.

But Palmer, like his fellow deists, considered atheism an ultimately unacceptable position. He repeatedly condemned disbelief in a deity, claiming that such a denial would fly in the face of empirical evidence and reason. Fortunately, Christianity and atheism were not the only options. There was a third way: deism. So far as Palmer was concerned, it was the only real alternative for a rational human being.

This central conviction obviously reflects Palmer's allegiance to the New Learning. Following Locke's example, he believed (along with his fellow deists) that reason and experience are the twin standards by which all knowledge claims are properly evaluated. Reason—"righteous and immortal reason"—reaches it highest human expression in the natural sciences. They shed light upon the physical realm by bringing to conscious awareness the manifold operations that constitute reality. Moreover, despite the rational faculty's occasional susceptibility to error, its discovery and elucidation of nature's laws is progressive. As Palmer the Enlightenment optimist says,

It is true that the natural imbecility and imperfection of our faculties, and the extensive nature and variety of those moral and physical combinations, from which science is to be deduced, evince the strong probability that man may frequently be erroneous in the conclusions which he draws from certain premises, because the [present] force of his faculties is not adequate to a full and complete investigation of the compounded and diversified relations of existence; but these natural obstacles to the clear deductions of science, are neither of a discouraging or an insurmountable nature. The nature of the human mind is prodigious in the disclosure of natural principles, and its activity must be measured on a scale of endless progression.[22]

Foremost among the natural principles disclosed by reason is the revelation that reality itself is rational. Taking his cue from Newton, Palmer maintained that the perceived regularity of phenomena must be the result of natural laws that are immutable as well as universal. True, these natural laws themselves are not directly experienced. But they can be inferred from the orderly, patterned, and predictable behavior of matter in motion. When this experienced regularity is coupled with the absolute lack of empirical evidence for the postulation of spiritual or nonphysical causes, only one conclusion is feasible: "The solar system is guided by laws, of which mathematical science has taken the most indubitable cognizance. The productions of the earth are subject to no supernatural derangement; they are exhibited with a constancy and specific similarity which disregard every idea of perversion in physical laws."[23]

But science does more than merely reveal the rational nature of reality. It also irresistibly points to the existence of a divine First Cause who set in motion the clockwork-like universal machine. Newton, after all, had established that reality is a vast network of causal relationships, thereby leaving no room for gratuitous or chance events. For Palmer, it followed that this principle likewise applies to reality as a whole. Just as no event in observable nature is without an antecedent cause, so nature itself is the effect of a prior cause: God.

Science, then, provides the foundation for a rational belief in the existence of God, a foundation that falsifies the claims of atheism. The light it sheds upon the nature of physical reality also enables humans to come to some understanding of the Deity's attributes. For Palmer, it is a self-evident principle that an effect is similar to its cause; it embodies and continues at least a semblance of the qualities of its origins. Consequently, if the physical order is itself the product of a First Cause, which

Palmer clearly believes, it follows that an examination of the essential features of observable reality will disclose truths about the essential features of its divine origin. Thus, laws of nature are both rational and immutable. The Deity, consequently, likewise possesses those attributes. Humans are capable of love and virtue. Ergo, the Deity is perfectly endowed with similar qualities. A scrutiny of nature reveals that it has been intelligently designed for the maximum advantage of mankind. It follows that benevolence can be attributed to God.

In short, a reasoned appraisal of the nature of causation leads to the conclusion that reality displays characteristics that must be "in strict conformity to the essential properties of [God's] existence." This means that nature, not Scripture, is the true revelation of God, and scientists, not theologians, are its proper interpreters. Any concept of the Deity (such as Christianity's) that denies the divine qualities disclosed by reason and nature is not merely false; it is also a scandalous example of infidelity. "There can be no errors more pernicious than those which destroy the conformity of operation in the physical world, and despoil the Creator the honour of governing the universe by immutable laws. . . . [Nature's] author is insulted and the scientific deduction of human intellect perverted or destroyed."[24]

It is clear that Palmer's deistic God is more akin to the classical than the Christian concept. The Supreme Architect is the God of philosophy not of Abraham, Isaac, or Jacob. He does not arbitrarily violate motion, nor is he capable of whimsical or wicked commands. Moreover, the essential rationality of his nature precludes self-contradictory attributes such as Christian trinitarianism, just as immutability prevents him from changing his necessary nature, contrary to the Christian myth of the Incarnation. God is the distant but sustaining cause of reality, and any permutation of his essence would destroy the universe.

But although Palmer's God lacks many of the anthropomorphic qualities of the Christian God, God is not thereby relegated to the status of a cold, abstract metaphysical principle. The essential immutability and rationality of the deistic God make him worthy of veneration and awe, but the benevolence that he displays in the providential design of the world commands love and worship. Palmer, like all deists, was no friend of religious enthusiasm. But he had no wish to portray God as an unapproachable and inaccessible cipher. That such was not his intention is admirably expressed in one of the most eloquent passages in the *Principles*.

Deism declares to intelligent man the existence of one perfect God, Creator and Preserver of the Universe; that the laws by which he governs the world, are like himself immutable and, of course, that violations of those laws, or miraculous interference in the movements of nature, must be necessarily excluded from the grand system of universal existence; that the Creator is justly entitled to the adoration of every intellectual agent throughout the regions of infinite space; and that he alone is entitled to it, having no copartners who have a right to share with him the homage of the intelligent world. Deism also declares, that the practice of a pure, natural, and uncorrupted virtue, is the essential duty, and constitutes the highest dignity of man; that the powers of man are competent to all the great purposes of human existence; that science, virtue, and happiness are the great objects which ought to awaken the mental energies, and draw forth the moral affections of the human race.[25]

RECIPROCAL JUSTICE AND UNIVERSAL BENEVOLENCE

"The practice of a pure, natural, and uncorrupted virtue, is the essential duty, and constitutes the highest dignity of man"—such was one of Palmer's deepest-held convictions. Although the entire deistic tradition placed a high premium on morality, arguing that virtue is the most sublime mode of worship, it was Palmer and Palmer alone who took the claim seriously enough to back it up with a consistent ethical system. Other American deists had touted the importance of ethical behavior, but had done so (like Franklin and Paine) in a piecemeal, haphazard fashion, or (like Jefferson) had merely endorsed a de-supernaturalized version of Christian morality. But Palmer recognized that neither alternative was sufficient. Virtue had to rest upon a more solid basis than a set of aphorisms that edified without instructing. Moreover, it had to be grounded in the naturalism that provided the deistic worldview with its first principles. It was the formulation of such a normative justification that Palmer undertook in his *Principles*, the subtitle of which designated it as an inquiry into the "moral causes of happiness and misery among the human species." While Palmer's criticisms of supernaturalist Christianity as well as his discussions of deistic first principles were rather conventional in method and argument, his ethical system broke entirely fresh ground. It was the only comprehensive ethic to emerge from American deism. It not only provided a cogent foundation for deism's emphasis upon moral behavior but also revealed Palmer to be one of the early Republic's most creative philosophical minds.

Palmer's starting point was the assumption that morality is a subset of natural science, founded upon naturalistic first principles derived from reason and experience. He denied that the scientific principles of a rational ethic were directly dependent upon divine command or supernatural revelation. Instead, morality "rests upon the relations and properties of human life," and consequently can be deduced from a careful scrutiny of biological and psychological laws. An individual totally ignorant of the existence of the God of nature is capable, through rational reflection upon these laws, of discovering the ground of virtue. This is because the "essential principles of morality are founded in the nature of man, they cannot be annihilated, they are as indestructible as human existence itself." As such, an understanding of these principles depends neither upon a mysterious revelation, the authority of sacred writ, nor the miraculous intervention of God. It requires only a rational appraisal of the evidence provided by ordinary experience.[26]

Palmer's entire ethical system is ultimately grounded in what he called the "law of sensation," a psychological postulate derived from his observation of organic behavior. "Every organized being," he asserted, "whether of a high or low station in animal existence, is susceptible of pleasure and pain."[27] Moreover, the attainment of the one and the avoidance of the other are the two primary psychobiological drives that motivate sentient creatures. In the case of humans, happiness—the ultimate aim of each person—is measured by how successfully pleasure is maximized and pain minimized. This inference in turn suggested to Palmer that human felicity rests upon two preliminary factors: first, the perpetuation of the individual's survival, since continued existence obviously is a necessary condition for all subsequent attributes; and second, that individual existence is pleasurable, or at least relatively pain-free.

Sentience, then, is the key to understanding human motivation and well-being. But humans, unlike other forms of organic life, are not exclusively sentient. They are rational as well. Even though their behavior is ultimately motivated by the sensate drives for pleasure and pain avoidance, they are also capable of rationally reflecting upon which acts and decisions truly enhance pleasure. The unreflective person might conclude that his survival and happiness are exclusively dependent upon personal aggrandizement, and that the best way to maximize his chances for both is to strong-arm his way through life, taking what he wants when he wants it. But a rational individual knows better, realizing that such roughshod strategies for promoting self-interest are in fact destructive. After all, if everybody strives for pleasure maximization at the expense of their fellows, thereby setting in motion a Hobbesian war of all against all, each individual's potential for a happy existence would be severely diminished. As Palmer cautioned, "If I assume to myself the pretended right of injuring the sensations . . . or general happiness of my neighbour, he has, undoubtedly, an equal right to commit the same violence upon me."[28] It does not take the genius of a Hobbes to realize that such a state of affairs inevitably renders life nasty, short, and brutish.

The psychological drive for gratification, ameliorated by the rational realization that certain strategies for insuring survival and enhancing pleasure are self-destructive, in turn gives rise to the insight that reality is "a vast assemblage of living creatures, whose relations are reciprocal and reciprocated under a thousand different forms." Each organized being, regardless of its "high or low location" on the biological ladder, is intimately and irrevocably related to all others. As such, each perforce "is interested in the whole, and the whole is interested in the preservation and diversified modification of the parts."[29] In the case of humans, this means that the reflective individual comes to see that his personal happiness depends upon the nature of the environment in which he exists, and that his personal welfare is determined by the social and interpersonal relations he establishes or fails to establish. Consequently, the rational person prudently tempers his native sensate drive for gratification by accommodating his behavior to the necessities of social existence. This deliberate amelioration of the psychobiological law of sensation may go against one's natural inclinations, but it is not impossible of realization.

It is, no doubt, extremely natural and even absolutely necessary that each individual should feel an anxiety extremely impulsive respecting the preservation of his own existence, and the means by which it is to be rendered tranquil and comfortable; but this sensation, the first which is experienced by a sensitive creature, does not preclude that expansion of mind which would . . . extend the circle of man's affections and duties, and which also prepares for himself an additional portion of exalted enjoyment.[30]

Palmer draws two corollaries from his discussion of the law of sensation, both of which carry normative weight. The first is that no human enjoys an innate privilege or superiority over other humans. From a biological perspective, all humans share identical fundamental attributes. "Whatever be the active power, the moving cause that directs the universe, this power [has] given to all men the same organs, the same sensations and the same wants." Thus, "in the order of nature, all men are equal." Moreover, inasmuch as this natural equality of sensations and wants "has given to every man the ability of preserving and maintaining his own existence, it clearly follows that they are created free, that no man can be subject, and no man sovereign, but that all men are the unlimited proprietors of their own persons."[31] Equality and liberty, then, are as "essential attributes of man" as is reason. They are not spiritual qualities attributable to a mysterious ensoulment, but rather natural ones linked to humanity's physical nature. Together, they serve as the proper foundation of social relationships, a foundation as "essential and immutable" as the "physical properties of inanimate matter."

[F]rom the principle that every man is the unlimited master of his own person, it follows that one inseparable condition in every contract and engagement is the free and voluntary consent of all the persons therein bound; farther, because every individual is equal to every other individual, it follows that the balance of receipts and payments in political society, ought to be rigorously in equilibrium with each other.[32]

The naturalistic grounding of liberty and equality sets the stage for the two explicitly normative principles upon which Palmer's ethical system rests: reciprocal justice and universal benevolence. The concept of reciprocal justice follows from Palmer's earlier contention that human actions are ultimately directed toward the attainment of happiness, with happiness defined as pleasure enhancement and pain avoidance. In any contractual arrangement—and Palmer, in keeping with the Enlightenment tradition, holds that all social relations are essentially contractual—no participant enjoys a protected isolated position. There is always an implied quid pro quo. It follows, then, that the prudent individual recognizes that it is in his own best interest to avoid harming others, since his welfare is intimately linked with theirs. Survival and personal happiness can only be attained if individuals cooperate with one another by guaranteeing to respect each other's interests. Such mutual respect, ultimately grounded in self-interest, is the basis of justice: fair and equitable treatment of equal participants in the social contract. As Palmer put it, "It is the reciprocation of sensation, the mutuality of condition, of powers and wants, that constitute the immortal basis of justice, and lead to the establishment of rules, whose operation must ever be in strict accordance with the happiness of the human species."[33]

But the principle of reciprocal justice, although a necessary condition for social justice and individual responsibility, is not by itself sufficient. Palmer recognized that it provided a theoretical foundation for the well-being of present generations of humans. But he was also anxious to extend concern to the well-being of *future* generations. It is this vision that prompted the postulation of universal benevolence, the second of his two fundamental ethical principles. The principle is distinctively Palmerian, and is one of the more creative ideas to emerge from the early Republic.

Humans are not solitary creatures. Each person's activities necessarily affect the well-being of other people. Consequently, individuals have both a rational and a prudential obligation to treat others with consideration: this much has been established by the principle of reciprocal justice. But the rational person realizes that his present course of action helps to establish and perpetuate institutions, policies, and customs that will affect future generations as well. It may well be that these institutions maximize pleasure and minimize pain for the present generation, but their true value cannot be appraised by such short-term considerations. They must also be evaluated in terms of their foreseeable long-term impact. If it is reasonable to suppose that future generations will exist, and if those generations will exhibit essential human qualities such as independence, equality of attributes and sentience, and finally if the possession of those qualities will posit the psychobiological need for pleasure-maximization and pain-minimization, then the ethical obligations of the present generation extend beyond its own situation into the future. In short, the recognition that the present actions of humans inevitably affect future events should lead to an attitude of universal benevolence that imposes limitations upon present behavior, even when that behavior promises immediate gratification for the present generation. In order to widen the social contract to include inhabitants of the future, then, currently existing humans should display

> respect for the aggregate of existence to which [they belong]. . . . The successive changes through which [humankind] is destined to pass, and the impossibility of relinquishing [its] connection with nature should inspire [the individual] with feelings of universal sympathy, and with sentiments of universal benevolence. Human reason has an important duty to perform in the institutions which it establishes; for these institutions will affect in succession, all the [sentient] portion of matter destined to pass through an organized predicament.[34]

It is obvious, continues Palmer, that the present generation "suffer[s] from the cruel lash of ancient institutions"—ecclesiastical oppression, political and civil tyranny, slavery, the subjugation of women—established by prior generations.[35] But a right-thinking person, aware of the necessary equality of all humans, present and future, will not desire to perpetuate such harmful institutions. Consequently, there are prudential and rational incentives for working toward their abolition. In doing so, the individual acts in his own present self-interest, enhances the potential for his fellows' happiness, and prevents recurrences of the injustices from which his generation suffers. As Palmer says, "If man had a comprehensive view of the successive changes of his existence, and a correct view of the nature of sensation continually resulting from the renovation of organic forms, sympathy or universal benevolence, would become irresistibly impressive upon his moral powers, and form the basis of his subsequent conduct."[36]

The principles of reciprocal justice and universal benevolence, then, are the twin pillars of Palmer's ethics. It is important to note that they are not theological postulates, much less expressions of revealed divine commands. Instead, they are firmly grounded in the necessary physical and psychological nature of the human race. As such, they are immutable as well as universal, and applicable to present and future generations alike. Palmer saw them, in short, as normative natural laws. Comprehension of and conformity to them is just as necessary for happiness and human well-being as is the understanding of physical laws. The latter enable humans to master nature, the former lead to mastery of self and the perfection of society.

The universality of Palmer's twin principles underscores his deistic conviction that reality in all its aspects is modeled on a rational cosmic blueprint. Moreover, their naturalistic origins emphasize his fundamentally humanistic belief that human destiny is ultimately in human hands. The felicity and progress of the race depend in the final analysis on human decision, not divine providence or predestination. Both virtue and moral evil are the products of human behavior. Conformity to the principles of universal benevolence and reciprocal justice is promotive of the former; the latter is a necessary consequence when they are disregarded. Human suffering, then, is not the product of original sin. Instead, it is caused by deviation from the laws of morality, a deviation that inevitably leads to the "establishment of a cause which must sooner or later work ruin to [a person's] sensation, or essentially disturb the tranquillity of his mind."[37] But such self-destructive tendencies can be expunged if humans follow the dictates of reason.

The depth of Palmer's humanism, as well as the extent to which he pushed his naturalistic orientation, is revealed by his denial of personal immortality. Most of the American deists believed—or at least wrote as if they believed—in the existence of an otherworldly realm in which disembodied souls would be rewarded or punished for earthly actions. Moreover, this postulation, whether meant to be taken literally or not, functionally served, to their way of thinking, as a necessary incentive for virtuous behavior. But Palmer, loyal to his naturalistic account of human virtue, rejected the possibility of a "spiritual, immaterial and indestructible soul." Self-awareness, if it occurs, is the epiphenomenal consequence of the permutations of matter in motion. It is not the result of a mysterious ensoulment. Consequently, the only semblance of immortality that can be rationally expected is of an impersonal variety. Humanity as a species survives, but individuals do not. It follows, then, that promises of future reward or punishment held out as incentives for present virtue are intellectually dishonest, archaic remnants of supernaturalism. Rational self-interest, which reveals to humans the central importance of conformity to universal benevolence and reciprocal justice, is the only prod to virtue available to the race. And, for Palmer, it is a sufficient one.[38]

THE DOUBLE DESPOTISM

Palmer's naturalistic ethic gave deistic moralizing the philosophical rigor it previously had lacked. It was also—and, for Palmer, preeminently—a theoretical justification for the social reformism his militant brand of deism advocated. It established that there was an observable equality in rationality and fundamental needs among persons, thereby bestowing on humanity a common set of rights and responsibilities. The zeal with which Palmer proselytized for natural religion was powered by his conviction that Christian supernaturalism and ecclesial authority violated these rights and responsibilities by retarding the exercise of reason and, consequently, the flourishing of human well-being. His condemnation of social injustice and political oppression was grounded along similar lines. If deism's purpose was to free humanity from the shackles of fear, ignorance, oppression, and superstition, it was not enough to decry the abuses of the Church or the irrationalisms of Christianity. It was also necessary to denounce those social practices and political institutions that worked hand in hand with the Church to shatter the human spirit. As Palmer said as far back as 1793 in his Independence Day speech, the amelioration of humankind's wretched condition depended upon destroying the "double despotism" of "priest-craft" and "king-craft."

To that end, Palmer's career as a crusader for deism necessarily meant that he likewise became the ardent foe of unjust institutions such as slavery and the subjugation of women. Differences in physical appearance or accidents of birth were no excuse for unequal treatment, let alone exploitation, for all humans shared the same needs and accompanying rights. In the *Principles*, Palmer expressly condemns the institution of slavery along precisely these lines.

> Among the species, there is evidently a great diversity of external appearance; the white and the black man are as different in some other

respects, as they are in the color of their skin; the long straight hair of the one, and the curled wool of the other, is a verification of this remark. [But] both races are intelligent, and it is presumed that the intellectual powers are not in any essential degree dissimilar. Improvement has made more difference than nature, and the immoral opinion, that the whites have a right to enslave the blacks, is a complete abandonment of the principle of reciprocal justice, and a violation of the fundamental laws of Nature.[39]

In a 1797 oration titled "An Enquiry relative to the Moral and Political Improvement of the Human Species," Palmer champions political and social equality for women by once again appealing to the notion of the innate equality of needs, wants, and abilities.

> Among those causes of human improvement . . . that are of most importance to the general welfare, must be included, the total annihilation of the prejudices which have established between the sexes an inequality of rights, fatal even to the party which it favors. In vain might we search for motives by which to justify this principle, in difference of physical organization, of intellect, or of moral sensibility. It had at first no other origin but abuse of strength, and all the attempts which have since been made to support it are idle sophisms.[40]

Like most thinkers in the modern liberal tradition, Palmer believed that steady progress could be made toward the amelioration of social injustices such as these through universal education and open debate. Anticipating John Stuart Mill's later discussion of the self-regulating marketplace of ideas, Palmer argued that the unimpeded and public exchange of opinions presents no threat to human well-being. As he wrote in *The Political World*, a manuscript left unfinished at the time of his death, "It is an old maxim, and a true one too, that guilt needs no accuser; it condemns itself." Mischievous ideas or destructive opinions, then, will fall of their own accord when exposed to public scrutiny. Their censure is a greater evil than any harm their publication might temporarily inflict. It follows that Palmer was an ardent and unreserved champion of an absolutely free press. "The press should never be prevented from declaring and publishing the boldest truths, whether these truths relate to the humble citizen, or to the man that is high in office.

Citizens of America! . . . If the press be shackled, your liberties are in danger; if the press be silenced, your freedom is gone, it is annihilated for ever, and you will bury in one common grave, THE HOPE AND HAPPINESS OF THE HUMAN RACE."[41]

But for all his faith in the liberating effects of universal education, Palmer was not so naive as to suppose that education, by itself, was capable of destroying the double despotism of church and state. After all, the fundamental strategy of the ecclesial and political partnership was to consolidate its power by convincing people that they were too stupid to forgo authoritative supervision of their consciences and actions. "You are too ignorant to govern yourselves, exclaims the fanatic; you must come under our protecting and paternal control, says the civil tyrant; we pity your ignorance, we commiserate your misfortune, and we will take upon ourselves the trouble of conducting your affairs." In a word, "interested despotism has determined to hold, in a state of . . . bondage, the life of man."[42]

Given the tenacity with which the double despotism holds them in thrall, then, Palmer refused to rule out the possibility of countervailing measures stronger than education and freedom of the press. Human felicity and progress, he warns in the *Principles*,

> will never succeed extensively till the civil and religious tyranny under which they groan shall be completely annihilated. This will lead to the application of force in the political revolutions of the world; an expedient, however, the rectitude of which some benevolent philosophers have called in question. . . . [But] despotism gives no encouragement to any kind of improvement, and the hope of human amelioration from this quarter will ever prove to be fallacious. Reason, righteous and immortal reason, with the argument of the printing types in one hand and the keen argument of the sword in the other, must attack the thrones and hierarchies of the world, and level them with the dust of the earth. If civil and ecclesiastical despotism were destroyed, knowledge would become universal, and its progress inconceivably accelerated.[43]

With inflammatory calls to arms such as this, it is little wonder that Palmer was seen by his contemporary detractors as a dangerous menace to religious orthodoxy and to political and social stability. Their fears, of course, were well founded. Palmer's militant crusade for deism had no less of a goal than the complete emancipation of humans from any form of authority that retarded the exercise of reason and robbed people of their chance for a meaningful existence; and such emancipation demanded, in his mind, the overthrow of ecclesial and civil authority. To have settled for less would have been a betrayal of the God of nature.

THE CHIEF OF THE AMERICAN DEISTS

In Philadelphia, in the summer of 1791, Elihu Palmer first crossed swords with Christianity by unsuccessfully attempting to deliver a discourse against the divinity of Jesus. Run out of town in the "style of an ancient apostle" by an outraged mob, he returned to Philadelphia two years later, only to become blind and widowed in the space of a few days. On April 7, 1806, while once again back in Philadelphia on a speaking engagement, Palmer succumbed to pneumonia. One can only imagine that the dying Palmer grasped the irony of his situation: his career ending where it began, in a city that had always been his nemesis.

Palmer died broken in body and penniless. His thirteen-year crusade for deism had wreaked havoc on his always frail constitution, and most of his personal financial resources had been consumed by the numerous deistic newspapers and societies he had launched. His second wife would have been left indigent by his death, in fact, had not Tom Paine generously provided for her. But despite all this, Palmer left a rich legacy. Through his efforts, deism had become a household word in the young Republic. His theological and social militancy had enraged and horrified many, but it had also served as the conscience of the nation, forcing people to reflect deeply and sometimes with agony about their traditional commitment to supernaturalist Christianity and their tolerance of social injustices.

It is not too much to say that Palmer irrevocably influenced the character of nineteenth-century religious thought in America. After his deistic crusade, orthodox apologists realized that their defenses of Christianity could no longer credibly bypass textual criticism or ignore natural science. They did not, obviously, convert to deism, but they did incorporate in their theologies many of natural religion's methodological principles. In short, Palmer's doggedly militant challenge to the Christian worldview was too serious to ignore. It is because of this that he so richly deserves the title bestowed him by a twentieth-century commentator: "the chief of the American deists."[44]

This is not to say that there are no shortcomings in Palmer's deism. Stylistically, for example, he obviously was not in the same league as Franklin, Paine, Jefferson, or Freneau. His journalistic pieces were often tossed off in such a white heat that they tended to be either too sketchy or too obvious. His *Principles of Nature*, although written in an easily accessible, jargon-free manner, occasionally lapses into long-windedness and redundancy. Part of the book's repetitiveness can be attributed to the fact that it was dictated by a man who was blind. Nonetheless, it is undeniable that Palmer, in spite of the reputed eloquence of his oratory, was not a master of the written word.

More serious than his relative lack of literary flair is the charge made by several commentators that Palmer's crusade to disseminate deism smacked of religious revivalism. An essential Palmerian strategy for the propagation of natural religion was the consolidation of its advocates into a nationwide organization that would very much resemble the internal structure of New England Congregationalism. The local chapters of this deistic federation would have each possessed their own ministers as well as magnificent temples of reason at which the faithful could worship the God of nature with liturgies and ceremonies reminiscent of traditional religious services. But such an institutionalization of the religion of nature, had it gotten off the ground, might well have amounted to little more than the replacement of one ecclesial hegemony with another. The evangelical zeal with which Palmer campaigned for a national religion of nature, in short, struck some as the confused aspirations of an apostate who still clung fervently to the external trappings of Christianity. Whether or not Palmer's vision would have resulted in the emergence of a burdensome ecclesial structure, with the rigidity characteristic of such institutions, is, of course, academic. Despite his grandiose plans, not a single temple of reason was built. But the federation of deistic societies dreamed of by Palmer struck even many of his admirers as strangely dissonant with his republican ideals and passionate advocacy of absolute freedom of conscience.

When measured against the broader backdrop of Palmer's achievements, these two caveats appear insignificant. Regardless of his eccentricities of style or attachment to the ceremonialism of traditional forms of worship, Palmer succeeded in launching a national crusade against what he took to be the enemies of reason, happiness, and progress. In the process he not only pushed deism into the national spotlight; he also bestowed upon it an intellectual legitimacy that gave the Christian establishment no choice but to take it seriously. Although zealous in his assault upon ecclesial and political usurpation of private conscience, his confidence in the inevitability of reason's victory prevented him from sliding into either hollow cynicism or embittered dogmatism. Toward the end of his *Principles*, he gives voice to the idealistic vision that sustained him throughout the hardships of his crusade.

> The period is at hand, in which kings and thrones, and priests and hierarchies, and the long catalogue of mischiefs which they have produced, shall be swept away from the face of the earth, and buried in the grave of everlasting destruction. Then will arrive the era of human felicity, in which the heart of the unfortunate man shall be consoled; then will appear the moment of national consolation, and universal freedom; then the empire of reason, of science, and of virtue, will extend over the whole earth, and man, emancipated from the barbarous despotism of antiquity, will assume to himself, his true predicament in nature, and become a standing evidence of the divinity of thought and the unlimited power of human reason.[45]

No passage in the *Principles* better expresses Palmer's central vision. Few passages in any book state better the noblest aspirations of humanity.

NOTES

1. John Fellows, "Memoir of Mr. Palmer," in *Posthumous Pieces, By Elihu Palmer, being three chapters of an unfinished work intended to have been entitled "The Political World." To which are prefixed a memoir of Mr. Palmer by his friend Mr. John Fellows of New York, and Mr. Palmer's "Principles of the Deistical Society of the State of New York"* (London: R. Carlile, 1828), p. 4. Fellows's "Memoir of Mr. Palmer" is the only extended biographical treatment of Palmer's life. I have relied heavily

on it in this section. See also Roderick S. French, "Elihu Palmer, Radical Deist, Radical Republican: A Reconsideration of American Freethought," in *Studies in Eighteenth-Century Culture*, vol. 8 (Madison: University of Wisconsin Press, 1979).

2. Ibid.

3. James Riker, *The Annals of Newtown, In Queens County, New York* (New York: D. Fanshaw, 1852), p. 232.

4. John Fellows, "Memoir of Mr. Palmer," p. 6.

5. Ibid., pp. 6–7.

6. *Extracts from an Oration, delivered at Federal Point, near Philadelphia, on the Fourth of July, 1793, by Elihu Palmer, citizen of Philadelphia; and published by request of those who heard it*, in *Political Miscellany*, ed. G. Forman (Philadelphia, 1793), pp. 22–26.

7. All quotations are taken from Kerry Walters, *Elihu Palmer's "Principles of Nature": Text and Commentary* (Wolfeboro, NH: Longwood Academic, 1990). The text in this critical edition is based on the 1806 printing of the *Principles*, which was the last one Palmer himself corrected and revised. The quote is from page 78.

8. Ibid., p. 214.

9. Ibid., pp. 138, 142.

10. Ibid., p. 164.

11. Ibid., pp. 96, 131.

12. Ibid., p. 109.

13. Ibid., p. 114.

14. Ibid., pp. 103, 104.

15. Ibid., p. 114.

16. Ibid., p. 107.

17. Ibid., p. 114.

18. Ibid., p. 120.

19. Ibid., p. 150.

20. Ibid., p. 186.

21. Ibid., pp. 174–75.

22. Ibid., p. 234.

23. Ibid., p. 133.

24. Ibid., pp. 133, 136, 192.

25. Ibid., pp. 261–62.

26. Ibid., pp. 221, 222.

27. Ibid., p. 223.

28. Ibid., p. 242.

29. Ibid., p. 223.

30. Ibid., p. 224.

31. Ibid., pp. 243, 244.

32. Ibid., p. 244.

33. Ibid.

34. Ibid., p. 225.

35. Ibid.

36. Ibid.

37. Ibid., p. 190.

38. Ibid., pp. 203–12, 265–70.

39. Ibid., pp. 124–25.

40. Elihu Palmer, *An Enquiry relative to the Moral and Political Improvement of the Human Species. An oration, delivered in the City of New York on The Fourth of July* (New York: Printed by John Crookes, 1797), p. 32.

41. Elihu Palmer, *The Political World*, in *Posthumous Pieces*.

42. Ibid.

43. Ibid., p. 175.

44. Alan Heimert, *Religion and the American Mind: From the Great Awakening to the Revolution* (Cambridge, MA: Harvard University Press, 1966), p. 538.

45. Palmer, *Principles of Nature*, p. 263.

CHAPTER SEVEN

DEISM'S POET

PHILIP FRENEAU

The major American deists were, for the most part, accomplished literary stylists. Writing with the eloquent economy characteristic of eighteenth-century letters, they penned defenses of the religion of nature that pleased the ear while challenging the intellect. Franklin, for example, was the master of the homespun aphorism that compressed volumes into a few words. Paine excelled in coining pithy slogans that lodged in the memory and stirred the imagination. Jefferson's sentences were as painstakingly chiseled as those of the classical authors he so admired. Palmer specialized in prose that was easily readable but philosophically profound. Even Ethan Allen occasionally infused his somewhat cumbersome prose with a pleasing and infectious energy. But Philip Freneau was master of them all. He was a born poet, and brought a poet's sensitivity to his espousal of natural religion. There were deists who argued their points with more intellectual rigor than Freneau, just as there were deists who enjoyed a wider readership. But none of them matched, much less surpassed, the eloquence and sometimes haunting beauty with which he poetically celebrated nature and nature's God. He was the undisputed poet laureate of American deism.

Along with Ethan Allen before him, Freneau belongs to the second rank of American deists. His ideas about the religion of nature were for the most part borrowed from like-minded eighteenth-century predecessors. He was not a militant champion of natural religion like Palmer, or a fiery smasher of Christian idols like Paine. He displayed, on the contrary, a deep-seated aversion to embroiling himself in the heated deistic debate that rocked the early Republic, preferring the role of the quietly supportive fellow traveler to that of the outspoken crusader.

Still, Freneau is worth consideration here for at least two reasons. The first has just been mentioned: the lyrical beauty with which he celebrated nature's God. The second is that Freneau was the last noteworthy American champion of Enlightenment deism. He is a bridge, as it were, between eighteenth- and nineteenth-century free thought. Born just twelve years before Palmer, he survived all the major deists of his day, as well as, indeed, the deistic movement itself. By the time he died in 1832, the heyday of American deism was a good two decades in the past. Other challenges to orthodox Christianity, most notably romanticism, had replaced Enlightenment rationalism. But whereas Jefferson, Palmer, or Paine would have been intensely uncomfortable with romanticism's scorn of reason's promise, Freneau was sympathetic with the new current. His youthful poetry, in fact, anticipated and in many respects paved the way for nineteenth-century American idealism, and in his later poetry there is a romantic melancholy underlying his characteristically deistic locutions.

Freneau, in short, was a man caught in the shift from one worldview to the next, and his poetry understandably reflects tendencies from both. Just as Benjamin Franklin's early deism was an ambivalent amalgamation of ideas drawn from Calvinism and rationalism, so Freneau's late deism tensely juggled opposing elements from romanticism and rationalism. The dissonance generated by the attempt to wed disparate worldviews lent a certain poignancy and depth to his thought that is absent from the writings of many of his predecessors. From a psychological perspective, Freneau is a much more complicated individual than his sometimes one-dimensional fellow deists. Yet in spite of the tension between romanticism and rationalism apparent in his thought, Freneau, like Franklin before him, by and large remained rooted in the ideals and principles of eighteenth-century American deism. There would be other freethinkers in the United States after Freneau, but none who subscribed like him to the classical Enlightenment perspective. Freneau was the last of his line, and his death signaled the end of deism in America.

THAT RASCAL FRENEAU

Of all the American deists, Freneau's beginnings were the most propitious. Even Jefferson, the son of a wealthy Virginia landowner, was not as fortunate. Born into a prosperous merchant family in New York on January 2, 1752, Freneau grew up in an atmosphere of books, art, and intellectually stimulating conversation. Many of New York's leading artistic and intellectual luminaries frequented Mount Pleasant, the aptly named estate his father had bought shortly after Philip's birth. Exposure to their cultivated table talk, as well as excellent training by a series of private tutors, so prepared the precocious Philip for higher education that he entered the College of New Jersey (later Princeton) with sophomore standing at the age of sixteen. The results of his entrance exams were so impressive that President Witherspoon himself took notice of the boy. Nor did Philip disappoint Witherspoon's expectations. His performance as a student was brilliant, and his early poetry and scholarship were admired by fellow students and professors alike.

There was only one temporary fall from grace. In his second year at college, Freneau succumbed to the spell of Bishop Berkeley and, for a time at any rate, was a convinced idealist. This youthful allegiance inspired one of his earliest poems, "The Power of Fancy." This paean to Berkeleyan idealism concluded that sense phenomena are "But thoughts on reason's scale combin'd, / Ideas of the Almighty mind."[1] President Witherspoon, a staunchly orthodox Presbyterian, was neither edified nor amused by his prize student's conversion to British idealism, but he need not have been overly concerned. It was a phase through which Philip quickly passed. This early lapse into heterodoxy is significant, however, for it reveals that Freneau, even at an early age, was interested in philosophical speculation and preferred to go his own way in matters intellectual.

Like many other eighteenth-century youths of promise, Freneau was expected by his parents to study for the ministry. Although apparently not enthusiastic about the prospect of a clerical career, he was not particularly opposed to the idea, either. Consequently, in the years 1773 and 1774, he bowed to his father's wishes and applied himself to the study of divinity, conscientiously plowing his way through weighty theological tomes such as Burnet's *Expositions of the Thirty-nine Articles* and Pearson's *Exposition of the Creed*. Always the industrious student, he even began a notebook in which he dutifully scribbled down lengthy quotations from his reading, interspersing them with pious adolescent interjections. The opening pages of this notebook show the young Freneau to be a conventional and unimaginative student of theology, apparently cured of his Berkeleyan infection. But a change in tone soon appears. While jotting down his *Innuendo sermonibus,* or "Themes for Sermons," he began almost unwittingly to foreshadow the general humanistic orientation of his future deism. In his notes for a sermon titled "Where Is Hell?" he settled on the conclusion that punishment of earthly transgression originates and ends "in the conscience of the man." The wages of sin are not eternal damnation, but rather a physical existence stunted by pain and frustration. This unorthodox conclusion spelled the beginning of the end for Freneau's budding clerical career. Like Palmer before him, his investigation into the mysteries of theology eroded rather than strengthened his lukewarm fidelity to conventional Christian doctrine. Although he seems to have made an effort to quell his growing skepticism, his thirty-page theological notebook abruptly ends in 1774 with the following memorandum: "You have collected a considerable variety of extract and hints but it was lost labour; it never answered the trouble. Farewell to the study of Divinity—which is, in fact, the Study of Nothing!—and the profession of a priest is little better than that of a slothful Blockhead!"[2]

The brutality of this concluding entry may be chalked up in part to Freneau's relief at finally severing his ties to a course of study that had become increasingly distasteful. But it also reflects a fundamental reversal in his intellectual allegiances. Even as he immersed himself in orthodox apologetics, he had also explored the more heady philosophical waters of liberal Christianity and rationalist philosophy. In his notebook, for example, he mentions studying Robert Jenkin's *The Reasonableness and Certainty of the Christian Religion* (1743), a treatise that tried to reconcile scriptural claims with the "late Discoveries in Natural Philosophy." He also dipped into less orthodox authors such as Hume, Lord Bolingbroke, the "heavenly Pope," and the "godlike" Addison. He had at least a secondhand acquaintance with Newton's *Principia.* Finally, it is during this period that Freneau discovered the Roman philosopher Lucretius, and was immediately and permanently won over by his forceful defense of atomistic materialism. (It is also a safe bet that Freneau was impressed with Lucretius' philosophizing in verse.) When compared to the limpid arguments of these thinkers, traditional Christian doctrine struck the unenthusiastic divinity student as, indeed, the "Study of Nothing." After two years of reading dogmatic theology and Enlightenment rationalism side by side, Freneau emerged a confident believer in the God of nature and an equally confident opponent of supernaturalism and scriptural authority.

Upon calling an end to his theological studies, Freneau drifted for a time, occupying himself with halfhearted attempts at school teaching while constantly scribbling poetry. He had come to regard himself as a man of letters, but somehow couldn't seem to find a direction for his talents. It took no less than the outbreak of the American Revolution to fire his imagination and set his course. In the first months of the conflict, aflame with patriotic fervor, he published a series of poems full of passionate invective against the British aggressors. The poems were not very good, but they struck the exact tone Freneau's fellow patriots wanted to hear, skillfully combining a sense of pious indignation with bellicose posturing. A typical example is "Libera Nos, Domine," written in June 1775:

> From a Kingdom that bullies, and hectors, and swears,
> We send up to heaven our wishes and prayers
> That we, disunited, may freemen be still,
> And Britain can go—to be damned if she will.[3]

In spite of the pious pretensions of this and other poems from the same period, Freneau was not above striking out at the Church of England and those Anglican priests who balked at insurrection against the authority of King George. Addressing himself to these loyalist divines in another of his revolutionary poems, Freneau made no attempt to hide the contempt he felt for the sophistries of revealed religion.

> I interfere not with your vast design.
> Pursue your studies, and I'll follow mine.
> Pursue, well-pleas'd, your theologic schemes,
> Attend professors, and correct your themes.
> Still some dull nonsense, low-bred wit invent,
> Or prove from Scripture what is never meant,
> Or far through Law, that land of scoundrels, stray,
> And truth disguise through all your mazy way.[4]

There is no reason to doubt the sincerity of the patriotic sentiments expressed by Freneau in his revolutionary poetry. But it cannot be denied that the initial edge of his zeal quickly became blunt. Although he was perfectly capable of dashing off poetry brimming over with martial ardor, he lacked both the temperament and the staying power of a warrior. He was too mercurial in his moods as well as interests to remain bellicose for long. As soon as his initial revolutionary enthusiasm had been cooled through poetic expression, he dropped his career as a polemicist and set sail for the West Indies in search of adventure. For the next three years he lived in Santa Cruz, serving as a private secretary to a leading plantation owner and all but forgetting the conflict between the North American colonies and Britain. The island's wild beauty tapped hitherto submerged creative springs in Freneau, and some of his best poems, including "Santa Cruz," "The Jamaica Funeral," and the gothic "House of Night," were written under its spell.

An unhappy romance drove Freneau back home in early 1778. Prompted, perhaps, by an uneasy conscience, he went so far as to join the New Jersey militia in June of that year. But wanderlust and the promise of adventure exerted too strong a pull on the young man, and he soon shipped out again, this time sailing to the Azores. He returned a few months later and immediately made plans to revisit the West Indies, only to have the war finally catch up with him. The ship on which he booked passage had barely pulled out of New York when it was stopped by a British man-of-war. Freneau, as a member of the New Jersey militia, was declared a prisoner of war, and so it happened that about the time Ethan Allen was being released from his three-year British captivity, Freneau was incarcerated in the prison ship *Scorpion*. While a prisoner, starvation and harsh treatment so ravaged him that he was first transferred to a hospital ship and then released, nearly dead, in a prisoner exchange. He later described the nightmarish ordeal, which taught him that "Death was better than the prisoner's fate," in "The British Prison-Ship" (1781), one of his most popular poems.

Freneau's near-fatal imprisonment on the *Scorpion* seems to have knocked the wanderlust out of him—at least for a time. Following his recovery, he served, albeit in a desultory sort of way, as an employee of the Philadelphia post office. Freneau probably took the job because it promised him ample leisure time to write poetry. He rediscovered his earlier revolutionary fervor and penned dozens of satirical diatribes against the British and their loyalist supporters, and just as many hymns to the suffering and noble triumphs of his fellow patriots. This poetry, much of which appeared in the *Freeman's Journal* (which Freneau also helped to edit), was often transparently jingoistic. Some of it even sank to the level of crude doggerel. But occasionally Freneau turned his poetical talents to reflective appraisals of the human condition in general, appraisals that reflected his fidelity to Enlightenment ideals. In a piece from this period titled "Philosophical Reflection," for example, he eloquently expresses his commitment to the principle of individual liberty.

> Curs'd be the day, how bright so'er it shin'd,
> That first made kings the masters of mankind;
> And curs'd the wretch who first with regal pride
> Their equal rights to equal men deny'd;
> But curs'd over all, who first to slav'ry broke
> Submissive bow'd and own'd a monarch's yoke,
> Their servile souls his arrogance ador'd
> And basely own'd a brother for a lord;
> Hence wrath and blood, and feuds and wars began,
> And man turn'd monster to his fellow man.[5]

The obvious message of this poem is that individual happiness and social progress are in the hands of individuals, not the gods. If the natural rights of liberty and equality are lost, it is at least partly because individuals have allowed them to be usurped by unscrupulous despots. This sentiment, of course, is squarely within the Enlightenment tradition. But Freneau's optimistic rationalism, even at this early stage in his career, was mixed with a more tragic, less hopeful vision of reality. In an essay published shortly after "Philosophical Reflection," he allows this other side of his thought to surface:

> Discord and disorder are interwoven with the nature and constitution of the human race, and I am well convinced that we may as reasonably expect to see an ocean unruffled by tempests, or the sky perpetually clear of the iron glooms that so often infest it, or to find individuals without private quarrels, jealousies and bickerings, as the world delivered from rapine, dissention, tyranny, discord, violence and bloodshed.[6]

Freneau's thought constantly leaped back and forth between the poles of Enlightenment optimism and proto-romantic weltschmerz, and his spirit was just as restless. He found it difficult to stay at any one place in any one occupation for long. It was no surprise to those who knew him best that he abandoned both post office and *Freeman's Journal* at war's end in 1784, and once again took to the sea. This time he went as master of the brig *Dromelly*, bound for Jamaica. Before reaching its destination, Freneau's ship sailed into a hurricane that destroyed most West Indian shipping and so damaged the *Dromelly* that she barely made it into port. Freneau captured the near-tragic moment in a poem titled "Verses, Made at Sea, in a Heavy Gale." In it he marvels at the majestic indifference of nature to human well-being, and concludes (most un-deistically) that in the face of natural forces "skill and science both must fall, / And ruin is the lot of all."[7]

Five years later, after having sailed the oceans in fair weather and foul more than most of his countrymen, Freneau returned home, this time to stay. He settled first in New York, where he married and became the editor of the *Daily Advertiser*. In 1791 he relocated to Philadelphia, the Republic's nerve center, to manage the *National Gazette*. The *Gazette's* political sympathies were ardently republican, and Freneau rarely missed an opportunity to browbeat Federalist statesmen such as Alexander Hamilton or even, when the occasion warranted it, to attack such venerable figures as Washington. Many Federalists in the early Republic assumed that the *Gazette's* editor was little more than Thomas Jefferson's hired gun, particularly since the young secretary of state had given Freneau a minor bureaucratic appointment upon his arrival in Philadelphia. But both the sincerity of Freneau's convictions and his independence of mind became apparent after news of the French Revolution reached the American shore. Freneau was so extreme in his support of the revolution's principles that even like-minded associates such as Jefferson were embarrassed by his enthusiasm. Freneau's radical republicanism made him so many influential enemies—including Washington, who dismissed him as "that rascal Freneau"—that when Jefferson temporarily retired from public office in 1793, Freneau found it expedient to resign his government post. Moreover, the *National Gazette* was forced to suspend publication in October of that year because of financial difficulties. Freneau was unbroken by these professional setbacks. He seems to have recaptured some of the elan of his revolutionary youth, and happily occupied himself with organizing demonstrations in support of French republicanism and furiously writing poems and essays that defended the human right to liberty, equality, and self-determination. His uncompromising republicanism later prompted Thomas Jefferson to remark that Freneau "saved our Constitution from galloping into the arms of monarchy."[8]

After the demise of the *National Gazette*, Freneau spent a few more years as a journalist/editor, first with the rural *Jersey Chronicle*, and later with New York's more influential *Time-Piece*. Although his activities were not at the political center stage, as they had been during his years in Philadelphia, Freneau's writings during this period lost none of their republican fervor. Moreover, many of his poems returned to his youthful anticlericalism. As he wrote in "On the Causes of Political Degeneracy," for example,

Left to themselves, where'er mankind is found,
In peace they wish to walk life's little round,
In peace to sleep, in peace to till the soil,
Nor gain subsistence from a brother's toil,
All but the base, designing, currying few,
Who seize on nations with a robber's view,
With crowns and sceptres awe the dazzled eye,
And priests, that hold the artillery of the sky;
These, these, with armies, navies, potent grown
Impoverish man and bid whole nations groan.[9]

As the eighteenth century gave way to the nineteenth, Freneau felt the need for a less hurried, more contemplative life. He retired to a farm near Monmouth, New Jersey, where he continued to write poetry and essays on politics, religion, current events, and deism. He also edited his past work, published as well as unpublished, and issued it in two major collections: *Poems Written and Published during the American Revolution* (1809) and *A Collection of Poems on American Affairs . . . Written between the Year 1797 and the Present Time* (1815). But Freneau's life in his pastoral retreat was soon plagued by financial hardship. As an old man of seventy, he was forced to work on New Jersey's public roads in order to meet his taxes. Most of his farm was sold, lot by lot, to pay off creditors, and in extreme old age Freneau even wandered from house to house, offering his services as a tinker and handyman. It is little wonder that "Winter," the last-known poem he wrote, dismally asks whether there can be any pleasures left to the "cold months" of old age.[10]

Freneau's end was strangely fitting for an individual who, throughout his long life, so often had defied nature's fury. In mid-December 1832, he tarried late in a village some two miles from his farmhouse. Some say he lost track of the time in the town library, others insist it was the village tavern. In any case, Freneau set out for home in the dark, and had scarcely left the village when a sudden blizzard overtook him. He attempted a shortcut through a boggy meadow, but evidently lost his way in the blinding snow. His body was discovered the next morning. One of Freneau's obituaries described him as "a staunch whig, a good soldier, and a warm patriot."[11] But he was much more than that. He was also the bard of American deism.

REASON'S SCOPE

The American deists never tired of trumpeting the powers of reason, and Freneau was no exception. Like them, he considered the rational faculty to be the necessary condition as well as the ultimate guarantor of social progress and individual felicity. Like them, moreover, he believed that human reason was ultimately a reflection of Divine Reason, and hence enjoyed a degree of the Deity's necessary perfection. This typically deistic confidence in the divine origin and utility of reason is expressed in his poem "On the Powers of the Human Understanding."

> This human mind! how grand a theme:
> Faint image of the Great Supreme,
>   The universal soul,
> That lives, that thinks, compares, contrives;
> From its vast self all power derives
>   To manage or control.
> What energy, O soul, is thine:
> How you reflect, resolve, combine,
>   Invention all your own!

Material bodies changed by you
New modes assume, or natures new
    From death or chaos won.[12]

This rather gushing hymn to reason should not be taken, however, as an unambiguous endorsement of reason's purview. For all his confidence in reason's promise, Freneau was also convinced that there were definite limits to its ability to comprehend and manipulate nature. True, reason served as the foundation of the sciences because it enabled humans to discern the presence of immutable laws behind transient phenomena. But in the final analysis, the incredible complexity of nature was such that its workings are ultimately unfathomable. The most humans could hope for, Freneau believed, is a limited knowledge of observable phenomena and an even less exact appreciation of the laws governing them. That the universe did in fact conform to universal and immutable law Freneau never doubted. He was too much a child of the New Learning (as well as an admirer of Lucretius) to have reservations on that score. But he was also impressed by early romanticism's insistence on the fragility of human reason and its essential inability to penetrate through to the heart of reality. Consequently, Freneau tempered his deistic enthusiasm for reason with a rather un-deistic skepticism:

Vain wish: to fathom all we see,
For nature is all mystery;
The mind, though perch'd on eagle's wings,
With pain surmounts the scum of things.
Her knowledge on the surface floats,
Of things supreme she dreams or doats;
Fluttering awhile, she soon ascends,
And all in disappointment ends.[13]

It would be a mistake, however, to attribute Freneau's hesitancy to endorse Enlightenment pan-rationalism to his romantic tendencies alone (although the influence of his romanticism cannot be discounted). Ironically, his skepticism can also be seen as arising in part from the very empiricism he imbibed from New Learning luminaries such as Bacon and Locke. Freneau took these thinkers at their word when they insisted that all human knowledge originates from sense experience. True, the champions of classical empiricism had then gone on to argue that trust-worthy generalizations could be inferred from scrutiny of sense data. Such generalizations in turn served as the foundation of science. But Freneau was wary of the strength of such inferences. Taking the principles of empiricism seriously—perhaps too seriously—he believed that the only truly reliable knowledge a rational person can accept is what comes immediately from the senses. This meant that all abstract inferences from that data, such as those that posited objective natural laws, were merely hypothetical in nature and hence provisional. Consequently, for Freneau, the Enlightenment's (and deism's) claim that reason is capable of exhaustively charting reality is suspect—and can be shown to be so in terms of the Enlightenment's own empiricist first principles.

It can be argued that Freneau's Humean, almost positivistic inter-pretation of empiricist standards is too narrow, but it is not difficult to discern the psychological factors that led him to conclude that the New Learning tended to inflate reason's purview. His youthful absorption and subsequent rebellion against theological speculation, as well as his short-lived courtship of Berkeleyan idealism, had soured him on elabo-rate, abstract models of explanation. He saw them as ethereal and self-indulgent, too far removed from the concrete testimony of ordinary experience. Instead of remaining faithful to the bedrock of cautious observation, they inevitably spun off into reified speculations that obfus-cated more than clarified the nature of really. Such conclusions as they generated, therefore, were always suspect. It was his radical empiricism, then, that prompted him to place limits upon reason's scope, and in turn nudged him in the direction of romantic skepticism. Echoing Bacon, he dismissed abstractions as syllogistic play that distanced the observer from experience. Better to focus upon phenomena, he concluded, rather than logical contrivances spun from words and concepts. As he poetically admonished a "student of dead languages"—here a clear allusion to overly abstract speculation—"He better plans, who things, not words, attends, / And turns his studious hours to active ends."[14]

Freneau's moderate appraisal of reason's scope, then, can be seen as the product of two disparate influences. His strict interpretation of empiricist principles—one which bordered on positivism—led him to suspect abstract generalization as straying too far from the evidence of immediate experience. This skepticism in turn pushed him in the direction of the romantic insistence that human reason was incapable of fully comprehending reality. Freneau never doubted that reality itself was fully rational; he simply denied that human reason was powerful enough to fathom the exact architecture of the cosmic machine. His skepticism was consequently grounded upon epistemic, not metaphysical, considerations. Whether this agnosticism was congruent with his fundamentally deistic orientation is a question to which we will turn shortly.

Still, if it only remains within the circumscribed limits proper to it, reason is capable of shedding a great deal of light upon both physical reality and the nature of knowledge itself. Reason, as Freneau defined it, is essentially an analytical device that allows its practitioners to investigate knowledge claims. Its raw material is the data of experience. With this data, as Freneau says in "On the Powers of the Human Understanding," it performs two types of operations. First, it "compares" and "combines," checking for consistency and inconsistency, and classifies sensory testimony on the basis of such comparison. Second, it "contrives" and "resolves" by provisionally suggesting generalizations it infers from its classifications. This primarily logical function of reason enables humans to differentiate between plausible and implausible knowledge claims. It also, to a certain limited extent, allows for speculation about the overall nature of reality. But the further removed reason is from direct sensory evidence, the less reliable are its contrivances. Of "things supreme," reason only "dreams or doats." Abstract flights and metaphysical fancies "all in disappointment" end. In the final analysis, then, reason is a tool for evaluating the reach of legitimate human belief. Its operations are essential but limited.

Given this characterization of reason, its most immediately obvious virtue is its capacity for disabusing humankind of the superstitious ignorance that traditionally has hampered the advancement of science and the progress of society. Like all deists, Freneau sees institutional Christianity as the chief instigator of the spread of "Dread superstition," the "worst plague on the human race." Orthodoxy's endorsement of supernaturalist and irrational doctrines such as trinitarianism, the Incarnation, original sin, and predestination perverts what should be the noblest expression of human hope—religion—into an oppressive system that feeds on the race's fear of the unknown. As Freneau laments in "On Superstition,"

Implanted in the human breast,
Religion means to make us blest;
On reason built, she lends her aid
To help us through life's sickening shade.
But man, to endless error prone
And fearing most what's most unknown,
To phantoms bow that round him rise,
To angry gods, and vengeful skies.[15]

Perniciously, supernaturalism's "angry gods" encourage not only fear and superstition. They also insist upon dominion over individual conscience and belief. As an outraged Freneau thunders,

What human power shall dare to bind
The mere opinions of the mind?
Must men at that tribunal bow
Which will no range to thought allow,
But his best powers would sway or sink,
And idly tells him what to THINK.
Yes! there are such, and such are taught
To fetter every power of thought;
To chain the mind, or bend it down
To some mean system of their own.[16]

So far as Freneau is concerned, enslavement of the mind "to some mean system" such as supernatural religion is not only the most egregious affront to the dignity and progress of the race but also a thwarting of the faculty of reason. Reason, even in the limited sense in which Freneau defines it, has as its special function the careful evaluation of evidence. Belief in any proposition or doctrine is justifiable only when the mind has freely examined the available testimony. There is no demerit in suspending judgment until such testimony has been considered. Contrary to Christian dogma, the rational individual is one who refuses to allow himself to hold a belief until he is rationally convinced of its truth through a scrutiny of the available evidence.

On mere belief no merit rests,
As unbelief no guilt attests:

Belief, if not absurd and blind
Is but conviction of the mind.

Nor can conviction bind the heart
Till evidence has done its part:
And, when that evidence is clear,
Belief is just, and truth is near.[17]

For Freneau, then, the distinctive characteristic of human reason is its ability to question received wisdom, to examine data, and to decide, on the basis of its established standards of logic and consistency, the truth or falsity of a given proposition. Although the rational faculty cannot transparently reveal all of nature's secrets, it can disencumber humankind of ignorance and superstition by refusing to endorse any proposition "Till evidence of the strongest kind / Constrains assent, and clears the mind."[18] Given the destructive consequence of unjustified beliefs as well as reason's logical capability of cutting through the mare's nest of superstition and ignorance perpetrated by orthodoxy, it follows for Freneau that free inquiry is the necessary condition for human improvement. Even stronger, such inquiry is a natural right of mankind, and any system of doctrines, secular or religious, that seeks to usurp its prerogative is illegitimate. Disbelief of orthodox platitudes, then, is not an option; it is a fundamental privilege.

Not to believe, I therefore hold
The right of man, all uncontrol'd
By all the powers of human wit,
What kings have done, or sages writ.[19]

NATURE, NATURE'S GOD, AND RELIGION

Given Freneau's abiding reluctance to engage in abstractions far removed from the data of sensory experience, it might be expected that his philosophy of nature as well as his doctrine of God would be minimal. But a close examination of his poetry reveals that such an assumption is only partially correct. It is true that he refrains from the elaborate speculation typical of the natural religion of, for example, Ethan Allen and Elihu Palmer. But it is also the case that he poetically defends certain general claims about both nature and God that, although perfectly in keeping with the deistic tradition, come perilously close to overstepping the bounds of legitimate belief that his own narrow empiricism dictates. These claims, basically, are three in number. The first is that the physical realm is regulated by orderly and immutable natural laws. The second is that such laws point to and reflect the nature of a divine source. The third is that physical creation is best interpreted as an overflowing of divine love. Freneau's first two points fall squarely within the mainstream of deistic thought. The third, while sharing some affinity with the deistic notion of providence, is a refreshing and intriguing novelty. It illustrates the romantic undercurrent in Freneau's ruminations, and underscores the lyrical and at times almost visionary nature of his reflections. Unlike Franklin, Jefferson, Palmer, Paine, or even Allen, Freneau was not a philosopher so much as a poet. He sought to voice intuitions and express insights, not to chisel out painstakingly precise formulae, and this orientation is nowhere better seen than when he muses over the nature and function of divine love.

Freneau's most representative statement about the orderliness of nature is to be found in his poem "On the Uniformity and Perfection of Nature." In keeping with his radical empiricism and conventional deistic methodology, his starting point is the "simple" observation of nature. But it is clear from the following stanza that Freneau, no less than any other avowed positivist, is incapable of remaining loyal to his stated aim of pure description unadorned with interpretative presuppositions.

> Who looks through nature with an eye
> That would the scheme of heaven descry,
> Observes her constant, still the same,
> In all her laws, through all her frame.

The giveaway here is Freneau's injunction to observe nature with a discerning eye—that is, with the deliberate attempt to infer the lawlike constancy behind the panorama of individual phenomena. To "read" natural data through such a filter is clearly to beg the question, but Freneau appears not to have noticed that he has stacked the deck from the outset.

Instead, he believes that the lawlike frame of nature is immediately discernible. Moreover, he quickly moves from the putatively observable fact of nature's constancy to the equally "observable" fact that its regularity is synonymous with rationality.

> On one fix'd point all nature moves,
> Nor deviates from the track she loves;
> Her system, drawn from reason's source,
> She scorns to change her wonted course.

The immutability of nature that Freneau posits, one must conclude, is derived more from his absorption of the natural philosophy of Lucretius and Newton than from a naked observation of ordinary experience. Still, it is likely that he genuinely believed his ascription of uniformity and rationality to the physical realm was indeed a description rather than an interpretation. But even Freneau recognized that his next move was an inference rather than the statement of a pellucid, observable fact. From his insistence that "on one fix'd point all nature moves," he goes on to conclude, in opposition to Christian orthodoxy, that the concept of miraculous ruptures within the fabric of reality is incoherent and demeaning to the dignity of nature.

> Could [nature] descend from that great plan
> To work unusual things for man,
> To suit the insect of an hour—
> This would betray a want of power,
>
> Unsettled in its first design
> And erring, when it did combine
> The parts that form the vast machine,
> The figures sketch'd on nature's scene.

For Freneau, then, the natural order reveals itself—at least to one who "would the scheme of heaven descry—to be a "vast machine" with operations guided by natural laws, immutable and rational. The machine neither needs nor brooks interference. To admit the latter as a possibility, in fact, would do such violence to the perceived integrity of the whole that the reliability of nature itself would be called into question. It would be to presume that the universe is inherently flawed. But such a suggestion is not only contrary to reason; it also violates ordinary experience. For the discerning student of the natural world, "No imperfection can be found / In all that is, above, around."[20]

It is at this point in his argument that Freneau feels justified in making one of the few speculative inferences that the radically empiricist side of his thought will allow as legitimate: the inference of the existence of a Divine Architect. The justification he appears to have in the back of his mind is a version of the design argument. Experience reveals that reality is a comprehensive whole, the parts and functions of which operationally relate with perfect symmetry and absolute precision. Such a dramatic display of orderliness immediately suggests that the clocklike nature of reality is the result of intelligent design rather than blind change or spontaneity.

> We see, with most exact design,
> The WORLD revolve, the planets shine,
> In nicest order all things meet,
> A structure in ITSELF complete.

But if the "nicest order" observable in nature is such that it inescapably points to the presence of design, reason dictates that reality be the product of an intelligent designer:

> Great Frame! What wonders we survey,
> In part alone, from day to day!
> And hence the reasoning, human soul
> Infers an author of the whole:
>
> A power, that every blessing gives,
> Who through eternal ages lives,
> All space inhabits, space his throne,
> Spreads through all worlds, confined to none;
>
> Infers, through skies, o'er seas, o'er lands
> A power throughout the whole commands,
> In all extent its dwelling place,
> Whose mansion is unbounded space.[21]

On a first reading, these lines seem to suggest that the divine "author of the whole" Freneau has in mind is more akin to the god of pantheism than the detached supreme architect of deism; the divine power "inhabits" space, "all extent" is "its dwelling place," "space its throne." Nor can it be denied that occasionally, particularly in his more lyrical moments, Freneau indeed does employ locutions which suggest that his god is identical to reality itself and is a kind of Wordsworthian force that animates nature and is coextensive with it. But in spite of those passages in which Freneau's romanticism brings to mind a pantheistic concept of God, he is too squarely within the Enlightenment tradition to accept an identity between the divine and creation. It is better to interpret these and other stanzas that smack of pantheism as attempts on Freneau's part to express the typically deistic tenet that nature is God's revelation.

It will be recalled that the American deists were unanimous in their rejection of the orthodox notion of revelation—the notion that God discloses himself either through supernaturalist prophecy (as "recorded" in sacred scripture) or miraculous intervention. Instead, for the deist, the immutable rational character of the natural realm, its clear display of intelligent design and purpose, is the true manifestation of the presence and attributes of God. The book of nature, then, not the prophetic writings of supernatural religion, is the locus of God's self-revelation, and it is in this spirit that Freneau's remarks about God's "inhabiting" all space should be read. God's presence is obvious in all creation, not because the divine is identical to creation, but because he manifests himself in his works. As Freneau continues in the poem quoted earlier,

> THOU, nature's self art nature's God
> Through all expansion spread abroad,
> Existing in the eternal scheme,
> Vast, undivided, and supreme.[22]

Elsewhere, in his "On the Universality and Other Attributes of the God of Nature," Freneau makes the same point:

> All that we see, about, abroad,
> What is it all, but nature's God?
> In meaner works discover'd here
> No less than in the starry sphere. . . .

> His system fix'd on general laws
> Bespeaks a wise creating cause;
> Impartially he rules mankind,
> And all that on this globe we find.[23]

Again, the "universality" attributed to God here is not the pantheistic identity of the divine with everything that is. Instead, it is a lyrical expression of the deistic claim that God as the supreme cause of reality imparts exemplars of his nature to creation. Intelligence, which points to the divine origin of reality, is discernible everywhere, in the "starry sphere" as well as in "meaner works."

Nature, then, reveals itself to the discerning mind as a systematic whole whose operations exhibit an underlying orderliness and rationality—or, in Freneau's estimation, design. This in turn suggests the inference that nature is the creation of an intelligent designer God who has imbued it with vestiges of the divine attributes. In reading the book of nature, humans discover much more than the network of natural laws that regulates physical phenomena. They also arrive at a knowledge *that* God exists, as well as some indications of *what* God is. True, neither God nor nature is completely fathomable by human reason. But in Freneau's judgment characteristics of both are sufficiently discernible to warrant the assertion that reality is rational and unblemished by any intrinsic mysteriousness. There is no essential incomprehensibility to reality, even though there is a necessary limit to the human ability to know and fully describe it.

Human reason is capable of discerning yet another essential attribute of nature and nature's God: love. Freneau, in keeping with the deistic tradition, argued that an examination of the realm of experience reveals hints of divine benevolence—what, in Enlightenment's language, was usually called "providence." The design apparent in nature points to more than just a rational cosmic plan. It also indicates that the plan is designed and consummated by the Divine Architect with the intention of providentially supplying the maximum opportunity for human felicity and growth. As Freneau puts it,

> In all the attributes divine
> Unlimited perfections shine;
> In these enwrapt, in these complete,
> All virtues in that centre meet.
>
> This power who doth all powers transcend,
> To all intelligence a friend,
> Exists, the *greatest and the best*
> Throughout all worlds, to make them blest.[24]

God manifests himself in nature to render humans "blest." This assumption is based partly upon Freneau's postulation of lawlike orderliness in nature, a uniformity that prohibits chaos or unpredictability (which obviously would preclude the possibility of science and the harnessing of natural resources). But it also rests upon Freneau's almost mystical vision of the divine creative act as an overflowing of love, whereby God freely and lovingly empties himself in and for his handiwork. This vision is best expressed in a stanza from Freneau's "On the Universality and Other Attributes of the God of Nature."

> All that he did he first approved
> He all things into *being* loved,
> O'er all he made he still presides,
> For them in life, or death provides.[25]

This virtually Neoplatonic notion of divine emanation is unique to Freneau's deism and is particularly interesting when compared to the conventional deistic assumption that the Supreme Architect is somewhat distant from his creation. Following the generally mechanistic natural philosophy characteristic of Enlightenment thought, most deists tended to view reality as a cosmic machine that, although constructed and set in motion by the Deity, is irreducibly other than God. True, natural law within the cosmic mechanism reflects essential attributes of the Deity such as rationality and benevolence. But the general impression one gleans from reading the works of American deists is that God is an impersonal, aloof First Cause whose original creative act is more an act of intellect than an act of love. Consequently, although reality mirrors its divine source (albeit imperfectly), it does so in a rather distant, somewhat washed out way.

The remorselessly rational concept of God suggested by this model guarantees that reality is uniform and lawlike, but tends to posit a psychologically alienating gulf between human and existence. Freneau was clearly sensitive to this dilemma, and attempted to overcome it with his poetical suggestion that nature is the product of divine love overflowing itself. A deity who "all things into being loved" is a radical departure from the aloof deity who serves as reality's distant archetype. The mechanistic separation of humans and God is lessened without sliding into the postulation of supernaturalist interventions. Freneau's God, in short, remains the supremely rational principle that undergirds reality, but his loving act of creative overflow renders him less distant, more accessible, than the impersonal First Cause of mainstream Enlightenment deism. Freneau's concept of God, then, retains the deistic emphasis upon panrationalism, but enlivens its rather static mechanism by incorporating a proto-romantic notice of divine vitalism.

The upshot of Freneau's lyrical ruminations upon reality and God is that true religion is founded upon God's self-revelation in nature. Religious belief does not entail a blind fidelity to ecclesial or scriptural dogma, nor does it require that humans suspend the exercise of their God-given reason by trusting in supernaturalist descriptions of either the deity or reality. Nor, for Freneau, is true religion a gloomy, fearful affair that centers around superstitions such as human depravity or the awesome unpredictability of God. Instead, religion—which "means to make [humanity] blest"—is an affirmative and even joyful awareness of the God of reason and love, an awareness acquired and strengthened through the rational study of nature rather than the perusal of abstract theological tomes. Scrutiny of nature will not reveal to finite human reason the full scope of either reality or the divine, but it does eradicate the shackles of fear and superstition which historically have bound the human spirit. Freneau is confident that true religion, the religion of nature, will eventually give rise to a world in which reason, freedom of thought, scientific progress and individual happiness will all flourish. This vision is eloquently expressed in the closing stanzas of his poem "On the Religion of Nature."

Religion, such as nature taught,
    With all divine perfections suits;
Had all mankind this system sought
    Sophists would cease their vain disputes,
        And from this source would nations know
        All that can make their heaven below.

This deals not curses to mankind,
    Or dooms them to perpetual grief,
If from its aid no joys they find,
    It damns them not for unbelief;
        Upon a more exalted plan
        Creation's nature dealt with man—

Joy to the day, when all agree
    On such grand systems to proceed,
From fraud, design, and error free,
    And which to truth and goodness lead:
        Then persecution will retreat
        And man's religion be complete.[26]

CURIOSITY, VIRTUE, AND HAPPINESS

One of the distinctive features of Freneau's lyrical brand of deism, as already indicated, is its insistence that although reality is a completely rational system with fixed and universal laws, the human intellect is too meager to fully comprehend it. Consequently, unlike his fellow deists, Freneau cautions that it is a "Vain wish, to fathom all we see, / For nature is all mystery. . . ."

Clearly this statement indulges in a bit of poetical license, for we have seen that, for Freneau, some aspects of nature as well as nature's God are discernible—enough, in fact, to infer the overall cosmic plan, even if many of the particulars are out of reach. Still the fact remains that Freneau was much less confident in reason's ability than the other proponents of American deism. But while this relative devaluation of reason's scope may have been an occasion of concern for some, Freneau more optimistically took it as the divinely ordained catalyst for moral growth.

Freneau, like Aristotle some two millennia earlier, took curiosity to be an essential human trait. In "Science, Favourable to Virtue" he asserts that

The mind, in this uncertain state,
Is anxious to investigate
All knowledge through creation sown,
And would no atom leave unknown.[27]

Scientific knowledge can assuage this innate wonderment to a certain extent, but given the inability of human reason to discover all of nature's secrets, it cannot ultimately satisfy it. This limited capacity of reason necessarily engenders a sense of frustrated expectation: just when reason believes itself on the edge of victory, "all in disappointment ends."

This inevitable frustration of reason's ambition can be looked at in two ways. One can either conclude from it that reality, far from being a benevolently designed system, is one in which God maliciously endows humans with a longing that cannot be appeased; or one can assume that the inevitable frustration of human curiosity, like every other facet of existence, is premeditated by the divine mind and hence purposeful. Freneau, predictably, opts for the latter alternative.

And yet this proud, this strong desire,
Such ardent longings to aspire,
Prove that this weakness in the mind
For some wise purpose was designed.

But for what purpose? According to Freneau, the frustration that reason's investigations inevitably run up against serves as an incentive to human virtue—a spur, as it were, to normative growth. It encourages fortitude and discipline, both of which Freneau deems essential to a rational person, and in the process slowly (albeit painfully) weans humanity from its "brutal instincts" of sloth, pride, and complacency. There is an obvious element here of the romantic conviction that Sisyphean endurance in the face of adversity ennobles and dignifies human existence. But it is also clear that Freneau sees a more pragmatic and immediate advantage to such a state of affairs: the continuous striving for truth serves as a necessary catalyst for scientific progress and the growth of human knowledge. The inability of reason to attain its goal completely, then, is part of the divine plan to inculcate individual virtue as well as break the pernicious hold of superstition and ignorance. Disconcerting as it is, the psychological pains of frustrated intellectual endeavor is the birth-pang of normative and scientific progress.

> To him who rules the starry spheres,
> No evil in his works appears:
> Man with a different eye, surveys,
> The incidents in nature's maze:
>> And all that brings him care or pain
>> He ranks among misfortune's train.
> The ills that God, or nature, deal,
> The ills we hourly see, or feel,
> The sense of wretchedness and woe
> To man may be sincerely so;
>> And yet these springs of tears and sighs
>> Be heaven's best blessings in disguise.[28]

It is important not to miss Freneau's point in these verses. He is not denying that human beings experience pain, a "sense of wretchedness and woe." No one who endured the prison-ship privations Freneau did would dare to make such an obviously false and insensitive claim. He is arguing for two quite different conclusions, one explicit and the other only implied. The more explicit one has already been discussed: the "ills we hourly see, or feel" arising from reason's frustrated attempts to fathom nature's secrets serve as prods for human fulfillment and continuous intellectual and normative growth. Granted, the psychological sense of defeat that reason's limitations bring is unpleasant, but it is temporary and serves a higher, more permanent purpose.

Implicitly, Freneau seems to be arguing that the physical pains and misfortunes that beset humanity are fair trade-offs for the system of natural laws the Divine Architect has set in motion. Humans are part of physical reality, and hence necessarily conform to its laws. One of those laws, for example, dictates that all organic, sentient creatures are transient. They come into being, flourish, age, succumb to illness, and perish. Physical suffering is a necessary consequence of such impermanence, and so a human life inevitably will be beset with the burdens impermanence brings. But for Freneau, this limited quantity of necessary pain is a small price to pay for existing in a universe that conforms in a rational, predictable, and immutable way to divinely established physical laws. The alternative would be to forgo immutability and dwell in a world in which chaos, spontaneity, and divine whimsicality reigned supreme. We may in moments of desperation wish for a supernatural intervention or a miraculous rupture in the established order of cause and effect, but reflection tells us that, were such wishes fulfilled, the ensuing state of affairs would be disastrous. Better to live in a world regulated by immutable causal patterns and endure the natural pains they entail than to dwell in a reality that is purposeless and unpredictable. The most rational response to physical misfortune is the adoption of a stoical attitude of endurance which recognizes that individual ills are a necessary consequence of the natural order that makes human existence possible. The influence of Lucretius' materialism upon Freneau's thought is especially apparent here. But it is also the case that this interpretation of physical ills was defended by other deistic thinkers, most notably Elihu Palmer.

It is, then, an error to presume that the supreme principle of benevolence, which "into being all things loved," either willingly or inadvertently created a reality hostile to the well-being of humans. True, physical as well as psychological pain exists, but only as an inevitable consequence of natural law, on the one hand, and as an incentive to excellence, on the other. Still, it is clear that physical and psychological frustration does not exhaust the range of misfortunes that beset humanity. People also suffer from the effects of what might be called moral evil. Once again, however, the God of nature cannot be held accountable. Moral evil is the result of human actions in the world. Unlike physical and psychological pain, which at best can only be ameliorated but never eliminated, moral evil is vanquishable. It is caused by unjust social, political, and economic institutions. Consequently, the removal of these institutions necessarily results in the elimination of moral evil.

Freneau's ardent hatred of social injustice first expressed itself in his youthful revolutionary poems. In them, he opposed any form of tyranny that sought to violate what he took to be the natural equality of humans. The passage of years did little to quench his outrage at forms of government or systems of thought that consolidated their power through fear, ignorance, and exploitation of "brutal instincts." No person is born with ethical privilege. Consequently, no political or ecclesial authority is justified in setting its interests above those of the whole. In a late poem titled "On False Systems of Government," Freneau loudly condemns such abuses:

> How can we call those systems just
> Which bid the few, the proud, the first
>   Possess all earthly good;
> While millions robbed of all that's dear
> In silence shed the ceaseless tear,
>   And leeches suck their blood.
>
> Great orb, that on our planet shines,
> Whose power both light and heat combines
>   You should the model be;
> To man, the pattern how to reign
> With equal sway, and how maintain
>   True human dignity.
>
> Impartially to all below
> The solar beams unstinted flow,
>   On all is poured the RAY,
> Which cheers, which warms, which clothes the ground
> In robes of green, or breathes around
>   Life;—to enjoy the day.

The impartiality with which nature and nature's God (poetically symbolized here as the "Great orb") bestow blessings upon mankind should serve as the model for political institutions. Unfortunately, however, history shows that established authority, whether sacred or profane, fails to heed nature's lesson.

> But crowns not so;—with selfish views
> They partially their bliss diffuse
>   Their *minions* feel them *kind*;—
> And, still opposed to human right,
> Their plans, their views in *this* unite,
>   *To embroil and curse mankind.*

Ye tyrants, false to *HIM*, who gave
Life, and the virtues of the brave,
    All worth we own, or know:—
Who made you great, the lords of man,
To waste with wars, with blood to stain
    The Maker's works below?[29]

But the unjust institutions that have destroyed individual happiness and retarded human progress can be overcome. There is, says Freneau, a "moral track to man assign'd / A transcript from the all-perfect mind."[30] A key insight provided by this "transcript" is "That in the course of human things / Felicity from virtue springs."[31]

A necessary condition for the full emergence of human happiness and fulfillment, then, is virtue. For Freneau, virtue minimally entails that individuals as well as social and political institutions strive to embody in their codes norms that reflect the natural equality observable in nature. Reason, impartiality, uniformity, and benevolence are the essential characteristics of nature. Consequently, they also serve as normative exemplars for human behavior.

Let laws revive, by heaven designed,
To tame the tiger in the mind
    And drive from human hearts
That love of wealth, that love of sway,
Which leads the world too much astray,
    Which points envenomed darts:
And men will rise from *what they are*;
Sublimer, and superior, far,
    Than SOLON guessed, or PLATO saw;
All will be just, all will be good—
Then harmony, "*not understood*,"
    Will reign the general law.[32]

The republic of peace, harmony, and felicity, the reign of virtue and benevolence, is not an unattainable pipe dream so far as Freneau is concerned. It is an eminently likely possibility, grounded as it is in the natural order and the hearts and minds of people. The key to a new world order of justice and equality lies in the inauguration of social and political institutions that promote such ideals. And if humans seek exemplars for inspirations and guidance, they need but turn to the divinely established system of nature that surrounds them. Reality's raison d'etre is the maximization of human happiness and progress. The only thing needed to bring this goal to fruition is human cooperation.

AN INCOMPLETE EMPIRICISM

Freneau was a fascinating, multifaceted man, both personally and intellectually. Like so many other complex individuals, his richness often manifested itself dichotomously. He was born wealthy but died impoverished. He was an ardent champion of the revolution but, at best, a summer soldier. His poetry sometimes rose to the level of the sublime, but he was also willing, when occasions warranted it, to indulge in polemical doggerel. His adventurous spirit felt the allure of exotic places and cataclysmic natural phenomena, but there was also a side to him that distrusted and feared the unknown and the wild. He was a believer in the deistic worldview, but also admitted to a proto-romantic skepticism about the ability of reason to fathom reality. He admired the mechanistic natural philosophy of Lucretius and Newton, but attempted to wed it with an almost mystical vision of a divine emanationism that "loved" the world into being.[33]

As indicated at the beginning of this chapter, the tensions in at least his intellectual worldview can be explained partly by the fact that he was a poet rather than a philosopher, and partly by the historical accident of his living in a time when Enlightenment deism began to be superseded by nineteenth-century romanticism. But these explanations notwithstanding, it is still reasonable to ask whether the seemingly disparate poles of his thought are so irreconcilable that they represent an inconsistency in his thought. The most obvious of these tensions is Freneau's denial that reason is ultimately capable of comprehending reality, alongside his steadfast conviction that reality is nonetheless rational.

On the surface, there is not necessarily a contradiction here. All Freneau seems to be asserting is that the finitude of human reason renders it incapable of knowing everything, and that consequently the best it can hope for is to discern general patterns while forgoing a meticulous cataloging of the particulars. This appears reasonable. Though one has not experienced the death of each and every organism, one may safely say, for example, that all organic entities die. Without knowing on a firsthand basis each and every individual, one may safely say that all living humans have bodies. Inductive inferences that lead to general statements are the relatively unproblematic stuff of which both science and everyday knowledge is made.

The problem is that Freneau's narrow concept of rationality appears to undercut the strength of most generalizations. Recall that for Freneau reason properly can be said to possess but two functions. On the one hand, it collects the data of experience and "compares" and "combines" them in order to check for similarity and dissimilarity. On the other hand, it "contrives" and "resolves" this classified data into hypotheticals that are always subject to reformulation or outright rejection. The further removed these hypotheticals are from the raw data of observation, the more speculative and hence unreliable they become.

While it seems that Freneau's methodological assumptions render some generalizations uncontentious—that is, people die, people have bodies—those same assumptions necessarily disenfranchise other generalizations as being too speculative to take seriously. It might be argued that his rigorous interpretation of empiricist criteria disallows any generalization that is not in principle experientially verifiable. If this is the case, one such improper generalization would be his claim that reality is rational, subject everywhere and at every time to immutable and uniform natural laws. Had Freneau shown fidelity to his own standards, the most he would have been able to say is that reality *as it is experienced* by fallible humans *appears* to be rational. As for the rest, he would have had to adopt an agnostic position: reality itself *may* be rational, but such a sweeping generalization is unverifiable even in principle, precisely because of the finitude of human reason.

It is not surprising that Freneau failed to see he had undercut his own empiricist first principles by illegitimately indulging in "speculative" flights. He was too much a child of the Enlightenment, in spite of his romantic leanings, to forgo the deistic article of faith that the natural order is unequivocally rational in character. To have done so would have knocked the props out from under his worldview. The ensuing collapse would have taken with it his assurance that reality is governed by immutable natural law, and would have seriously undermined his insistence that reality, loved into existence by a compassionate God, is benevolent. Freneau was willing to admit that human reason, that sacred cow of the Enlightenment, was limited in scope. But beyond that he was not prepared to go. He pushed against the boundaries of deism's pan-rationalism more strenuously than any American deist before him. But, as with his youthful attraction to the West Indies hurricane, the initial allure of the unknown and uncontrollable quickly repelled and frightened him.

NOTES

1. Philip Freneau, "The Power of Fancy," in *The Poems of Philip Freneau. Written chiefly during the late war* (Philadelphia: Francis Bailey, 1786). References to this collection hereafter cited as *Poems*, 1786.

2. Philip Freneau, "Theology Note Book," quoted in Jacob Axelrod, *Philip Freneau: Champion of Democracy* (Austin: University of Texas Press, 1967), p. 51.

3. Philip Freneau, "Libera Nos, Domine," *Poems*, 1786.

4. Philip Freneau, "MacSwiggin, A Satire," *Poems*, 1786.

5. Philip Freneau, "Philosophical Reflection," *Freeman's Journal*, July 17, 1781.

6. Philip Freneau, "The Pilgrim," *Freeman's Journal*, June 19, 1782.

7. Philip Freneau, "Verses, Made at Sea, in a Heavy Gale," *Freeman's Journal*, April 13, 1785.

8. Quoted in Lewis Leary, *That Rascal Freneau* (New Brunswick, NJ: Rutgers University Press, 1941), p. 233.

9. Philip Freneau, "On the Causes of Political Degeneracy," *Time-Piece*, July 7, 1798.

10. Philip Freneau, "Winter," quoted in Leary, *That Rascal Freneau*, p. 362.

11. *New York Mirror*, January 12, 1833.

12. Philip Freneau, "On the Powers of the Human Understanding," in *Poems Written and Published during the American Revolutionary War*, vol. I (Philadelphia, 1809). Hereafter cited as *Poems*, 1809.

13. Philip Freneau, "Science, Favourable to Virtue," in *Poems*, 1809.

14. Philip Freneau, "Epistle to a Student of Dead Languages," in *Poems Written between the Years 1768 and 1794* (Monmouth, NJ, 1795).

15. Philip Freneau, "On Superstition," in *A Collection of Poems*, vol. 1 (New York, 1815). Hereafter cited as *Poems*, 1815.

16. Philip Freneau, "On the Abuse of Human Power, as Exercised Over Opinion," in *Poems*, 1815.

17. Philip Freneau, "Belief and Unbelief," in *Poems*, 1815.

18. Ibid.

19. Ibid.

20. Philip Freneau, "On the Uniformity and Perfection of Nature," in *Poems*, 1809.

21. Philip Freneau, "Reflections on the Constitution, or Frame of Nature," in *Poems*, 1809.

22. Ibid.

23. Philip Freneau, "On the Universality and Other Attributes of the God of Nature," in *Poems*, 1815.

24. Ibid.

25. Ibid.

26. Philip Freneau, "On the Religion of Nature," in *Poems*, 1815.

27. Philip Freneau, "Science, Favourable to Virtue," in *Poems*, 1809.

28. Philip Freneau, "On the Evils of Human Life," in *Poems*, 1815.

29. Philip Freneau, "On False Systems of Government, and the Generally Debased Condition of Mankind," in *Poems*, 1809.

30. Philip Freneau, "On Happiness, as Proceeding from the Practice of Virtue," in *Poems*, 1815.

31. Ibid.

32. Philip Freneau, "On False Systems of Government, and the Generally-Debased Condition of Mankind," in *Poems*, 1809.

33. Nelson F. Adkin, *Philip Freneau and the Cosmic Enigma: The Religious and Philosophical Speculations of an American Poet* (New York: New York University Press, 1949) traces the influence of Lucretius on Freneau. Adkin's book—really little more than an essay—is the only secondary source devoted exclusively to Freneau's deism.

CHAPTER EIGHT

ZION RESTORED

THE DECLINE AND FALL OF AMERICAN DEISM

Philip Freneau, deistic bard, celebrator of the God of nature, had the unhappy distinction of being the last of America's Enlightenment deists. By the time the unexpected squall overtook him in 1832, deism as an integrated, influential, and militantly outspoken movement had been finished, for all practical purposes, for at least two decades.

Still, all in all, American deism had a good and productive run, lasting for some eighty-five years. Although the year was somewhat arbitrarily chosen, in chapter 2, I designated as its date of birth 1725, the year in which Benjamin Franklin published his *Dissertation on Liberty and Necessary*, the "youthful folly" he later regretted and repudiated. For the next fifty-odd years, Franklin, Jefferson, and a host of lesser-known and scarcely remembered thinkers steadily pondered and wrote about the religion of nature, at first with some ambivalence and hesitancy but, as the years progressed, with growing conviction and increasing stridency. The upshot of this progression was that deism made such an impact on the popular imagination that by midcentury orthodox spokespersons such as Ezra Stiles and Uzal Ogden saw it as a genuine threat to American Christianity. Toward the end of the century, deism as a widespread movement came into its own. Ethan Allen published his *Oracles of Reason* in 1784, Paine's *Age of Reason* shook the faithful in 1794/5, and Elihu Palmer propelled deism to its high-water mark in the years 1793 to 1806 with his militant and tireless crusading. After his death, deism's influence began to diminish, and the movement soon faded into a tired old age. Its final spurt of energy came in 1810 when the New York Deistical Society of Theophilanthropy, a reconstitution of the Parisian fraternity in which Paine had been an active member some fifteen years before, launched the last national newspaper devoted to rational religion. It was called the *Theophilanthropist*, and boldly announced in its inaugural prospectus that its pages would be devoted to the correction of "false opinions," the promotion of "the progress of reason," and the increase of "the sum of human happiness." Its first issue appeared in January 1810, but the project never really got off the ground. Plagued by financial difficulties and poor management, as well as an evident lack of vision, the *Theophilanthropist* appeared only irregularly, and even then tended to reprint articles rather than solicit new and fresh contributions. It finally ceased publication altogether toward the end of 1811. The *Theophilanthropist's* sporadic and uninspired career was the rather pathetic swan song of American deism. Its end signaled the end of deism.

Why did a movement that exercised the American imagination for two generations end in such a dismal way? There are several explanations. To begin with, the leading voices in the movement died out one by one, and no new generation of deists arose to take their place. Palmer, the firebrand who launched the national crusade for deism, died in 1806; Paine in 1809. Jefferson lingered on until 1826, but was no more public about religious matters in his old age than he had been in earlier years; if anything, he was even more reticent. A sprinkling of deistical societies founded in several states by Paine and Palmer continued for a time, but their older members gradually died off and there were few or no new recruits. By the time the *Theophilanthropist* made its halfhearted effort to revitalize the movement, the leadership as well as the rank and file of rational infidelity were pretty well depleted.

This depletion occurred largely because the ideal of rational religion had lost currency in the minds of many. It no longer spoke to those dissatisfied with conventional Christianity, no longer offered an alternative to supernaturalism that was deemed viable. There was an out-of-step, antiquarian air to its optimistic endorsement of eighteenth-century rationalism that somehow didn't quite suit the mentality of early nineteenth-century infidels. For make no mistake about it: infidelity at the time of Freneau's death still challenged Christian orthodoxy. But the arguments it appealed to and the language it used differed from the substance and style of the earlier generation of rational infidels. Figures such as Abner Kneeland, Robert Owen, and Frances Wright represented the new generation of infidels, a generation whose radicalism was more influenced by the utopian socialism of the Comte de Saint-Simon and Charles Fourier than by the Enlightenment New Learning of Bacon, Newton, and Locke.[1] Moreover, the infidelity inspired by romanticism— a movement represented by American transcendentalists such as Emerson and, later, Thoreau—was also beginning to make itself felt, and there is scarcely a worldview more alien to deism's ideal of "reason, right-eous and immortal reason" than transcendentalism. In short, Freneau lived to see the Enlightenment-spawned natural religion of his youth supplanted by new expressions of heterodoxy that, for one reason or another, more ably spoke to and for the new generation. Ironically, as seen in the preceding chapter, Freneau himself was caught in this transi-tion between the old and new forms of infidelity.

In addition to the emergence of a new style of infidelity that no longer spoke the language of Enlightenment rationalism, deism's demise as the predominant locus of American dissent was hastened by the growth of what one historian calls the "democratization" of religion in the early Republic.[2] Partly as a conservative reaction to deism's challenge to super-naturalism, partly as a consequence of the splintering of Calvinist hege-mony, a wave of Christian revivalism swept through the country between, roughly, 1780 and 1830. This movement, characterized by an emphasis upon personal piety, salvationism, and anti-intellectualism, was led by charismatic men accomplished in organization and rhetoric. It came to be known as the Second Great Awakening.[3] This revivalist movement, very much like its twentieth-century American counterparts, stressed biblical fundamentalism, the primacy of a personal, saving experience of the divine, and social and political conservatism. Like all successful revivalist crusades, it strategically targeted and relentlessly attacked what it consid-ered to be the enemies of true piety, virtue, and social order. Its foes were predictable: liberal Christianity, deism, and radical republicanism. The first betrayed the message of the Gospels, the second represented nothing less than perverse atheism, and the third inexorably led to excesses such as those witnessed in the French Terror—or so the revivalists preached.

The fifty-year crusade of the Second Great Awakening to recapture the soul of America was remarkably successful. Between 1820 and 1830, for example, Methodist membership doubled. In the three decades following the American Revolution, Baptist membership increased tenfold, and the number of Baptist congregations mushroomed from five hundred to over twenty-five hundred. The number of preachers per capita exploded in the same time period, swelling from some eighteen hundred in 1775 to almost forty thousand by 1845.[4] Religious populism in the early nineteenth century, in short, overwhelmed the nation, eclipsing the deistic threat that had so effectively challenged eighteenth-century orthodoxy. It is not surprising that Alexis de Tocqueville was impressed in the 1830s by the predominance of religious enthusiasm in the early Republic. He arrived on the American scene during the heyday of the religious backlash to militant deism.

The Second Great Awakening captured the popular imagination for many reasons. Its anti-intellectualism was appealing, and so was its insistence that an unemotional, rationalistic religiosity was antithetical to Christianity. Both points were aimed directly at deism. For all the attempts of Paine and Palmer to transform the religion of nature into a popularly based movement, deism never quite managed to throw over its aura of intellectual elitism. Although it exerted what, in retrospect, can be seen as a remarkably popular influence in its heyday, it nonetheless tended to remain a "thinking person's" religion. It appealed most to students, savants, the upper class, and social reformers who were often looked upon by their more conventional contemporaries as misfits and cranks. Fidelity to it required at least a passing acquaintance with the methodological presuppositions of the New Learning as well as some familiarity with natural philosophy; and such requirements smacked of an intellectual elitism that came to be deeply resented by the populace at large. As de Tocqueville noted in the nineteenth century and Richard Hofstadter reaffirmed in the twentieth, the American ethos of egalitarianism ill tolerates its intellectual sons and daughters, who speak in voices different from the crowd's.[5] The Second Great Awakening's appeal, as well as its final demolition of American deism, fed in part upon ingrained and sometimes rabid anti-intellectualism.

CRACKS IN THE MACHINE

Of course, the explanations just given for the decline and fall of American deism still only scratch the surface. The more fundamental questions they raise remain to be answered. Why, for example, did no new generation of American rational infidels replace the eighteenth-century deists? What were the *precise* reasons for deism's ultimate failure to endure as an alternative to American Christianity? In order to answer these questions, we must examine more closely the philosophical, theological, and methodological presuppositions upon which deism built its case. Although these presuppositions were ably defended by many American and foreign-born deists, weaknesses in them that were not readily discerned in the eighteenth century became increasingly obvious to nineteenth-century critics of deism. The emerging recognition of these weaknesses, in fact, was the catalyst in the transition from Enlightenment-based infidelity to what might be described as the post-Enlightenment infidelity of an Abner Kneeland or Robert Owen. Moreover, the realization of these weaknesses contributed to the resurgence of more orthodox views of the world and religion. In short, American deism collapsed in part because the foundation upon which it stood ceased to exercise the intellectual authority and appeal it once had. In broad terms, the reason for this breakdown was that the deistic worldview, founded squarely upon the New Learning's allegiance to mechanism and rationalism, began to be perceived as too simplistic, and hence a distortion of reality.

The deistic worldview, it will be recalled, revolved around two fundamental principles, one metaphysical and the other epistemic.

Deism's metaphysical assumption was that the universe could be exhaustively explained in terms of Newton's mechanistic schema. Physical reality was analogous, if not identical, to a cosmic machine whose various constituents causally interacted with one another with mathematical precision. This interaction was determined by immutable and absolute natural laws set in motion by a supremely rational and all-powerful deity. There was no possibility of physical phenomena deviating, in even the slightest way, from the preordained cosmic blueprint. The series of causal relations definitive of reality, in other words, was deemed necessary. Physical reality was a kind of perpetual motion machine, exhaustively explicable in terms of the laws of causality, motion, and inertia, and totally void of any non-mechanistic (or supernatural) attributes.

The eighteenth-century deists had been exhilarated by the stream of scientific discoveries and inventions that seemed to corroborate Newton's system. In their eyes, this system represented a clear advance over the traditional Aristotelian model of reality, which seemed to obfuscate more than clarify. But as the eighteenth century gave way to the nineteenth, cracks began to appear in the system that were difficult to ignore. One of these was philosophical in nature, the other psychological.

The philosophical crack was Hume's trenchant criticism of the assumption that our ideas of causality actually conform to objective phenomena. Although Hume originally published the attack in his 1739 *Treatise of Human Nature*, it attracted little notice for a generation. As Hume himself ruefully recalled some years later, the book's original edition "fell deadborn from the press." But subsequent editions reached more receptive and discerning audiences, and a result of this wider attention was that one of the fundamental principles of the Newtonian system was called into question.

The mechanistic worldview defended by Newton rested on the postulate that the relations between objects were causally determined by natural laws, and that individual instances of such causation were empirically observable, just as the entire network of necessary causal relations was mathematically expressible. But Hume, appealing to the very same empiricist principles that so impressed Newton as well as his deistic admirers, argued that the very "fact" of causality was suspect.

Hume acknowledged that humans possessed an idea of causality, but then went on, in good empiricist fashion, to inquire into the origins of such an idea. Following Locke's argument that all ideas are derived from sensory impressions, the traditional Newtonian and deistic response was that the idea arises in our minds because of our *experience* of causality. This experience was thought to be one arising from the relationship between objects or events. An unprejudiced examination of ordinary experience reveals just three types of relations: *contiguity*, or proximity; priority *in time*, or the phenomenon of A (the "cause") preceding B (the "effect"); and *constant conjunction*, the perception that one event is always conjoined with another. All three of these relations were affirmed by Newtonianism. Furthermore, because of the determinism posited by its mechanistic analysis, it insisted that all such relations were *necessarily* connected with one another, such that the occurrences of physical phenomena were mathematically predictable given a sufficient database. But such a "necessary connection" between events or objects is never experienced, concluded Hume. It is merely inferred on the basis of our impressions of contiguity, temporal priority, and constant conjunction. This inference is itself the result of a psychological "habit of association" produced by repeated experiences of the three relations. Necessary causal relations, then, are neither observable nor deducible from scrutiny of experience, according to Hume; and this conclusion struck at the very heart of Newtonian mechanism.[6]

It would be too much to say that Hume's argument dealt a devastating blow to late eighteenth- and early nineteenth-century advocates of the Newtonian worldview. Awe over its comprehensive and systematic vision and the apparent corroboration of its conclusions by the achievements of applied mechanical sciences tended to reduce the impact of Hume's abstract philosophical caveat. Hume himself acknowledged that a practical person would do well to act as if necessary causality was in fact an objective phenomenon. Nonetheless, Hume's challenge cracked the hitherto unblemished casing of the cosmic machine model that served as the basis of the deistic worldview. Given the closed and presumably immaculate perfection of the system, as well as the centrality to it of necessary causality, this crack was enough to undermine the entire Newtonian superstructure.

The second crack in the system was more psychological in character than philosophical. While Hume's assault on the notion of objective causality may not have perturbed many outside the philosophical community proper, the effects of the psychological crack were more far-reaching.

Newton's mechanistic system assured eighteenth-century natural philosophers (or those, at any rate, who ignored Hume's challenge) that the deterministic nature of the cosmic machine was a guarantee of the advance of science and the progressive flourishing of humankind. After all, if nature is nonwhimsical, as Newton insisted, then it is possible to learn enough about the laws governing causal relations to harness them in the interests of humanity. Bacon set the stage for this optimism by insisting that his new logic provided a calculus for the invention of "arts"

and "works." Subsequent investigations into nature's ways only reinforced the eighteenth-century's confidence that the cosmic clockwork
constituted the best of all possible worlds, a veritable cornucopia of technological possibilities providentially filled by the benevolent Supreme
Architect. True, wits such as Voltaire occasionally lampooned this exuberant optimism, but for the most part, eighteenth-century rationalists
were satisfied that the physical order that surrounded them, mathematically precise and immaculately rational as it was, provided a safe and
fecund home for human striving. This optimism became a central article
of belief for the American deists. Given enough time, tolerance, and
rational inquiry into nature's mysteries, there was no limit to human
accomplishment.

But as the eighteenth century gave way to the nineteenth, and the full
implications of Newtonianism became more apparent, an uneasiness
arose. In the minds of many, the mechanistic worldview increasingly
came to be seen as an austere, cold, lifeless, and generally forbidding
structure; in spite of all the talk about providential design, the vast, silent
expanses of the universe seemed indifferent to the human condition.
How could a machinelike universe act any differently? Pascal had already
voiced this discomfort in the seventeenth century with his plaintive cry
that the eternal silence of infinite space filled him with terror. At the time
his was a voice crying in the wilderness, but in the nineteenth century
more people began to feel the same. The impersonal perfection of the
cosmic machine began to alienate more than enrapture. Edwin Burtt
admirably expressed the particulars of this alienation when he wrote that
its overpowering presence tended to reduce humanity's self-image to that
of a

> puny irrelevant spectator (so far as a being wholly imprisoned in a
> dark room can be called such) of the vast mathematical system whose
> regular motions according to mechanical principles constituted the
> world of nature. . . . This world that people had thought themselves
> living in—a world rich with color and sound, redolent with fragrance,
> filled with gladness, love and beauty, speaking everywhere of purpo-
> sive harmony and creative ideals—were crowded now into minute
> corners of the brains of scattered organic beings. The really impor-
> tant world outside was a world hard, cold, colorless, silent and dead.[7]

The psychological sense of displacement, of existential forlornness expressed in this passage, was unbearable for a growing number of intellectuals in the early nineteenth century. The Newtonian machine metaphor not only reduced humans to unimportant units in the machine, describable in impersonal, mathematical terms; even more obviously, as Burtt points out, it rendered them irrelevant. It is not too much to suggest that the resurgence of Christian revivalism and the emergence of transcendentalism in the early nineteenth century were both, in their separate ways, reactions to the psychological malaise prompted by the forbidding austerity of the deistic worldview. Metaphysical caveats such as Hume's could be overlooked or safely shunted aside to the abstract realm of philosophical speculation. But the overpowering burden of dwelling in a frozen, indifferent universe could not so easily be dismissed. Even some of the American deists themselves, most notably Freneau, began to tremble at the impersonal sterility of the cosmos, and sought assurances that the universe was not the cold, aloof machine they had portrayed it as.

Deism's wholehearted and sometimes unreflective endorsement of the mechanistic worldview gradually led, then, to an awareness of certain weaknesses internal to it, and these in turn diminished its intellectual appeal. Moreover, the mechanistic assumption went hand in hand with the belief that the ultimate criterion for belief about reality was reason. This too came to be called into question.

The deists, it will be recalled, can be described as pan-rationalists. For them, physical reality was imbued with divine reason in such a way as to render it perfectly accessible to rational investigation, and humans were capable of such inquiry because they too participated in divine reason through their intellects. Careful empirical observation and rational analysis were therefore the necessary and sufficient conditions for an adequate understanding of divine, physical, and human nature. The light of reason banished all shadows and penetrated into every dim corner of the universe—or at least was capable in principle of doing so.

This assumption of reason's adequacy as a basis for human knowledge inspired the eighteenth-century thinker with the optimistic confidence that progress in the natural and human sciences was an inevitability. But as the nineteenth century started, this confidence began to cool. A growing number of individuals came to doubt the adequacy of reason's ability to fully reveal the secrets of either physical reality or the human condition. Epistemic skepticism, reawakened in part by Hume's pushing of the empiricist method to its logical conclusion, raised questions as to whether a "rational" appraisal of experience disclosed anything save facts about psychological laws of association. After all, if there was no guarantee that human impressions of perceptual data actually corresponded to events in the real world, then even the most coherent cosmological model could be dismissed, or at least challenged, as nothing more than an elaborate, abstract speculation. But this, of course, was precisely the kind of "syllogistic" construct Bacon had railed against in the seventeenth century. Similarly, the rise of romanticism strongly challenged the Enlightenment assumption that human nature and social behavior could be exhaustively explained and manipulated by rational analysis. Inspired by romanticism, the transcendentalist movement argued, to the contrary, that there were depths within the human soul inaccessible to rational investigation, and that a surer, although by no means certain, route to self-knowledge was through a harkening to one's moods, intuitions, and passions. Once again, it was Pascal who anticipated this move. "What will become of you, O man," he wrote, "who try by your natural reason to discover what is your true condition? . . . Know then, proud creature, what a paradox you are to yourself. Be humble, impotent reason; be quiet, imbecile nature: *know that man surpasses man infinitely.*"[8]

Pascal's contemptuous dismissal of reason as "impotent" was a far cry from Elihu Palmer's enraptured "righteous and immortal reason," but it better fitted the mood of the early nineteenth century. It also pointed to what in retrospect can be seen as one of the most fundamental weaknesses of the deistic worldview. For all the sincerity of their humanistic ideals, the American deists endorsed a philosophical anthropology that simplistically objectified the human spirit. Given their fidelity to mechanistic Newtonianism and its accompanying pan-rationalism, such a view of human nature was perfectly consistent. But consistency notwithstanding, it must be confessed that the perspective was shallow. In their efforts to extend the domain of scientific method to all arenas of investigation, they tended to ignore or dismiss those elements in experience that resisted such incorporation. In the case of their analysis of what it meant to be human, this resulted in a radical de-subjectivization of persons: humans were little more than animated physical objects that, like all other objects, necessarily conformed to immutable natural laws. The sole obstacles to humanity recognizing its determined place in the vast scheme of things were superstition and ignorance. Remove these hindrances, and individuals would naturally accommodate their thoughts and actions to the rational order of which they were a part. The cosmic machine would then operate perfectly at the human level, and individual felicity and social progress would inevitably ensue.[9]

But this type of humanism, very much like the cosmological mechanism that served as its foundation, in fact was rather lifeless and flew in the face of ordinary experience. Humans are not predictable, rational cogs in a complex world machine, and this fact became increasingly apparent to critics of Enlightenment deism. Instead, as Kant acknowledged in his *Critique of Pure Reason*, humans are better seen as occupying a unique place in the scheme of things. They are, to a certain extent, bound by the same rational laws as all other elements of nature. But, Kant continued, humans also possess freedom and an interior existence that distinguishes them in kind from the physical system of bodies in motion. They are in one respect akin to the "starry heavens above," but they are also to a certain extent unpredictably free of mechanistic restraints. This paradoxical combination of disparate dimensions filled Kant with "ever new and increasing admiration and awe," as well it should have. It also echoed Pascal's point when he said of man, "What a paradox you are to yourself." But the fact that humans cannot and should not be regarded as just another class of rationally analyzable material bodies by and large escaped the American deists. In their zeal to liberate people from the burdens of superstition and irrationality, they unwittingly reified humans into exclusively rational entities very much reminiscent of the embodied thinking substances in Descartes' description.

In summary, deism in America began to fail when the Enlightenment view on which it was founded was seen to have severe shortcomings. Its cosmology was based on the assumption of the objective existence of causal relations, and this objectivity was called into question by David Hume. Its portrayal of reality as an impersonal system of deterministic relations bred a sense of uneasiness and alienation, and the individual came to see himself or herself as adrift in a world, as Burtt put it, devoid of "color and sound . . . , gladness, love and beauty." The assumption that reason was a sufficient instrument for the illumination of nature grew increasingly unacceptable, and new thinkers began to emphasize the importance of moods, affections, and intuition. It began to look like deism reduced reality, reason, and the human condition to a limpid but one-dimensional set of explanations. The richness of experience, in all its bewildering diversity, was being sacrificed for the sake of a deceptive lucidity.

CLUMSY EXEGESIS AND A TOO-DISTANT GOD

The one-dimensional simplicity of rational religion's first principles also expressed itself in the deists' criticism of Christianity and their more positive reflections on God and religion.

The deistic criticism of Christianity took as its primary target the notion of biblical authority. This concentration upon Scripture was a logical first step in the campaign against supernaturalism, since the deists correctly perceived that the Christianity they so despised regarded the Bible as the ultimate foundation of its doctrinal beliefs. To cast doubt upon the Bible's authority, then, was to undermine the basis of the Christian worldview. Moreover, all of the American deists were well acquainted with the Bible, and hence eminently qualified to speak of it. Allen and Paine could recite long passages of Scripture from memory; Palmer and Freneau studied the Bible as part of their training for the ministry; Franklin grew up in a "pious" family that regularly read the Bible; and Jefferson spent a good many years editing a version of the New Testament that highlighted its moral teaching while omitting its supernaturalist accounts of miracles and prophecy. Each of these men knew sacred writ at least as well as many colonial and early Republic clergy.

But for all their familiarity with biblical narrative, their hermeneutic technique was rather uninspired (although Jefferson, up to a point, is an exception to this rule). The deists by and large read Scripture in the same way they perused a book of history—that is, they assumed that sacred writ was nothing more than a straightforward, discursive work that purported to give a literal description of events that had occurred two millennia and more earlier. This assumption led them to dismiss as false or meaningless any biblical account that violated the canons of reason or the lessons of ordinary experience. By approaching the Scriptures in such a simplistic, literal way, they appear to have had no appreciation for the rich functional diversity of human discourse. It never occurred to them, for example, that at least some tales in the New Testament can be read allegorically, or that certain Old Testament stories that do not conform to reason or experience might nonetheless serve to express a point metaphorically or symbolically. For them, scriptural texts communicated at only the discursive level. Given this rigid, literalistic mode of reading, it is not surprising that they had little difficulty in picking passages apart and emphasizing their strangeness.

Elihu Palmer was especially guilty of such a one-dimensional interpretation of Scripture, though in many cases he was just appealing to examples of a style of exegesis already defended by Allen and Paine. A couple of illustrations of his method will serve to point out the narrow, literalistic way in which deists tended to interpret biblical stories.

At one point in his *Principles of Nature*, Palmer examines the story in Matthew 8:28 about the Gadarene swine. Jesus rid two men of the demons that possessed them by sending the demons into swine, which then "ran violently down a steep place and perished in the waters." Now, surely one way of interpreting this account is to assume it is a parable conveying a message about the self-destructive nature of unbridled human passions. Reading it this way, one can profit from the story without bruising one's rational faculties by taking it as a record of a literal, historical event. But the possibility that the story may convey a deeper meaning never occurs to Palmer. He insists upon reading it as if it is a straightforward historical description. As a consequence his exegesis is pedantic: "Were the devils in this case drowned with the hogs, or did they make their escape the moment they were immersed in water? . . . In any view of the story, it is marked with injustice, and inhumanity, injustice toward those who were the rightful owners of these swine, and inhumanity or cruelty toward the swine themselves."[10]

In another chapter of *Principles of Nature*, Palmer reflects upon the Genesis account of the expulsion from Eden, and particularly upon the following passage: "And the Lord God said unto the serpent, because thou hast done this, thou art cursed above all cattle, and above every

beast of the field; upon thy belly thou shalt go, and dust shalt thou eat all
the days of thy life" (Gen 3:14). Palmer ignores the possibility that the
story of the expulsion can be read as a parable of the wages of pride or
self-will. Instead he makes the obvious point that the passage just quoted
raises perplexities when read literally.

> It is a question of magnitude, which ought to engage the attention of
> theological doctors to inform us, in what manner the serpent per-
> formed locomotion, previous to his transgression, for which he received
> the condemnatory sentence of a going upon his belly. Did he walk about
> erect like a man? If so, he must have cut a curious figure, travelling
> about upon the point of his tail; and the condemnation which brought him
> to a horizontal position, was rather in his favour than against him.[11]

In these and many other examples of deistic exegesis, there is a narrowness of interpretation, a rigid concentration upon literalism at the
expense of connotative meaning, which reduces much of rational religion's criticisms of Scripture to the level of insipidity. Doubtless part of
the simplicity of their exegesis stems from a polemical motive. It is
obvious in Palmer's commentary upon the Genesis passage, for example,
that he wished to cast doubt upon scriptural veracity by employing sar-
casm, and such a ploy always requires oversimplification if it is to pro-
duce the desired effect. In addition, it must be noted that a literal reading
of the Bible was the usual mode of interpretation by many of the deists'
Christian contemporaries. Consequently, the deistic belaboring of
obvious absurdities or inconsistencies in Scripture was an understandable
and effective strategy of dissent within the context of eighteenth-century
orthodoxy, even though it seems tediously irrelevant to the twentieth-century mind. Finally, it should be noted that "scientific" exegesis
of scriptural texts, which attempts to examine sacred writ from both a
historical and a philological perspective, was largely (though not exclusively) a nineteenth-century phenomenon. It is somewhat anachronistic
to criticize the American deists for failing to employ the hermeneutical
techniques of historical criticism when the latter arrived only later on the
theological scene.

Still, it can scarcely be denied that the attacks against Scripture
launched by the American deists are unsatisfying. They smack of the

tunnel vision of a village atheist who is versed in the letter but totally ignorant of the spirit and function of religious discourse. The literalness with which the advocates of rational religion approached biblical texts parallels the narrowness of their cosmological and epistemic first principles. For the deists, reality, knowledge, and styles of communication were unambiguous, simple, and straightforward. There was a complete denial—or, more accurately, a total ignorance—of the possibility that reality and human discourse are multileveled and diverse in aspect and function, and that a single methodological approach does not fit all contexts equally well. The possibility that biblical texts and at least some Christian dogma are more properly read as symbols than as linear statements of fact was alien to their interpretative assumptions. As a result, their criticism of "supernaturalism" often missed the mark. Such an approach was more or less sufficient so long as the Enlightenment view remained comparatively intact. But as soon as problems arose with the philosophical and psychological aspects of the worldview, the method of criticizing Christian scripture and dogma revealed itself as overly simplistic. Emerson's well-known statement that a foolish consistency is the hobgoblin of little minds can be seen as aimed at the rationalistic perspective. To at least a certain extent, it is also applicable to the methodological presuppositions behind the deistic appraisal of Christianity and its uncritical acceptance of the mechanistic cosmos.

Finally, the deistic concept of the God of nature, which clearly was the central tenet upon which the rational infidels based their case, became increasingly unsatisfactory to deistic sympathizers and critics alike. This God, it will be recalled, was envisioned by the deists as a distant First Cause, a removed Principle of reason and uniformity who sets in motion the system of natural laws that reflect his essential attributes but who also refuses to intervene actively in either physical events or human actions. The deists insisted that this deity was both good and loving, as evidenced by his having created a physical reality conducive to the well-being and flourishing of the human race. But given the overall character ascribed to the deistic Supreme Architect, two suspicions began to emerge as the eighteenth century drew to a close. The first was that the God of nature was too aloof to sustain, much less encourage, a personal response from the very humans he supposedly loved and benefited. The second, which emerged somewhat earlier in deism's career, was that the deistic God was, in point of fact, a superfluity, a kind of *deus ex machina*. His only real purpose, when it came right down to it, was to supply a convenient "explanation" for the existence of reality.

One recent commentator has described deism as the most "masculine" of all religious sensibilities.[12] This appraisal is based upon the perception that deism's religion of nature is remorselessly intellectual in character and almost completely lacking in those affective elements that seem to be such a vital aspect of living religious traditions. For the deist, God is, of course, the necessary condition for creation's plenitude. He is the supremely generative principle without which nothing would be. But, much more fundamentally, the deistic God is also the ground of that cosmic reason that permeates reality. He is the source of immutable order, of intractable precision in the cosmic machine, of the absolute and eternal laws that implacably regulate the actions of inanimate bodies as well as humans. Seen from this pan-rationalistic perspective, the God of nature is more akin to a mathematical axiom or a metaphysical power holding the universe together than to a deity of love and compassion whose self-giving elicits from humans personal trust and adoration. God is a distant, inaccessible, impersonal, monarchical Principle that engenders, perhaps, awe and fascination, but not affective reverence. True, God reveals himself in nature, and hence is not totally out of human reach. But such a mode of revelation, at least as the deists interpreted it, only underscores God's impassive, rational character. To experience the divine presence in nature was not, as it would later be for the American transcendentalists, to discern intuitively an enduring ground beneath the stream of ephemeral appearance, a ground that would evoke an emotionally overwhelming sense of the sublime. Instead, the deistic account of natural revelation stressed an intellectual awareness of the existence of a cold, immaculate, supreme agency that manifested itself, in a mathematically perfect way, in physical laws. There was no place in this rational framework for what the deists contemptuously referred to as "enthusiasm." Indeed, an underlying assumption of their concept of religion was that emotional responses in spiritual matters inevitably bred superstition and dogma, and hence were sources of irrationality better forsaken than encouraged. To worship God was to imitate his nature, and this could only be done by comporting one's thoughts and actions to the immaculately rational nature of God and God's creation. It is little wonder that Paine, speaking for all the American deists, proclaimed natural philosophy, the dispassionate scientific study of physical phenomena, as the foundation of "true" theology.

It hardly needs to be said that such a concept of God and religious experience is, in the minds of many persons both then and now, psychologically distressing and theologically suspect. The image of a God detached from creation and but little, if at all, concerned with or responsive to the supplications, fears, insecurities, and hopes of humanity is every bit as alienating as the coldly deterministic character of his handiwork, the mechanistic cosmos. Such an abstract deity might meet the religious and emotional needs of a disembodied intellect, but it is scarcely sufficient for most flesh-and-blood humans, who long for and require a more personal relationship with the divine. Even some of the American deists themselves attempted to reduce the seemingly unbridgeable gap between this distant First Principle and humanity. Franklin, recall, was reluctant to let go of the conventional theological belief in special providences. Freneau sought to soften the abstract otherness of nature's God by proto-romantically stressing the divine's presence in the world of human experience. Even the more stalwart of deistic thinkers such as Allen, Jefferson, Paine, and Palmer argued that the Supreme Architect was essentially benevolent, as evidenced by his infusion of rationality into the physical realm and the human intellect. But such attempts to render the deistic God more accessible were, in the long run, both unconvincing and dissatisfying. At best, all they suggested was that God had thoughtfully designed reality in such a way as to provide a suitable home for humans. But having done this, the Deity then stepped back and assumed the attitude, as it were, of an absentee landlord, whom no amount of prayer or personal longing could reach.

In short, the God of the deists was too transcendent, too removed from the realm of ordinary human needs and aspirations, to provide individuals with that experience of communion which is vital to a fulfilling religious life. One can be fascinated and awestruck by such a deity, but one can hardly adore it, much less love it. To invoke Pascal once more, the deistic Supreme Architect was the God of the philosophers, not of Abraham, Isaac, or Jacob. An awareness of his existence could possibly satisfy the intellect, but not the heart.

Along with the problem of whether the deistic God was too distant to meet the needs of popular religion was the philosophical problem of whether such a deity was in fact necessary. The first person to level the charge that it was not was Baron Henri d'Holbach (1723–1789), the leading Enlightenment proponent of atheistic materialism. In his *System of Nature*, d'Holbach examined the central claims of rational religion and concluded that its attempt to provide an alternative to traditional theism on the one hand and to atheism on the other was unsuccessful. D'Holbach argued that the mechanistic cosmology endorsed by the deists provided a sufficient account of both physical and human reality; there was no need to posit the existence of a divine First Cause in addition to it. One could speculate as much as one wished about the origins of the machine, but all such reflection, d'Holbach warned, was idle. Human reason could never arrive at an adequate solution to questions concerning the origins of the universe; and even if it could, the answer would not shed any more light upon natural law than already had been acquired through natural philosophy. Reality existed, and operated in conformity to immutable law. That was all that needed to be known (or in fact could be known), and the postulation of the existence of a divine First Cause behind observable phenomena contributed no new, essential insight into reality. Consequently, concluded d'Holbach, the deistic concept of God is a "useless" one.[13] As Laplace would say a generation later, the closed universe of mechanism is explicable in terms of self-regulating physical principles intrinsic to it. There is no need, then, of the "God hypothesis."

Such a conclusion was not one the American deists were willing to accept. Each of them, as demonstrated in previous chapters, believed in the existence of God. Some of them—Palmer and Freneau come immediately to mind—did so fervently. It will also be remembered that the immediate impetus for Paine's *Age of Reason* was his consternation over the rise of atheism during the French Revolution. But given the concept of God defended by the deists, d'Holbach's criticism was both insightful and, to a large degree, appropriate. Taken to their logical conclusions, the pan-rationalistic worldview of the deists, their scorn of speculative reflection, and their insistence upon experience-based knowledge, all tended to eliminate or at least greatly diminish the need for God as an explanatory principle. When this fact is coupled with the observation that the abstract, impersonal concept of God they defended apparently satisfied none of the affective needs so important to religious sensibility, d'Holbach's challenge is especially striking. The deistic God recedes to the shadowy status of a rather superfluous *deus ex machina*.

There are, then, a number of explanations for the early nineteenth-century demise of American deism. It attracted no new leaders, and was eventually swamped by the religious revivalism of the Second Great Awakening and by the rise of transcendentalism because its Enlightenment-based worldview ceased to strike resonant chords in either intellectuals or laypersons. Its mechanistic cosmology reeled from the blows of Humean skepticism. Its pan-rationalistic attempt to reduce all explanations to the epistemic standards of the New Learning ignored the complexity of modes of knowing and the complexity of human and physical nature. Its defense of both a deterministic universe and a distant, impersonal deity alienated secular as well as religious individuals. Deism's worldview and its religion of nature, in short, offered a formal, pristine, aesthetically classical vision of reality and God that ultimately failed to paint either a realistic or a psychologically satisfying portrait of the world. The rational infidels' attempt to replace traditional religion with rational religion was a noble experiment, but, in the final analysis, an unsuccessful one.

DEISM'S INFLUENCE ON AMERICAN CHRISTIANITY

To say that the deistic experiment was ultimately unsuccessful is not to say it was a total failure. It is true that the rational infidels were unable to replace Christian belief as the predominant religious orientation in the United States. It is equally the case that renewed attempts in the nineteenth century to challenge Christian orthodoxy were not deistic in either temperament or fundamental principles. But it would be incorrect to conclude that the deistic movement in the United States left no positive, enduring mark—that it was nothing more than a curious chapter in the history of American religious dissent. Deism passed out of vogue along with the Enlightenment ethos that birthed it, but it bequeathed to later generations a lasting and far-reaching legacy. Its influence was not as revolutionary as its eighteenth-century advocates had hoped, but its impact still had dramatic repercussions in subsequent theological, philosophical, and social thought in America.

To begin with, deism's challenge to orthodox Christianity helped to push the style of American theology in a new, fresh direction. Although its overly intellectualistic approach to religion ultimately failed to satisfy the human spirit or popular religious sensibility, deism's devastating assault upon supernaturalism could be neither dismissed nor ignored by churchmen. The criticisms leveled against the hallowed tenets of Christianity by rational infidelity had to be acknowledged and responded to in a convincing manner, and in the process Christian apologists absorbed something of the mood as well as the method of the very deists they railed against. As a result, the deistic challenge to orthodoxy infiltrated American theology and influenced its future course in at least three ways.

First, deism's insistence that theology and natural philosophy should be seen as compatible and, indeed, complementary, provoked champions of orthodoxy to focus more closely in their apologetics upon arguments derived from natural theology and reason than from revelation and personal piety. What was originally a strategic attempt to beat the deists at their own game slowly became an accepted theological modus operandi. This is not to suggest that deism was the sole catalyst for this change in method. As we saw in chapter 1, so-called liberal Christianity in the early eighteenth century was influenced by the Enlightenment's emphasis upon reason and experience before deism came into its own as a threat to American orthodoxy. Nor is it the case that the new emphasis upon natural theology was endorsed by all post-deistic Christian sects. Some theologians, particularly many of the leaders of the Second Great Awakening, scornfully dismissed rational apologetics as nothing more than disguised infidelity, and insisted on returning to a religious sensibility characterized by emotional fervor and scriptural literalism. But these qualifications notwithstanding, it cannot be denied that the deistic challenge was enormously influential in tempering the reliance of conventional American theology upon dogmatic supernaturalist approaches. The new theological style sparked by the need to respond to deism was especially obvious in denominations such as Universalism and Unitarianism, but it also struck root in more mainstream ones such as Episcopalianism and Congregationalism.

The deistic challenge encouraged a new regard for naturalistic arguments in Christian circles in two primary ways. First, it convinced many churchmen that religion needed to speak to the head as well as the heart, and that a viable and healthy theological tradition is one that does not balk from the enterprise of reinterpreting its central beliefs in the light of changing scientific and philosophical modes of explanation. In responding to the arguments of rational religionists, orthodox theologians learned that scientific discoveries about the physical realm, invoked by the deists in support of their Supreme Architect, could just as well serve to strengthen belief in the Christian revelation by rendering its tenets more palatable to reflective men and women. The Christian God revealed himself in nature as well as in Scripture and tradition, and a judicious utilization of the disclosures of natural philosophy, far from eroding faith, was soon seen as a prop to it. Traditional appeals to supernaturalist tenets such as miracles and prophecy were not, of course, renounced, but they ceased to be regarded as the sole vehicles to Christian belief.

Hand in hand with Christian theology's absorption of natural philosophy was an increased appreciation for the role of reason in religious inquiry. Calvinism's pessimistic dismissal of the human intellect on the grounds of its inherent depravity was eventually overshadowed in Christian circles by a confidence that the rational investigation of experience was both possible and conducive to strengthening religious conviction. This led to a new way of defining religious belief; as one twentieth-century historian notes, it "gravitated toward the connotation it had for the Deists: intellectual assent to a definable proposition."[14] Leonard Woods of Boston's Andover Seminary proclaimed in 1830 that the theological doctrine defended by Jonathan Edwards was "as demonstrable, as any proposition in Geometry," and that the ultimate test for the formulation of Christian beliefs was that they be expressed in "language which shall carry them to the mind of every enlightened Christian and philosopher with perfect clearness." Lyman Beecher, the American theologian who bemoaned the popularity of deism during his college days (as we saw in chapter 1), was later so convinced of the importance of reason in Christian belief that he contemptuously dismissed mysticism and rebuked those enthusiastic Christians who, he said, "love to dream amid the repetition of beautiful uncertain sounds, and glittering undefined images."[15]

Reverend Woods's use of the expression "enlightened Christian" indicates the extent to which eighteenth-century deism's ideal of rational religion infiltrated subsequent American theological speculation and changed its course. Nineteenth-century Christian leaders were both unwilling and unable to go as far as deism had in expunging all supernatural elements from religious belief. But they willingly and even enthusiastically endorsed an "enlightened Christianity" that took its cue from the rational infidels' high regard for the theological merits of scientific investigation and rational standards of appraisal. This nineteenth-century marriage of traditional revelation and reason would eventually give rise to tensions in the Christian community reminiscent of the ones that plagued eighteenth-century liberal Christianity; but it also revealed just how much mainstream Christianity had absorbed the spirit of rational inquiry.

Closely allied with the embrace of natural philosophy and rational method was a new attitude among American theologians in regard to scriptural exegesis, and this too can be attributed to the influence of deism. It will be recalled that proponents of rational religion systematically targeted what they saw as inconsistencies, historical inaccuracies, and outright nonsense in Scripture. They assumed that to cast doubt upon the received doctrine of scriptural inerrancy was to undermine the very foundations of Christian belief. But as we saw in the preceding section, their exegesis was often crude and literalistic, with little appreciation for either the subtlety of language or richly diverse levels of discourse.

In spite of the weaknesses inherent in deistic exegesis, the rational infidels' continuous onslaught against Scripture made some impression on nineteenth-century Christian scholars. Granted, biblical literalism would continue to be the standard of interpretation throughout the first half of the century, but the deists had pointed out problems that arose from reading Scripture at face value, and this forced many theologians into a sometimes reluctant reappraisal of scriptural claims. Churchmen reeling from the criticisms of the deists sometimes dug in their heels and rigidly insisted upon a doctrine of inerrancy, but many more became wary of the dogmatic assertion of the literal truth of all sacred writ, and slowly groped their way toward a deeper appreciation of the ethical, allegorical, and symbolical functions of biblical language. As one recent historian has put it, the impact of deistic and scientific assaults on biblical literalism "rarely destroyed Christian faith. Yet it certainly shook complacency; the Bible, hence Christianity, never looked quite so plainly and simply true afterwards."[16] The so-called higher criticism launched by German biblical scholars such as David Friedrich Strauss and Karl Richard Lepsius in the early nineteenth century would not make much of an impact on American theology until the second half of the century, although at least one theologian, the Reverend Moses Stuart of Harvard, daringly introduced his students to the new critical method as early as 1812. But it is not unreasonable to suggest that the loosening up of dogmatic biblical literalism by eighteenth-century deism prepared the way for the eventual reception in America of the German higher criticism.

Finally, the deistic challenge to orthodoxy served to modify the American Christian tradition's tendency toward what might be described as spiritual authoritarianism. If the deistic movement in the colonies and early Republic accomplished nothing else, it at least impressed upon the minds of sympathizers and detractors alike the hazards of sectarian dogmatism. It legitimized the sometimes disconcerting realization that there are a variety of different ways to think about ultimate issues such as the nature of God, providential design, theological method, and the purpose of the religious life. No single individual or even sectarian group of individuals could with propriety claim to hold a monopoly on religious truth. Credal formulations of belief, therefore, are better regarded as hypothetical attempts to symbolize spiritual intuitions than as written-in-stone propositions that demand literal acceptance. As such, they are always open to reinterpretation and redaction.

Benjamin Franklin set the tone for such a liberal reading of religious creeds as far back as the mid-eighteenth century, and the American deists who came after him followed suit. Nineteenth-century theologians were not prepared to throw over credal expressions of faith entirely, but the deistic influence did serve to soften the traditional definition of credal statements as "fixed forms of dogma." Horace Bushnell, the leading American theologian of the antebellum period, was particularly impressed by the deistically inspired move to reexamine the nature of religious creeds. He suggested that "words of thought or spirit are inexact in their significance," and concluded that Christians would do well to focus upon the underlying message rather than their strictly literal meaning. Mere theological definitions, he said, "cannot bring us over the difficulty; for definitions are, in fact, only changes of symbol, and, if we take them to be more, will infallibly lead us into error."[17] In arguing against a literal inter-pretation of religious creeds, Bushnell was certainly not aligning himself with either deism or, for that matter, even liberal natural theology. He remained, from a theological perspective, squarely within the orthodox Christian camp (although nineteenth-century conservative fundamentalists predictably excoriated his interpretative approach to religious statements). But Bushnell's appreciation of the dangers of a spiritual authoritarianism, born of an unreflective and uncritical acceptance of creed as fixed dogma, clearly reflects the tolerant spirit of the rational religionists.

American theologians, then, tended to absorb certain elements of the deism that they had sought to refute. Sometimes consciously, but more often unwittingly, they adopted to a certain extent the tolerant spirit, rationalist orientation, and naturalist temper of rational infidelity. There remained, of course, widespread and influential segments of the Christian community that refused to compromise, and retreated instead into dogmatic fundamentalism. But this resistance notwithstanding, eighteenth-century rational infidelity had set in motion a new way of approaching theological questions that could not be gainsaid by main-stream American theologians. John Macquarrie, a twentieth-century Anglican theologian, has expressed this point well. "In . . . important respects," Macquarrie asserts, "we remain inevitably children of the Enlightenment. Some of its lessons can never be unlearned. We cannot go back to the mythology of a former age, or to its supernaturalism, or to the spiritual authoritarianism of an infallible church or an infallible Bible."[18] These words could just as well apply to deism's influence upon nineteenth-century Christianity.

At least in the context of Christianity in America, the impossibility of such a retreat is partly due to the influence of the American deists. They failed to replace Christianity with rational religion, but their example served to moderate the extremism and refine the sensibility and method of American theology. Deism, in short, helped to awaken Christianity in the United States from its dogmatic slumber.

DEISM'S HUMANISTIC LEGACY

The legacy of deism in America extended beyond the theological sphere into the secular arena. Although the connections are a bit more difficult to trace, the generally humanistic orientation of rational religion certainly helped to consolidate and strengthen certain political and social ideals that have come to be associated with the American experience. There is no question that deism was but one of many factors at work in the early Republic that led to the democratization of American life, but the strident republicanism of its advocates made it a voice louder than most.

As indicated in previous chapters, deism was not simply a religious movement. It also carried along with it a reformist social agenda. Each of the American deists was ardently republican in his political sympathies. Each supported the revolutionary cause, and a few of them made great sacrifices for it. Allen and Freneau were both incarcerated during the Revolutionary War, and Paine bankrupted himself through his financial support of the cause. But the social activism of the deists did not cease with the attainment of American independence. Convinced as they were that the full exercise of reason and the inauguration of a golden age of scientific and social progress could only be nurtured by an environment that respected diversity of opinion and freedom of thought, they continued their efforts to bestir the conscience of America after the revolution as well. As we saw in chapter 1, their militant championship of republican and humanistic ideals probably won them as many enemies as did their crusade for rational religion. But for the rational infidels, the two were inseparable. Repression was repression, regardless of whether it was ecclesial or political in origin.

The humanistic tenor of American deism, with its insistence upon the ability of mankind to improve itself if left unshackled by priestly superstition and political oppression, bequeathed to the young nation a general legacy of pluralistic tolerance. In matters religious, the deists from Franklin to Freneau insisted upon absolute freedom of conscience, arguing that no church, social institution, or political authority had the right to dictate religious sentiment, coerce conformity, or punish dissent. As Paine so memorably said, a person's mind is his or her own church. Humans had to be allowed the opportunity to think religious issues through for themselves and arrive at their own conclusions, and it was the duty of a democratic government to guarantee that opportunity. Sectarian allegiances deserved protection from persecution, either civil or ecclesial, and freethinkers had an equal right to such protection. There was nothing to fear, in the deists' eyes, from this attitude of live-and-let-live pluralism. On the contrary, a healthy respect for doctrinal diversity could only serve to refine individual and collective religious sensibilities by acquainting the members of society with a variety of theological perspectives against which to weigh their own positions. It was this spirit of universal toleration for religious belief that grounded the American deists' untiring advocacy of the doctrine of the separation of church and state. Jefferson, Paine, and Palmer were particularly eloquent in the defense of the necessity of such a separation, but Franklin, Allen, and Freneau were not far behind.

A rational scrutiny of religious options is possible only if the citizenry of a pluralistic society has the opportunity to educate itself, and consequently the American deists campaigned for free and universal education as well as for absolute freedom of the press. It is true that some of the early, more moderate deists—especially Franklin—were somewhat wary of the prospect of universal education, seeing it as a double-edged sword that could promote social instability at the same time that it encouraged the advance of reason and toleration. But their reservations were not shared by most deists, who zealously campaigned against what they perceived as the deadly effects of illiteracy and censorship. Franklin, in spite of his reservations, founded the American Philosophical Society in 1743 for the "diffusion of useful knowledge" in the colonies, and encouraged the growth of subscription libraries in Philadelphia and elsewhere. Jefferson attempted to legislate free public education in Virginia, unsuccessfully worked to reform the curriculum of his alma mater, the College of William and Mary, and eventually founded the University of Virginia, which matriculated its first class in 1825, the year before his death. Paine and Palmer, the two most militant advocates of rational religion, both waged campaigns for the freedom of the press. One of the last treatises Palmer began (but unfortunately left unfinished at his death) was a systematic defense of the open press, based upon the proposition that the unimpeded interplay of ideas and opinions in the intellectual marketplace would inevitably bring the good ideas to the fore. He conceded that a completely unchecked press was capable of occasional harm, either through the printing of disinformation or the assumption of an ideological editorial policy. But the alternative of censorship, he argued, was the greater of the two evils. If given the opportunity to develop their critical faculties, readers were capable of discerning truth from falsehood.

From the deistic perspective, universal education and an uncensored press were more than just necessary conditions for the free exercise of religion and the promotion of toleration. They were also essential vehicles for the redress of social injustices, individual bigotry, and mean-spiritedness born of ignorance. One of the most fundamental convictions of the American deists was that all individuals are imbued with a spark of divine reason, and hence equally deserving of opportunities to cultivate and utilize their God-given abilities.

Moreover, as Palmer argued in his *Principles of Nature*, every human is sentient, and hence necessarily suffers from and is stunted by emotional distress, intellectual coercion, and obstacles to self-development. Consequently, he and the other deists insisted that all segments of society enjoyed the fundamental or "natural" right to exercise reason and avoid pain; and this conviction led them to champion the dispossessed and exploited who, because of their social station, were deprived of avenues for either personal growth or happiness. Jefferson and Palmer, for example, expressed concern over the institution of slavery in America and eventually condemned it. Franklin attacked the persecution of minor religious sects by their more mainstream Christian brethren. Palmer and Freneau deplored the often savage treatment of Native Americans by European settlers. In addition, Palmer argued (very much like Mary Wollstonecraft had in her 1792 *Vindication of the Rights of Women*) that the "gentler sex" possessed the same rational faculties as men and therefore deserved equal legal rights and social opportunities. The zeal with which the deists went about redressing what they perceived as social injustice, although infuriating to many of their more politically conservative contemporaries, was perfectly consistent with their humanistic religious orientation. As each of them in his own way said many times, the highest form of worship by which an individual can honor the Deity is the exercise of reason and virtue. And the deists—unlike, it must be said, many of their orthodox opponents—practiced what they preached.

The deistic movement in America, then, functioned as a gadfly that constantly irritated and occasionally stung the public conscience. It is too much to claim that the humanistic social agenda advocated by the deists was solely or even primarily responsible for subsequent social reforms in education, the separation of church and state, and recognition of the rights of Native Americans, slaves, and women. Too many other social, economic, and political factors were at play in each of these areas to establish a direct causal link between deistic agitation and eventual reform. But it is unquestionable that the impressive and eloquent example of the American deists' humanism helped to solidify an attitude of toleration and a sense of fairness that, sometimes circuitously, contributed to the rectification of at least some of the more blatant social ills of the eighteenth and nineteenth centuries. In the preceding pages, I suggested that the deistic assault upon religious supernaturalism, although ultimately unsuccessful, awoke American Christianity from its dogmatic slumber. It is not wide of the mark to add here that the deists' espousal of humanistic ideals and their often fearless campaigns for justice ultimately helped to jolt both politicians and private citizens from their rather complacent conformity to the social status quo.

A SUBTLE SUCCESS

When Freneau died in 1832, orthodox churchmen in the United States could well have triumphantly assumed that Zion, which they once feared would die groaning "without an helper," had now been restored. Freneau, the last of the rational infidels, had gone to meet the Calvinist God whose patience he and his fellow apostates had so tried, and Christianity again reigned supreme and unchallenged. But as I have argued in this chapter, such an appraisal would have been shortsighted. Enlightenment deism as a movement that captured the minds and sometimes hearts of a large number of people was no more, but it had irreversibly stamped its mark upon American theology as well as upon social attitudes and policies. Faith in the Christian message continued after the death of both Freneau and deism, but it was a faith tempered by—and to a large extent refined by—the challenge of rational infidelity.

Ironically, deism ultimately failed as a movement because it succeeded so well as a corrective. By this, I mean that its eighteenth- and early nineteenth-century assault on supernaturalism was such a potent antidote to religious dogmatism that much of the original urgency and appeal of deism's message became defused. In saying this, I do not mean to discount the philosophical and psychological difficulties intrinsic to the deistic worldview, difficulties that eventually served to discredit its mechanistic and pan-rationalistic foundations. My point is merely that deism's primary role in the history of American thought was as a purgative to the excesses of supernaturalist Christian thought.

The American deists themselves certainly saw rational religion as more than just a corrective to dogmatic supernaturalism. In their eyes, it was a comprehensive, superior alternative to the Christian religion, and none of them doubted that it would eventually supplant Christianity, thereby spelling the arrival, once and for all, of the Age of Reason. As we have seen, they were mistaken in this optimistic assumption. The Enlightenment ideal of a religion of nature, founded exclusively upon reason, experience, and virtue, lost currency at the beginning of the nineteenth century. But for almost one hundred years, deism spread in America the message of religious toleration and rational inquiry with a vigor, conviction, and dignified eloquence that could not help but influence the subsequent course of American thought. This legacy fell short of the one the American deists wished to bequeath to future generations. But, in the final analysis, it is no small inheritance.

NOTES

1. For overviews of post-Enlightenment forms of American infidelity, see Susan Jacoby, *Freethinkers: A History of American Secularism* (New York: Henry Holt, 2004); James Turner, *Without God, Without Creed: The Origins of Unbelief in America* (Baltimore: Johns Hopkins University Press, 1985), pp. 171–269; and Alice Felt Tyler, *Freedom's Ferment* (New York: Harper & Row, 1962), pp. 166–226.

2. Nathan O. Hatch, *The Democratization of American Christianity* (New Haven, CT: Yale University Press, 1989).

3. An interesting analysis of this revival is Donald G. Matthews's "The Second Great Awakening as an Organizing Process, 1780–1830," in *Religion in American History: Interpretive Essays*, ed. John Mulder and John F. Wilson

(Englewood Cliffs, NJ: Prentice-Hall, 1978). See also Jon Butler, *Awash in a Sea of Faith: Christianizing the American People* (Cambridge, MA: Harvard University Press, 1992); and Hatch, *Democratization*, pp. 220–26.

4. Hatch, *Democratization*, p. 3.

5. Alexis de Tocqueville, *Democracy in America*, trans. George Lawrence (New York: Doubleday, 1969), pt. 2, chs. 1, 2, 8, 19; Richard Hofstadter, *Anti-Intellectualism in American Life* (New York: Alfred A. Knopf, 1963).

6. David Hume, *A Treatise on Human Nature*, bk. I, pt. 3, secs. 1–4.

7. E. A. Burtt, *The Metaphysical Foundations of Modern Science* (Garden City, NY: Doubleday Anchor, 1955), pp. 238–39.

8. Pascal, *Pensees*, art. 8, quoted in Ernst Cassirer, *The Philosophy of the Enlightenment*, trans. Fritz C. A. Koelin and James P. Pettegrove (Boston: Beacon Press, 1951), p. 144.

9. I've discussed the Enlightenment assumption that the methodology of the natural sciences is appropriate to the human sciences at some length in *The Sane Society Ideal in Modern Utopianism: A Study in Ideology* (Lewiston, NY: Edwin Mellen Press, 1989), pp. 148–68.

10. Kerry Walters, *Elihu Palmer's "Principles of Nature": Text and Commentary* (Wolfeboro, NH: Longwood Academic, 1990), pp. 198–99.

11. Ibid., p. 196.

12. Susan Juster, "'In a Different Voice': Male and Female Narratives of Religious Conversion in Post-revolutionary America," *American Quarterly* 41 (March 1989): 34–62.

13. Paul-Henri Thiry, Baron d'Holbach, *Systeme de la nature, ou les Lois du monde physique et du monde moral*, vol. 2 (Paris, 1770), ch. 5.

14. Turner, *Without God*, p. 103.

15. Lyman Beecher, *Lectures*, Lecture 6, "The Attributes and Character of God," p. 139. Quoted in Turner, *Without God*, p. 103.

16. Turner, *Without God*, p. 146.

17. Horace Bushnell, *God in Christ*, pp. 48, 72. Quoted in Turner, *Without God*, p. 162.

18. John Macquarrie, *Jesus Christ in Modern Thought* (London: SCM Press, 1990), p. 26.

INDEX